John Wesley's
Life & Ethics

John Wesley's Life & Ethics

RONALD H. STONE

Abingdon Press
Nashville

JOHN WESLEY'S LIFE AND ETHICS

Copyright © 2001 by Abingdon Press

This book is printed on recycled, acid-free, elemental-chlorine–free paper.

Library of Congress Cataloging-in-Publication Data

Stone, Ronald H.
  John Wesley's life & ethics / Ronald H. Stone.
    p. cm.
  Includes bibliographical references and index.
  ISBN 0-687-05632-2 (alk. paper)
    1. Wesley, John, 1703–1791.   I. Title: John Wesley's life and ethics.   II. Title.

BX8495.W5 S73 2001
287'.092—dc21
[B]

2001033492

Scripture quotations, unless otherwise indicated, are from the King James Version of the Bible.

Scripture quotations marked (TEV) are from the Today's English Version—Second Edition © 1992 by American Bible Society. Used by permission.

Excerpts from *The Works of John Wesley,* vol. 18, ed. W. Reginald Ward and Richard P. Heitzenrater. Copyright © 1988 by Abingdon Press. Used by permission.

Excerpts from *The Works of John Wesley*, vol. 1, ed. Albert C. Outler. Copyright © 1984 by Abingdon Press. Used by permission.

Pages 221-23 are adapted from *The Ultimate Imperative: An Interpretation of Christian Ethics,* Ronald H. Stone (Cleveland: The Pilgrim Press, 1999), 149-55. Copyright © 1999.

01 02 03 04 05 06 07 08 09 10—10 9 8 7 6 5 4 3 2 1

MANUFACTURED IN THE UNITED STATES OF AMERICA

*For Hugh R. Stone,
brother and United Methodist pastor
in Iowa*

Contents

Preface

The completion of an intellectual journey begs the question: Why did you begin? The project was prompted a few years ago by my discovery that the works on John Wesley's ethics and social philosophy were going out of print just at the time I needed a book for my Methodist Social Ethics class at Pittsburgh Theological Seminary. Also, I wanted to try my hand at a biographical exploration of Wesley's ethics.

The insightfulness of John Wesley's tract "Thoughts upon Slavery" motivated me to find a way to give this popular powerful piece more attention than it was receiving among either Africans or Americans interested in Wesley. It was to me the best of the abolitionist pieces written in the eighteenth century by a person of influence. I wanted to tell the story of Wesley's social radicalness on the matter of slavery, and I hoped thereby to encourage Methodists and evangelicals to consider becoming risk takers against some of the social wrongs of our day, including economic bondage. As I entered more deeply into a study of Wesley, I discovered his model of personal-social transforming religion. He, of course, is a great believer in religious education and formation, both of which he thought best pursued within the framework of acceptance of justification by faith, nurture in a vital religious community, and commitment to social reform and philanthropy. Philanthropy and reform for him are not in tension. His realism recognizes that until God consummates the Kingdom, powerful forces will resist justice. The religiously renewed soul supported by community will engage the society for justice out of love. His model of care of the soul, renewal of the church, and reform of society seems appropriate, all-encompassing, and profound.

Further inquiry into his thought produced admiration for his struggle against poverty, for liberty, and for responsible government. North Americans will remain uneasy over his stubborn defense of the prerogatives of George III in the American colonies.

Their sympathy may be somewhat elicited by their comprehending Wesley's fear of social disorder and hatred of civil war.

Aspects of Wesley's ethics have become permanent gifts to the twenty-first century. These include realism, the emphasis on economics, his struggle with poverty, the focus on education, the welcoming of science, and his own method of using Scripture, traditions of the ancient church, reflection on experience (testimonies, social science, empirical observation), and rigorous reason as he understood it as tools for analysis.

Both faith and hope played important roles in his Christian ethic. He saw more clearly than most the centrality of love to Christian ethics, and yet his seeing it did not mean he necessarily always applied it. For example, his relationships with women were confusing to him, and he mixed religious sentiment with erotic feelings in ways unhelpful to his women disciples. Likewise, he could have expressed love to his preachers without the authoritarian dominance of them that he exhibited. These failures to achieve perfect love are part of the biographical presentation of this book.

The book reflects my methodological conviction that the ethical theory of a thinker should be developed in relationship to the theorist's life and history. Thus, personal material and eighteenth-century historical material are presented to comprehend Wesley.

The book is in part a gift of gratitude to the people of the First United Methodist Church of Humboldt, Iowa. This church was the most interesting place in town, and numerous members of that body nurtured and shaped my faith and ethics. The Methodist Church was my spiritual home through my twenty-fifth year, encouraging me through the Methodist student movement in college, the Navajo Methodist Mission in Farmington, New Mexico, employment by Goodwill Industries, and service as a local preacher in two Iowa churches. My undergraduate studies were at Morningside College, where the Methodist ethos and four great professors laid the foundations for this study. Professors Albert Sellen in history, Joseph Uemura in philosophy, and John Gingerich and Walter Benjamin in religion, mentored me there in the late 1950s. I was ordained a deacon in the New York-East Conference of the Methodist Church before I took up my academic vocation at Columbia University. I hope the book will encourage Methodists to rediscover the social messages and power of their founder and encourage them to find ways appropriate to their century to serve God and their neighbors near and far.

The search for the book involved two trips to England and one to the former slave coast of Africa. The Faculty Development Fund of Pittsburgh Theological Seminary and United Methodist Church sources funded this travel. Library work by student research assistants Anita K. Sattler and Rick D. Quinn enriched the book. Faculty secretary Sheryl Gilliland typed and retyped the manuscript while faithfully managing all of her other duties. The critique of Abingdon's editor led me to redraft the book, and then she contributed to polishing it further. I wish to express my deep thankfulness to these people and institutions.

Friends in England helped with the project. The Reverend Robert Morgan hosted my visit to Oxford, offering me orientation and a home on my arrival. His spouse, Prueh, and their daughter, Anna, provided family joy and comfort. Canon Trevor Williams, chaplain of Trinity College, graciously welcomed me to the fellowship of the college and to his Paul Tillich class. The Honorable Michael Beloff, Q.C., president of Trinity, had many hearty encouraging words, and I thank him and the wonderful Fellows of Trinity for the invitation to join them as a Visiting Fellow at the college. Librarians at the Radcliffe Camera, Bodleian Library, Regent's Park College Library, Trinity College Library, and John Rylands Library, Manchester, were all very kind in helping me track down Wesley's scattered works. A conversation with John Walsh led me to explore the deeper commitments of John Wesley to the poor. A special word of thanks is due Miss Moorah Al-Gailani, who helped in the location of Wesley's American war writings and books in his home at Wesley's Chapel and House and Museum of Methodism. The Reverend Tim Macquiban at Westminster College, Oxford, assisted in arranging attendance at the Wesley and Methodist Studies Centre Annual Day Conference. Martin Astell, librarian, arranged access to the archives at Westminster College. The three days in Epworth and Wroot were blessed by the hospitality of the warden of the Old Rectory and his spouse, Mr. and Mrs. Colin Williams. My daughter, Patricia Stone, serving in the Peace Corps in Benin, graciously guided me around the former slave coast of West Africa and provided translation of Fon and French sources.

My days in Oxford were spent in archival research as I tried to reconstruct Wesley's inspiration there two and a half centuries ago, and my own younger student days there three and a half decades ago. This is my first Oxford book, and I hope it is loyal to the space and traditions of that great university and to the spirit of one of its greatest sons.

Chronology

Queen Anne succeeds, 1702

War with Spain and France, 1702

John Wesley born, 1703

Earl of Marlborough's victories
1. Blenheim, 1704
2. Ramillies, 1706

Scotland and England united, 1707

Saved from burning, 1709

Tory victory, 1710

Treaty of Utrecht, 1713

Queen Anne dies, 1713

Enters Charterhouse School, London, 1714

George I succeeds, 1714

Whig victory, 1715

Jacobite rebellion, 1715–1716

War with Spain, 1719

Enters Christ Church College, Oxford, 1720

Robert Walpole, prime minister, and political stability, 1724

Ordained deacon by John Potter, bishop of Oxford, 1725

Elected fellow of Lincoln College, 1726

War with Spain, 1727

15

Ordained priest, 1728

Resident tutor at Lincoln, 1729

Samuel Wesley Sr. dies, 1735

Embarks for Georgia, 1735

Returns to England, 1738

Forms Fetter Lane Society, 1738

Heart warmed, 1738

Visits Moravians in Germany, 1738

Field preaching, 1739   War with Spain and France, 1739

Samuel Wesley Jr. dies, 1739

First classes, Bristol, 1742   War of Austrian Succession,
                                         1740–1748

Susanna Wesley dies, 1742   Robert Walpole resigns, 1742

"The Appeals to Men of Reason   George II at Battle of Dettingen,
and Religion," 1743   1743

First Methodist Conference, 1744

                                         Battle of Culloden, 1746

Sermons on Several Occasions, 1746

Marries Mary Vazeille, 1751

Notes upon the New Testament, 1756   Seven Years' War, 1756–1763

                                         George II dies, 1760

                                         George III succeeds, 1760

War with Spain, 1761

Peace of Paris, 1763

John Wilkes's riots, 1763

Stamp Act, 1765

"Free Thoughts on the Present," 1768   William Pitt resigns, 1768

George Whitefield dies, 1770

"Thoughts upon Slavery," 1774

"A Calm Address," 1775

American War of Independence, 1776–1781

Arminian Magazine, 1778

A Collection of Hymns, 1780   Gordon riots, 1780

Lord North resigns, 1782

Deed of Declaration and Ordinations, 1784

Charles Wesley dies, 1788

French Revolution begins, 1789

John Wesley dies, 1791

Introduction

This book is a historical study of John Wesley's ethics. Its task is to understand his moral philosophy critically. Its judgments are limited neither to the methods of history of religion nor to the methods of ethics; rather, the parameters of both limit the study and the possibilities of both expand the study. There are many fine biographies of Wesley's life, and there are a few studies of his ethics. Yet his ethical thought has not been studied historically.

As far as possible, the chronology of Wesley's life carries the development of the analysis of his ethical thought. This life covers most of the eighteenth century, and so to an extent the study of Wesley's ethics is a study of the eighteenth century as focused on the life and activity of Wesley, and particularly so as he reflected on those events ethically. The morals that guided Wesley's long life came from his family, the church, the culture, and the university. As he reflected upon these morals, he entered into the work of ethics. Neither his morals nor his ethics remained constant.

The historical study of ethics is one method of approach. It is one in which it is particularly helpful to place the ethics in context to understand the social and political meaning of ethical thought and applied ethics. The historical study of ethics does not assume that history determines ethics. It does not claim that ethics determines history. Ethical thought is one of the variables in history that at particular conjunctions of historical forces may exert strong factors into the direction of history. Wesley's thought did not determine major directions of the eighteenth century, but it did shape the minds of a significant number of people. Likewise, history did not determine Wesley's ethics; he significantly rearranged ideas from the history of morals and projected them into new meanings. Yet Wesley's influence in eighteenth-century England certainly marks him as one of the most significant people of the period. The influence of his mark on the evangelical movement—and in particular on the Methodist movement—is felt to this day. The church that he did not want to found became the second most important English sect of his century and contributed even more significantly in shaping the ethos of the United States, where it became in the nineteenth century the largest Protestant church body. This book at many points reflects this interaction of history and ethics. Wesley must not be expected to shape history where the character of history denies the possibility, but neither must the influence of ideas be denied when their shaping power of institutions acting in history seems obvious.

John Wesley's ethics are theological ethics. Sometimes the ethical insight shapes the expression of the theology, and sometimes the reverse happens. Occasionally, important ethical theories and recommendations are developed with only implicit suggestions of the theological presuppositions, and sometimes the theological arguments are developed while the ethical consequences are muted. This seems appropriate to Christian theological ethics that spring from the Great Commandment to love God and to love the neighbor. The formulation is similar to the division between the first four commandments that speak of particular ways to love God, and the last six commandments to love the neighbor through refraining from certain actions. In the Old Testament formulation and the New Testament formulation both neighbor and God are present. In human experience sometimes the theology determines the ethics, and sometimes the procedure is reversed. In Wesley's thought the two are held closely together, and one is inexplicable without the other. Thus, the themes of perfection and freedom help drive the theology, and the theology of grace shapes the ethic and worldly practice. The theme of antislavery is developed primarily on ethical grounds, even humanistic ethical grounds, whereas the doctrines of God's sovereignty and unity as well as his experience shape his views of monarchy for his political theory. Certainly, his belief in the free will of humanity that is a prerequisite for the loving God whom Wesley worships shapes his political struggles for liberation. Also, his doctrine of the sin of humanity drives his evangelical preaching and his political realism. His theology and ethics work in tandem.

This book follows Wesley's life, relating his ethical thought to the situation of the time. However, some aspects of his life are discussed little, for example, his music and poetry, though they are important to a total study of Wesley. The ethics hang upon the life story rather than standing as systematic treatises in ethical theory. The subjects of slavery and the revolutions of the eighteenth century are seen as important enough themes in social ethical theory to stand by themselves while depending upon the preceding chapter about the 1760s–1770s.

Chapter 1, "Origins," shows how the religious life of his parents shaped Wesley's moral formation. His particular character strengths were piety, discipline, rationalism, and moral seriousness, all of which he owed to his parents. He learned both free will and perfectionism from his mother, and her rejection of Calvinism shared with her former Calvinist husband determined central ethical trajectories of Wesley's mind. He was born into a long line of clergymen of dissent, and while his parents gave him their established religion, the dissent would emerge in Wesley's own way. The literate, religious seriousness came from the family as did his ease in both humble, rural settings and higher education. To a remarkable degree Wesley's life is understandable in terms of the loyalties and conflicts of his family. So the chapter concludes with a brief survey of his sisters' inability to secure solid marriages; with all the gifts Samuel and Susanna bestowed upon their children, their home life did not create a context out of which stable marriages flowed easily. John's love of and conflicts with women would threaten his vocation until late in his life. To the degree that ethics is reflection upon and the living out of relationships, his ethic was very troubled. His ethic would emerge out of love and rules.

Chapter 2, "Oxford," details the formation of Wesley in the environment of the university. His preparatory school in London led him to college education, which evolved into his vocation as an ordained young tutor. Though Oxford has been severely criticized for its academic laxity in the eighteenth century, for fifteen years it was for Wesley a place of rigorous learning. Besides his formal university studies, his attraction to Sally Kirkham led to his study of Thomas à Kempis and Jeremy Taylor, and to his journal writing. His rigorous religious self-examination was expanded through the community of the Holy Club founded by brother Charles and by William Morgan. The group found themselves living a strict religious morality dedicated to social service as well as regularized religious practices.

Refusing to settle into a parish, John had only a partially successful academic life. By 1735, after the death of his father, he was led to attempt to translate the Holy Club, with three of its members accompanying him, to the new world of Georgia. The outlines of Methodist religious rigor and social service were established in Oxford, even if the deep emotional commitments of the Wesleys to Christian experience were not yet realized. They would leave Oxford in 1735 still seeking the salvation of their souls.

John and his brother Charles were joined by two other members of the Oxford Methodist circle in their mission to the Native Americans of the Georgia colony. Chapter 3, "Georgia," details the unfitness of the Wesley brothers' Oxford Methodism for the New World. Their high churchmanship was resisted, and their ascetic discipline was rejected. Their naïveté with women led them to flee the colony. First, Charles lost influence with Governor Oglethorpe over misplaced charges of adultery. John fared little better, leaving the colony under a barrage of accusations related to his mistreatment of the niece of the leader of Savannah. The mission to the Native Americans was neglected and then buried under a tide of other assigned responsibilities. The lasting influence of the scholars' sojourn in Georgia was the recognition of a religious certainty in the Moravian brethren, which the Oxford men lacked. This recognition contained the spark that would ignite the Methodist evangelical movement on the return to England. Two other seeds that would bear later fruit were John's attempts to form devoted cells of religiously serious followers at both Frederica and Savannah, Georgia, and John's minor experiences with African slavery in Carolina.

The years 1738 to 1739 are presented as a single chapter, "Moravians." These were the years of Wesley's deepening, personal religious conviction under Moravian influence, the years of his trip to the Moravian center in Germany, the launching of his evangelical-preaching vocation, and the founding of his societies, which also reflected aspects of the United Brotherhood of the Moravians. Even his published hymnody reflected Moravian influence. Charles and John had to distinguish their position from their Moravian mentors in their first published volume of poetry and hymns because of the Moravian neglect of social ethics and public issues. They did not want the personal dimensions of much of their early hymnody, which in John's case were translations of Moravian hymns, to obscure the fact that Christianity was a social religion. By the end of 1739, John had found his vocation, his faith, and much of his society's organization. Five more decades would develop these trajectories, but the essential directions were in place for his life.

Chapter 5, "Reform," describes John's movement away from the Moravians. The Aldersgate "heart warming" experience remained foundational, but his efforts to reform church and nation differentiated him from the Moravian society. The previous ethic of seeking salvation by works of religion and charity was replaced. Now in faith, he accepted salvation and sought to do the gracious God's will through evangelization and the teaching of the love commandments. Controversy forced John into pamphleteering. All three of his pamphlets of 1742–1743—"A Brief History of the Principles of Methodism," "The Character of a Methodist," and "An Earnest Appeal to Men of Reason and Religion"—appealed to the tormentors of Methodism for understanding and appreciation. All three summarized the Methodist ethic as loving devotion to God and loving care for the neighbor. He never deviated from this ethic in his later ministry. The ethic is understood best as a form of rule-love ethic or, in William Frankena's terms, as a form of rule-agapism ethic. Wesley would later detail those rules, particularly in his discourses on the Sermon on the Mount. Here in 1743 in the "Appeal," he summarized those rules as the Ten Commandments as representing the constitution of the Church of England. The chapter also shows his characteristic practical bent with an appeal to the king and brief discussions of his social welfare work in poor relief, education, poor houses, and loans. Finally, he turned away at the end of the decade from his ascetic rejection of marriage. Abandoning his relative neglect of romance from the time of his "warm heart" experience of 1738, John fell in love with an inappropriate woman. Charles's interference broke this planned marriage to Grace Murray in 1748, and John's grief set him up for the sorrowful marriage to Mary in 1751.

At midlife, after losing his love and just before marriage, Wesley prepared and published his discourses on the Sermon on the Mount. For Wesley, the Sermon is the will of God, and his interpretation of its meaning is the detailing of his ethic for the English of the mid–eighteenth century. Once he had published these essays, he never felt the need to revise or change them, though he continued to preach often on the themes of the Sermon. These discourses or lectures in sermonic form on the Sermon on the Mount fill in the details of the meaning of his ethic of holiness, or perfection or love. They return again and again to the Beatitudes as expressions of love and to God's expectation of holiness from those who have accepted their salvation. The discourses receive greater emphasis in this book in chapter 6, "Sermon on the Mount," than other writings of Wesley because they show the details of his ethic grounded in the love commandments.

Chapter 7, "Marriage and War," covers the realities of Wesley's life in the midcentury decade of the 1750s. He preached joy, peace, and righteous justice as the fruit of the Christian life. But, in reality, he lived a sorrowful marriage in an England almost continually at war. The wars revealed the instability of too many nation-states in a small continent subject to the discordant governance of family dynasties. Wesley's marriage seldom rose above the discord of his father's separation from his mother over the legitimacy of dynastic succession in England. In 1754, the continental war broke out into a world war fought on five continents. These realities led Wesley, while reaffirming the life of holy love in *Genuine Christianity*, to also affirm strongly the fact of sin and a realism about human affairs. His reflections on these themes of love, sin, and war in particular reveal his affinities to the contemporary form of Christian ethics called Christian realism.

Chapter 8, "Maturation," discusses the growth and gradual acceptance of Methodism by the larger society in the 1760s and 1770s. It was a time of influence for John Wesley, and with the ascension of, in his opinion, the benevolent George III, his writings on public issues developed. This chapter includes his reflections on economic ethics. (However, the subjects of political liberty and slavery receive separate chapters. It is important to remember that while this study chooses to emphasize his writings in social ethics, he was also managing the movement, engaging in other scholarly writing, and furiously writing theological polemic.) He undertook two of his most strenuous theological debates for reasons of ethical emphasis. His writings on Christian perfection and against predestination were intended to ensure that Christianity remain morally rigorous. Perfection he advocated because he found it in the New Testament; predestination he denounced because it was not. But his moral reasoning and his reading of human experience convinced him that Christian perfection as a reading of total love and human free will were both essential to Christian ethics. The chapter suggests that in this case, he was more successful in defeating what he denied than he was in being persuasive about his affirmation.

His writings in this period, on natural philosophy, the history of England, and the Old Testament, reveal how much a person of Enlightenment reason he was. Christian revelation was compatible with Enlightenment reason at its best, and where it was not, it could correct the inadequacies of reason to illumine humanity's experience.

He managed the issue of women preaching in his connection with subtlety while resisting prophetic interpretation that would have forced the hand of the Church of England. Later successors to his mantle could not manage his insight and grace on this issue for another two centuries.

In the fields of economic ethics and Christian practice of charity and empowerment of the poor, there may not be his equal until the twentieth century within the ranks of church leaders. He regularly and systematically raised charity for the poor, he developed effective means of changing their situation, and he advocated policy changes on their behalf. This chapter is less critical of Wesley's economic ethics than some recent studies guided by liberation theology. It concludes that he was really very good in his relations with and writings on behalf of the poor.

Chapter 9, "Liberty," analyzes Wesley's political writings, which arose out of his own values and the threats of his times on liberty. He regarded the English, whether they were in England or America, as quite free. He particularly valued their freedoms in religious matters. The relatively free use of their property was also quite well protected, he argued, except for their obligations to pay taxes. He was quite probably correct that the English in the 1770s were relatively more at liberty than either their predecessors or other nationalities. Wesley respected the monarchy as a protector of those liberties, and he rose to defend the monarchy against radical demands for more liberty, whether from supporters of John Wilkes or the American Revolution. He was realistic about power and about the lack of political sophistication of the mob. He had no experience of a republican form of government succeeding in as large a polity as England or the colonies, and so he hoped for the victory of English monarchy over the American revolutionary. He hated war, but once it came, he hoped for English victory to restore order and to protect liberty.

Most of the arguments in the chapter, from defining liberty to the analysis of power and reflection on English rebellions and the American Revolution, are in Enlightenment political-philosophical terms. Behind this terminology rest John's theological convictions encouraging the sovereignty of God and monarchy and liberty in England and within an established church. The freedom that was required for honest worship was, in his mind, adequately guaranteed by king and church. Many of his Calvinist opponents, with less regard for the free will of humanity, wanted more freedom from both king and established church.

The theme of liberty continued in his writing on slavery in chapter 10. His participation in the abolitionist movement is his most radical social commitment. In this part of his work, he could be regarded as a thoroughgoing liberation theologian and activist. He wanted nothing less than the abolition of slavery and the dismembering of the economic system to which it was foundational. In this movement, he was more radical than the radical English or Americans he had opposed in their attacks on monarchy. His major treatise, "Thoughts upon Slavery," proceeds by stating the problem, studying its history and contemporary practice, exposing its evil practice, destroying the arguments defending slavery, arguing for a right to human freedom from natural law, and finally, appealing to those practicing slavery to give up their vile professions. His reliance upon Christian sources—the love of God, the apocalypse of Matthew 25, the Golden Rule, the commandment not to steal, and the commandment not to murder—is clear. The major arguments in this public theology are, however, in terms of natural law and not the particularized insights from the Christian moral tradition.

Chapter 11, "God Is with Us" (1780–1791), summarizes his final decade of life. He remained active on his itinerant preaching schedule until the end. The *Arminian Magazine* carried on his fight with the predestinarians and also expressed his political and social views. Just before his death in 1791, his movement numbered almost two hundred thousand; and it was second only to the Church of England in its influence. He held it within the church, while in America it moved from a Church of England society to an independent denomination. The persecution of the Wesleys had ended, and he was regarded as one of the spiritual leaders of the nation, being treated as a celebrity. From his position as a national figure, he continued to work on behalf of the poor and to end slavery. His ethic of Christian faith expressed in love through rules, education, counsel, discipline, and in works of mercy and justice remained constant.

The concluding chapter 12, "Ethics," summarizes the insights from his life and writing on ethics. Seven distinctive characteristics of his ethic are presented before the discussion of Wesley's relating of Christian love to moral law. The rule-agapism, deontological nature of his ethic is argued for, and then I show how this dominates his presentation of Christian character. His social ethic is demonstrated to be of a reformist rather than a revolutionary character. His passionate concern for the poor and for the reform of church and society is contrasted with the more harmonious view of society of his Glasgow contemporary, Adam Smith. Finally, his ethical theory is presented by a summarizing list of his moral practice for reform of church and society. Despite living through a transitional society usually at war and suffering from an inability to achieve a satisfactory married life, his ethic and his moral practice were very good. He remains a trustworthy guide when the eccentricities of his time are understood and relativized. His context is not our context, but it is important in understanding his particular Christian ethic. Those who follow his tradition or learn from his ethics have one of the wisest Christian ethicists from whom to draw moral wisdom.

1. Origins (1703–1714)

John Wesley's parents, Samuel and Susanna, emerged out of the fervor of the religious-political conflicts of seventeenth-century England. Both of them were born into Calvinist families that rebelled against the Church of England. They were married after the Glorious Revolution of 1688 promised to quiet the turmoil of British political-religious revolution and social conflict. They migrated into high-church Anglicanism, but they brought their Calvinist heritage of dissent with them.

These religious-social tensions of their time affected them deeply and nearly split their marriage. The Wesley adult children were aware that their parents' marriage included much conflict, the most famous occasion of which reportedly involved both their religious and their political loyalties. It was almost an archetypical case of the political becoming personal. In 1702, Susanna refused to say "Amen" at the morning prayer honoring King William III. She regarded him as a usurper of the Crown. Samuel, according to John, declared that if they served two different kings, they must have two different beds. Both parents remained inflexible. Soon Samuel left for London, where he represented the diocese of Lincoln at the church convocation. He remained there several months until after King William, or William, the Prince of Orange, as Susanna regarded him, died. Susanna and Samuel accepted Queen Anne as sovereign, so they reunited and their conjugal reconciliation led to John Wesley's birth in 1703.

Before the reconciliation Susanna had sought counsel and help from Lady Yarborough, also a supporter of clergy refusing the oath to William and Mary. Samuel had refused a reconciliation, for he had taken an oath not to touch her. She considered submission to her husband whom she addressed as master, but she could not surrender her conscience. A bishop, who as a non-oath-taking bishop had great authority in Susanna's group, ruled that Samuel's oath was not valid because it violated his previous marriage vows. Samuel had refused to refer the matter to arbitration. The counsel of another clergyman to Samuel and the burning of two-thirds of Epworth rectory finally led Samuel to return to the marriage bed. Susanna had seen in the fire "the finger of God."[1] Other conflicts characterized their marriage, but no other required the death of a king; the intervention of nobility, a bishop, and a cleric; and the burning of a rectory to resolve. It is hard to sympathize with Samuel's pride in the conflict; much of the time he was in London at Convocation spending funds that the family could ill afford to spare, while Susanna, also in her stubbornness, was stuck in Epworth with six children amidst hostility from community opposition.

John's birth in 1703 was in a thatch-roofed, timber cottage typical of England at the beginning of the eighteenth century. England was mostly rural, illiterate, and poor. The population was not more than five and a half million, and the towns were small. By the time of his death in 1791, England had grown to dominate a worldwide empire, and John regarded the whole world as his parish.

He knew the livestock of the family farm because his father served the farming parish of St. Andrew's in Epworth (probably meaning "Farm in the Hill") in rural Lincolnshire. He grew up playing with dogs, swimming in the canals, hunting, fishing, and boating. Though most English villages in 1703 were isolated, Epworth was particularly so because of its watery surroundings, which in winter reduced it to an island. The Isle of Axholme was surrounded by fen land that provided fishing and some pasturing to the peasant farmers of the Isle. St. Andrew's Church contains some architectural work from the twelfth century, and in all probability wooden churches preceded its construction. In Wesley's time the farmers still lived in the village of Epworth. They had been embroiled for a hundred years in struggles over the division and taxation of the former fen lands. The outlines of the island are still visible with the River Trent on one side and the low-lying fields, formerly fens, on the other side. In Wesley's day locals sometimes had to take a boat to get to the neighboring village of Wroot where Samuel served as curate, and where John served briefly after finishing his studies at Oxford. The landscape is still marked by the windmills of former days, and drainage canals still hint at the former wetlands of the area. Some of the rural roads are still on top of the dikes. The drainage of the fens begun in 1626 by the Dutch led to armed conflict. The fighting, destruction of drainage works, and lawsuits extended among the farmers into Samuel Wesley's tenure with them.

For all this, John's family was neither rural nor insular. His father and grandfather were Oxford educated. His mother knew London and came from a well-known family of Presbyterian clergy with connections to high society. Both families were connected to nobility.

John's great-grandfather and grandfather had been dissenting clergymen. His great-grandfather had also practiced medicine, as had his uncle. John published writings of both his grandfather and his father late in his own life, revealing how conscious he was of these traditions. The published dialogue between his namesake, Grandfather John, and the bishop was a disagreement about ordination and lay ministry. So, John's troubles with English bishops had roots in the two generations preceding his own father's return to the established church.

Samuel

Epworth, though not Samuel Wesley's first church, was to be his home for thirty-nine years (1696–1735). Samuel, the son and grandson of dissenting clergy, had found his way to Oxford (Exeter College) and to ministry in the Church of England. He combined a commitment to high-church Anglicanism with a dedication to church discipline more characteristic of his Calvinist heritage. The combination of the two would earn him much disfavor in Epworth and would plague his sons John and Charles in Savannah. Samuel regarded himself as a person of importance in communication with the wider English society, reform movements, and intellectual circles ministering to a sometimes beleaguered group of rural people. Samuel was too much for them. Comfort rather than challenge to their mores was their priority. His intellectual labors and publishing ventures were his outlet from the uneducated parishioners and a frustrated attempt at advancement.

Lincolnshire, where Samuel was called to minister, was among the more rustic counties of England. Amidst its crudity and backwardness Samuel aspired to be a poet. Some of his work found favor, but generally, he wrote too quickly to produce meritorious works in his publisher brother-in-law's opinion. Samuel's lack of financial skills contributed to their remaining in poverty, as did having to support such a large family. The expense of serving the church on behalf of Lincoln at Convocation in London, in addition to his already difficult financial burdens at home, landed him in debtors' prison.

In spite of the isolation, children, and poverty, Susanna maintained a literate household, even producing her own writings, and Samuel continued to work at editing a literary journal for a few years, publishing several of England's best writers. His life's work, a commentary on Job, was completed and published posthumously with many of England's notables as subscribers. Susanna revealed in a letter to her brother how difficult it was for Samuel to be isolated in a backwater like Epworth with his many gifts and talents. His attempts to escape failed, and he was passed over for appointment to an Irish bishopric.

Although there were frequent references to the poverty of the Wesleys in literature about the family, the present reconstruction of the brick rectory of the Wesleys seems to belie that portrayal. It was one of the most significant structures of a relatively modest village. Samuel Wesley indebted himself another £400 to construct the dwelling. They had lost most of their belongings to the fire, and reoutfitting seriously indebted the family. The church from its ancient foundations dominated the town from its hill. The assignment to the "Crown living" of Epworth is listed variously from £200 to £150 with another £60 added later from the curacy of Wroot. Though Susanna's testimony points to the difficulty of paying for bread, some of this lack is due to the legendary mismanagement of Samuel. He was liberated from imprisonment in debtors' prison by his bishop's intervention. The £200 figure, if accurate, would have been quite sufficient for a living that for the Wesleys was supplemented by the attached farm. Probably its return was closer to £100. Their resources extended beyond the church resources to their class connections, which provided their sons with the means to attend preparatory schools and then

Oxford University. These class and ecclesiastical connections placed their sons among the elite of the nation. The lack of land holdings or cash flow, however, did not make their daughters candidates for preferment for marriage. There are stories of the adult children being in a few cases unable to provide sufficiently for their nutrition. They had to settle for what they could win on their own without much financial support from the family.

The wider circle of acquaintances of Samuel Wesley included James Oglethorpe, a reforming member of Parliament. His engagement on behalf of reforming prisons and of founding the colony of Georgia was to become significant for the sons of Samuel. The first acquaintance was with Samuel Jr., who attended Oglethorpe's school in London. Samuel wrote and published poems praising Oglethorpe's ventures in both prison reform and colony founding, thanked him for previous financial help, mentioned his sons, and promised the completion of his work on Job. Oglethorpe responded by subscribing to nine copies of the promised work. Unfortunately, the rector of Epworth died before completing the work. Nonetheless, within seven months of Samuel's death in April 1735, John and Charles Wesley were employed by Oglethorpe and on board the *Simmonds* headed for Georgia. From the ship, John wrote Samuel Jr. about presenting their father's Latin commentary on Job to the disinterested Queen Caroline. She commented on its pretty binding and then returned to her amusements. John bowed his way out of the room.

Susanna as Puritan

Susanna grew up in the Puritan home of Dr. and Mrs. Samuel Annesley, a nonconforming clergyman. The home, conceived of as a little church, conducted its affairs methodically. Her father preaching to the House of Commons had challenged the members to make their homes well-ordered little Commonwealths.[2] Susanna learned to balance her recreational life with her personal devotional life and the taking of exercise. Her religious search led her at thirteen years of age to abandon church membership among the Nonconformists in order to move to the Anglican Church. Despite the hardships suffered by her learned father for his nonconforming, the transfer to a moderate Anglicanism was not a step that broke the family bonds. From her home she brought to Samuel Wesley the commitment to disciplined methodical living, home devotions, personal religion, and learning in secular and religious subjects. "The Annesley tradition was not lost upon the little Wesleys, and in one parsonage at least it was to prove true that if one scratched an Anglican, one would find a Puritan."[3]

The Puritan home of Dr. Annesley with its family devotions, Bible study, and prayer was handed on to the Wesley family through Susanna. Her home was not so much like a convent, as some have suggested, as it was the application of the strengths of the convent asceticism to the parsonage family. Her use of discipline and her successful efforts toward method, schedule, rule, productivity, learning, religion, and conscience all reflect Puritan training. Everything was lived in the presence of God with seriousness. Susanna's turn from nonconformity to conformity brought the Presbyterianism of her father into the Anglicanism of Epworth. From her father, Susanna was encouraged to keep a spiritual journal of her life.[4] This journaling could serve as the Puritan confessional. In keeping it, she set the context for John's and Charles's later adoption of the practice. Those diaries and journals surviving from John leave him among the most well documented of any of the Christian forebears. But originally for him, they were a method of spiritual record keeping toward holiness.

The best interpreter of Susanna Wesley, John A. Newton, records that after Wesley's Aldersgate experience, he no longer turned to her for spiritual advice. Before that John had sought Susanna's religious counsel on a variety of issues. A possible interpretation of the change is that at Aldersgate he found loving acceptance or what could be regarded as the feminine side of God. The mother who had provided so much discipline and encouraged much self-examination and rigorous seeking of holiness was replaced in psychic need by the loving acceptance ascribed to God. Alternative explanations for his not being so distracted by other women are also possible, but in the first few years of his religious enthusiasm he was freed from foolish behavior in the feminine presence. For a while it seemed as if he were a fit candidate for the celibate priesthood, which he was almost resolved to choose. Opposing this interpretation of John and Susanna is that she was quickly aging, over seventy, and grieving the death of her husband and, from 1734, the death of her first son. The revival's emphasis on personal faith was a different emphasis than that of her Puritan tradition. Susanna would gradually reconcile with the emphases of the revival, especially after her son Samuel's death. But to John's consciousness the faith in which he found comfort was different, though close to that he had learned from his mother at Epworth.

His mother would in 1739, on receiving Communion at the hands of her son-in-law Westley Hall, also feel her sins were forgiven. With this acceptance she moved into the Methodist camp completely. This was to accept part of Puritanism that her father, Dr. Annesley, knew but did not emphasize. Charles, penning her epitaph, put it rather starkly that for seventy years she had lived under law and only in this late-life Communion found personal assurance. Charles's bluntness is characteristic of him, but it says a lot of the brothers' perception of their family heritage. Newton's interpretation makes the point that in her late-life assent to her sons' emphasis, she returned to her Puritanism out of the Anglican rationalism in which she had lived.[5] Anglican rationalism would particularly criticize this Wesley need for personal assurance. Neither John nor Charles ever escaped her influence on the beginnings of their religious journey. She taught perfectionism in the love of God, as had her father before her. Her rationalism combined with biblical authority would remain a Methodist inheritance. John published her critiques of predestination and Whitefield. In her late days she came to the personal assurance preached by the revival. Most important, though, in her religious life of discipline, close to legalism at Epworth, she had set a standard that the brothers, unable to fulfill, would overcome in the acceptance of acceptance. She thereby united Puritan, evangelical revival, and Anglican as does Methodism at its best.

Home Schooling

The most well-documented aspect of life at Epworth was Susanna's schooling of the children.[6] In 1732 she wrote to John at his request and gave an account of her practice of self-teaching. At this time of writing she was sixty-three years of age and many years beyond the actual period of teaching. The results of her teaching were striking. The seven girls were taught to read before they were taught to sew. Some have speculated that their education made marriage to the rough men of the fen lands difficult. The three boys were prepared to succeed at the preparatory schools in London and then to move on to Oxford University and ordination.

Susanna was clear that the primary goal in her education was to save the souls of her children. She thought that few would care to follow her path in dedicating twenty years of their lives to such a demanding pursuit. The practice reflected emphases both from her father's Presbyterianism and from her own choice of Anglicanism. At places it echoed John Locke's philosophy from *Essay Concerning Human Understanding* and *Some Thoughts Concerning Education*. John's publication reflected his debt to her, but also his own agreement with the pedagogy. The extant versions we have of the letter reflect John's editing and abridging.

The letter emphasizes the regular method of living as the first principal rule she followed. The children's hours were so carefully regulated that the discipline of classes hardly differed from the rest of the day. The children were taught to "fear the rod," and they were permitted to cry only softly. Generally, she claimed the house was as quiet as if no children were there. As soon as they were capable, the children were limited to three meals a day with no eating between meals. Sleep was regularized quickly with supper at six, followed by prayers, washing and undressing with the assistance of the maid, and bed by eight.

The largest section of the letter is on the need to break the child's will for the sake of a religious education. Self-will she identified as the root of rebellion and therefore the root of sin. Forcing the child to surrender the will renders the child compliant to authority, parent, and God. From such compliance come peace and salvation. The will was regulated early, and thereafter religious observance, prayer, and politeness were insisted upon.

At age five they were taught to read. It was expected that the alphabet would be mastered on the first day of class. After learning the letters they began at Genesis. In commenting on Samuel, who was five years old on 10 February, she wrote that he could read a chapter by Pentecost. In using Scripture for the learning of reading and for the memorization of it, she ignored John Locke, who found the practice to be of no use. Each day they reviewed what they had learned. For six hours each day all the children worked hard, and Susanna was amazed at how much they could learn each day.

The letter as a whole has more on strict discipline and the breaking of potential self-will in it than it has developed pedagogical principles. This sense of hard work, discipline, and respect for authority of the letter also dominated the mind and thought of the twenty-nine-year-old son to whom she sent the letter.

The Wesleys were educated in Epworth outside their home also. Samuel Wesley Jr. studied at John Holland's Academy. Samuel Wesley Sr. was active in raising funds from his parishioners and the Society for Promoting Christian Knowledge for the establishment of a school. Even a hundred years later the school required all of the students to attend church services on Sunday morning with the schoolmaster.[7]

The hostility against Samuel's Tory politics and high churchmanship continued in threats and demonstrations from village protesters, with one leading to a nursemaid, kept awake during the night, rolling onto the three-week-old daughter, Susanna, and smothering her while Samuel was in debtors' prison in Lincoln Castle. At that time Susanna's remarkable courage held the family together through poverty and threat. The archbishop's intervention finally released Samuel from his three-month imprisonment. Susanna had known some wealth growing up in London, but in Epworth both money and polite society eluded her. Still she prevailed and protected her children, sheltering them from rough Epworth until the suspected arson of 1709 again burned the house down. Though young John was saved as "a brand plucked from the burning," the children were scattered, some in London with uncle Matthew Wesley, and others boarded in the village. Upon their reunion in the new, handsome brick rectory, which has since been restored, she set out to reform their manners and religious life with fresh zeal. The reformation and zeal were particularly focused on John. Two years after the fire she wrote under the label of "S. J.," meaning "son John," her prayer:

I would, if I durst humbly offer Thee myself and all that Thou hast given me, and I would resolve (Oh give me grace to do it) that the residue of my life shall be all devoted to Thy service; and I do intend to be more particularly careful of the soul of this child that Thou hast so mercifully provided for, than ever I have been, that I may do my endeavour to instil into his mind the principles of thy true religion and virtue. Lord, give me grace to do it sincerely, and prudently, and bless my attempts with good success.[8]

John would know of this special care, divine and maternal, and use the phrase "a brand plucked from the burning" to describe other escapes. One interesting use of it was to describe his escape from intimacy or marriage with Sophia Christianna Hopkey. There was grace in Susanna's love for John. However, the enforced discipline and internalized moralism would not serve him well. His early years reflected a dogged moralistic attempt to do well. The Puritanical expression within Anglicanism found expression in her methodical raising of the children and their expression of Methodism within Anglicanism. The later experience of grace at Aldersgate would finally, after much striving, bring him the relief he needed for the flowering of his generativity.

Despite all her admirers write about Susanna's equal education of the girls, the records seem to say that they were educated until they could read well and then their sewing work occupied equal time with their learning. The three boys went on to further schooling to prepare them for the best England had to offer, even if we should regard Oxford of the eighteenth century as educationally inadequate. The impact of the Wesley parents on the girls may have encouraged impossible ideals, as it seems to have in John and Charles, but it did not prepare them for their roles in life as wives of the men from the Isle of Axholme.

John was the child to express the fanaticism of a methodical approach to life most severely. Even his father noticed his extreme care to regulate his life by reason. Charles, a little more relaxed, was able to marry earlier and to produce brilliant children, and one of his grandchildren would make world-class contributions to music. Samuel seemed among the boys to be the least formed by his mother's methods, and both his career and his marriage were successful.

Daughters

The daughters, however, were notably unsuccessful in career and marriage. They lived in a desolate place with little opportunity for advancement except by marriage, and there were few family resources to promote the attractiveness of the marriages.[9] Through correspondence and face-to-face counsel, John shared many of their travails.

Emily's love affairs led nowhere. Her eventual marriage to a local druggist resulted in separation and her caring for their ailing daughter. She eventually came to depend on John as she ministered to the sick at the Foundry, where she remained until death at age seventy-nine in 1771. Susanna's quick marriage to Richard Ellison subjected her to violent abuse until she escaped the relationship. Mary Wesley probably had the happiest year of marriage, but she and her newborn son died and were buried in the Wroot church. Her husband, John's student, John Whitelamb, served out his unfulfilled life at Wroot. Hetty's love affairs led to her exile as governess to a family near Louth. She became pregnant and was forced into an unlikely marriage to an illiterate plumber. They set up shop in London but were beset by the early death of all the children and financial duress; she died at age fifty-three. Anne married successfully and seemed to do well. Their son they baptized John Lambert. After having several lovers, Martha married John's student, the Reverend Mr. Westley Hall, who proved unfaithful; and eventually, he left her to move to the West Indies. Kezzy never recovered from her broken engagement to Westley Hall, who married and deserted Martha. She lived for a while with various families including the Halls, but died at thirty-two years of age.[10]

None of the ten children made it out of the teaching or ecclesiastical worlds that had been the lives of their parents. Some of the girls worked for a while as governesses or teachers, but opportunities for advancement did not present themselves and almost all of their marriages failed. The education, discipline, and religion of the family seem to have prepared the family for success in professional religion, and that was an opening for the boys.

Their parents had been strong, but Maser's study focused on the sisters begins: "There was a unity about the Wesley family that was commendable, but it was not a unity cemented by love." After pursuing the seven sisters' mostly unsuccessful search for love in this world, he concluded, "Fundamentally, both Susanna and Samuel Sr. seemed to lack the spirit of love." Some of them did finally find rest in God's love, but their restlessness in seeking love confirmed Augustine's observation about remaining restless until finding rest in God. John seemed also not to have been given a sense of being loved by his parents. The strength of his mother and her ordering carried him well through school and university, but it encouraged a fanaticism noted by his critics.

Martha found her vocation with John. After her disastrous marriage to the Reverend Hall, who became polygamous, she helped administer the services of the Foundry. The education she had received and her development enabled her to hold her own with the famous conversationalist Samuel Johnson. Johnson commented on the similarity between John and Martha. The father's rejection of Hetty, after her seduction, put a strain on the whole family. But their journals and letters reveal a loving family that sometimes rallied to support one another in their times of loss. Samuel Jr. never wavered in his distaste for the enthusiasms of his brothers' revival. But Susanna found herself a convert with Martha, and at her death all of her living daughters were present. Maldwyn Edwards's interpretation of the family life at Epworth and beyond notes the discipline and the sternness, but he also records the ongoing caring communication among the siblings. He can find the winsomeness of John originating in the care and affection of the Epworth parsonage. Many loved John, and by the end of his career many of those who opposed him earlier held him in warm adulation.

It could have been hoped that one growing up among so many sisters could have worked out his relationships with other women better. His brothers did. Perhaps Edwards's generous interpretation contains one side of the truth: "Wesley never ceased from working out a strategy for the advance of God's Kingdom, and at the same time the sword never slept in his hand. No wonder that women grew exasperated with him. He had the power to attract them and win their affection, but whilst they asked so much, he could give them so little."[11] Even his sisters complained that he provided them with too little compassion and company. Neither the dominating discipline of the mother nor the failed marriages of his sisters bode well for John's seeking of a female life partner.

John's childhood development in the rectory in damp Epworth did not give him the emotional satisfaction he sought. He would find satisfaction years later in religious experience after overdeveloping his parents' disciplined religious life. Their discipline provided him with the opportunities at the all-male communities of Charterhouse and Oxford. The education at his mother's direction, surrounded in Epworth by social unrest, Dissenters from the established church, and political disturbances, supplied power for development. His father's literary and ecclesiastical ambitions for his sons contributed a drive to the maternal resources and social turmoil to create something new in England. John's rural boyhood years ended at eleven years of age when he was sent to London to Charterhouse School. London and Oxford would lend some sophistication to this son of rustic Lincolnshire.

2. Oxford (1720–1735)

Oxford was in a certain sense the birthplace of Methodism, for the leaders of the movement were first called Methodists there. But John's time at the university was preceded by some formative years at Charterhouse preparatory school in London.

The few letters that still exist between John Wesley and his family provide scant details of his scholarship at Charterhouse school in London (1714–1720). Charterhouse, only a few blocks from the site of his later Foundry Chapel and his burial site, was on the grounds of the former Carthusian monastery. Its name resulted from Anglicizing the French name of the order. As a scholarship student, John was with the sons of other clergy, lawyers, and the shadow elite educated to serve the landowners who ruled England. Charterhouse provided him with Greek, Latin, and classical learning preparatory for the place his achievements there won for him at Christ Church College, Oxford. Christianity and classical culture still lived in an easy synthesis in the Charterhouse curriculum, as they did at the other outstanding schools of Winchester and Eton.

Later in his life, John would regard his Charterhouse years as a time of religious laxness. It is a matter of perspective. His regular prayer, chapel attendance, and religious study probably prevented his peers from regarding it as lax. But Charterhouse was not so much of the Church of England as Oxford.

Oxford University always remained in Wesley's mind as one of the most beautiful places in England. Early in the eighteenth century before it became industrialized, Oxford graced the banks of the Thames River with its gleaming towers. It was fundamentally a college town with the architecture of the ancient university dominating the skyline of chapel towers and oak trees. Just before John's coming up to the university, it had enjoyed a renaissance in great architecture.

The age of Christopher Wren had glorified Oxford architecture, and the young Wesley from the plain north country could have been awed by the new, graceful spires of All Souls College, the rebuilt Queen's College, the Trinity College garden triangle and chapel, and Sheldonian Theatre. At John Wesley's college, Christ Church, the new library and Tom Tower from the 1680s signaled the power of the college, with its cathedral and bishop of Oxford. Christ Church was the largest, richest, and most politically powerful of the colleges. Its meadows flowing from the college wall to the river Thames provided the best walks in the town.

Oxford's graceful rural and park walks cast serenity among its privileged students in their walled and tower-topped colleges. From the protected colleges they would sally out in the eighteenth century to conquer more of the world than any previous people. They all read their Roman classics in Latin, and many of them dreamed of their role in the new empire. Wesley, too, could dream of the whole world in both Latin and Greek. Did not the thirteen heads of the Roman emperors look down on him whenever he left the Bodleian Library to go for his walks in the gardens of Trinity College? On the foundation of Greek and Latin classics, he would build pillars from the materials furnished by Christ Church College: patristics, reformation studies, science, rationalism, logic, music, and rhetoric. Passion for primitive Christianity developed there even if its particular evangelical experience awaited German imports and a London event. As his father had, he, too, became involved in a religious society in Oxford that combined social service with strong religious commitment. He arrived as a seventeen-year-old in 1720, and he remained there with a two-year leave until sailing for Georgia in 1735.

Like Cambridge University, Oxford of the eighteenth century was a seminary of the Church of England. Provision was made for the education of the laity as well, but a religious-academic commitment dominated. Three college chapels were built in the early part of the century: Hertford in 1716, Queen's in 1719, and Pembroke in 1732. All of the colleges required some chapel attendance, though actual attendance varied considerably. The instruction in divinity was provided by the colleges during Wesley's time in residence. Similarly, lectures in divinity and New Testament were required.[1]

It was to this Oxford that John and Charles followed Samuel Wesley. Charterhouse had guaranteed places at Oxford, but the efforts of the Wesley family were also instrumental in their going there. The parents sacrificed to find a few pounds for John's support, but equally important was Samuel's political role in pulling strings back in Lincolnshire to win his sons places at the university, as were the money and influence of Susanna's family. When John went up to Oxford, enrollment was down due to the severe recession of 1720. Charles would follow his brothers to Oxford and, fatefully for John and the world, initiate the group to become the Holy Club or the first Methodist society.

The monastic and clerical state of Oxford in the eighteenth century must be recognized to understand the ethos out of which Wesley's religious movement would come. None of the faculty or students was allowed to marry. Once elected to a fellowship, a faculty position, a don or professor could teach or not while receiving a stipend from the college. Many of the college fellows hung around the colleges until they could receive a "living" or a church call to a parish, at which time they could surrender their college stipend or fellowship and marry. Although the university was to continue its celibacy statutes and rules requiring all faculty to be Church of England members subscribing to the Rules of Religion into the twentieth century, some secularist tendencies were discernible in the eighteenth century.

Oxford University supported both the king and the church, and both king and church required the university's loyalty. Wesley's commitment to both, formulated in the home, was reinforced by the university from 1720 to 1735, and its rules of celibacy were applicable to him until his marriage in 1751 when he finally surrendered his stipend from Lincoln College. The whole university did not follow Wesley's loyalty, however; there was dissent from both the established church and the reigning monarch.

Forces of anticlericalism, rationalism, and secularism were developing in Europe. Though deism was largely outside the university, Matthew Tindal of All Souls had his work burned by Parliament in 1710. He did not have many followers in his time within the university. Gradually, deism began to disturb the moderation of Oxford's orthodoxy. A suicide attributed to questions raised by skepticism led to a prosecution of a Trinity College man by the bishop of Oxford. The prosecuted fled the country. Another expulsion from Trinity and two from Magdalen indicated the growing seriousness of theological dissent. John's elder brother was one of those to attack the Trinity College deists. The threat from deism would lead to many sermons against its opponents at St. Mary's, the official university church. Charles Wesley reacted against what he regarded as halfway measures to combat deism.[2] In part, the early fervor of the Holy Club was a reaction against the teaching of the radical transcendence of the Creator and the priority of reason over revelation in the religion of the deists. So also were the Wesley brothers' passion for real Christianity and the totally orthodox development of their early seriousness.

V. H. H. Green saw the Wesleyan movement as a response to the eighteenth-century crisis in England's religion. Deism and skepticism reduced the hold of the church on the learned mind. The monument to John Locke in Christ Church Cathedral testifies to the influence of his thought and not to his unitarianism. The defense mounted by Anglican rationalists did not protect the heart of the faith. Dean Swift estimated only one in a hundred of the learned people in the country took theology seriously. Daniel Defoe thought there had never been such opposition to Christianity since its founding. To the observation that Swift saw the gentry giving up the faith must be added that the masses were largely outside the active church life. Joseph Butler and George Berkeley made learned responses to the skepticism, and Butler's arguments for the faith's probability have stood well over the years since the eighteenth century. Few read their works or the skeptical writers of the Enlightenment, but the drift away from the church continued. Green's point is that while John Wesley did not make a credible intellectual response to the critics, he made a practical response, an evangelical and quite orthodox response to the human emotions rather than to reason. The authority for Christianity would, with him, rest on the experience of faith, according to Green.[3] Wesley continued to read philosophy, and he was passionately interested in science. He never was an eighteenth-century philosophical skeptic, but he did not desert reason; he remained an Enlightenment thinker. Wesley's great audience, though, was not the philosophers, but the poor; and his arguments to them were not the usual fare of Oxford discourse.

But religious doubts were less a threat to the Oxford of Wesley's day than political heresies. Oxford, like Wesley's family, was divided in its loyalty to the Stuart claimants and the Hanoverian dynasty for the monarchy of England. The university had alternatively celebrated and struggled with the Stuarts, but its loyalty to the Hanoverian house of Kings George I through III could not be assumed. Some of the entries in John Wesley's unpublished diaries from his Oxford years suggest that his mind was unsettled also regarding the claims of the Stuarts (the Jacobite party) to the Crown.

Although Oxford's elections to Parliament were often watched with interest, its direct political contributions were muted by distance from the Hanoverian monarchy, which dominated the eighteenth century. Its attraction to the Jacobite cause, which continued to renew itself until the Battle of Culloden (1746), reflected its earlier loyalty to the Stuarts and particularly Charles II, who had resided in Oxford in the seventeenth century. Although Wesley outgrew the Jacobitism of his mother and of Oxford colleges, his loyalty to monarchy and Anglicanism marked him as an Oxford man.

Riots occurred in 1715–1716 protesting the Hanoverian succession. Troops were sent to Oxford to assure order. Gradually, moderates supporting the government gained control. Yet much of the leadership of the university was more interested in church questions and independence than support of the government. Government favors to the university declined. Projects to bind the university closer to the government did not accomplish much. Lincoln College remained Tory. A piece of doggerel that John Wesley copied out in his first diary reflects Oxford's loss of favor with the government.

> King George, observing with judicious eyes
> The state of both his universities
> To Oxford sent a troop of horse; and why?
> That learned body wanted loyalty.
> To Cambridge books he sent as well discerning
> How much that loyal body wanted learning.[4]

Many of Oxford's critics were among its political enemies. Criticism of the university by Whigs may be regarded as partially political critique of the Tory domination of the university. But the university did indeed have its failings. Some lessening of the centrality of Aristotle and formal logic was needed. The system of preferment did little to encourage original scholarship, and other than some contributions in Hebrew, there was not much excitement in theological studies. The relationship of university lectureships to college studies was unclear; thus, the lectureships were neglected. The study of science had leaped forward in the seventeenth century, but lagged in the eighteenth. Against this background, the desire of Wesley, his brother, and three friends to supplement their academic preparation with their own reading group of the classics may understandably be seen as a critique of their assigned requirements.

Edward Gibbon's critique of Oxford as a waste of time is often quoted as a summary of its academic life in this period. One of Wesley's students taught him classics. Although Gibbon was young and unhappy during his short residence at Oxford, his views have cast a long shadow over the university's reputation at the time. Adam Smith's note in his influential *Wealth of Nations* (1776) that Oxford professors were not even pretending to teach has also defined Oxford's reputation. Even the university's publications in the twentieth century regarded the eighteenth century as a low point in Oxford's academic reputation. Felix Markham wrote of this period: "The average Fellow was a gentleman of leisure waiting for a living. Few Fellows were interested in teaching or even competent to do it."[5]

Of course, Dr. Samuel Johnson praised the instruction he received at Oxford. The rigors of William Halley in science, William Blackstone in law, and John Wesley in divinity represent another side of the issue. Serious study was possible even if the gentlemen students neglected it for their gambling and sporting lives. Samuel Johnson, at Pembroke College across the street from Wesley's college of Christ Church, served as a servant while studying. He said of his role as a "servitor": "The difference, Sir, between us Servitors and Gentlemen Commoners is this, that we are men of wit and not fortune, and they are men of fortune and no wit."[6]

As secular critics arose, they attacked Oxford, which, along with Cambridge, prepared Anglican clergy for their religious-political roles in England. Furthermore, Oxford's self-understood role in the eighteenth century was to protect and pass on to its students the rich traditions of the Anglican Church and the politics of the establishment. English stability in the eighteenth century owes a good deal to Oxford's continuing establishment role.[7]

There were needed attempts at academic reform in the eighteenth century, but they did not prevail. Oxford's promises of science from the seventeenth century went unfulfilled, and talent migrated to the Scottish universities and the dissenting academies. And how could they have come to anything when lectures were often not given, dons looked on their positions as property rather than assigned responsibilities, and examinations were lax? The academic discipline paralleled the torpor of the ecclesiastical life to which Oxford contributed access but insufficient learning. The British oligarchy, which controlled government, church, and university in the eighteenth century, did not feel the need to reform the system at that time, no doubt because the system preserved their own positions quite nicely! Reforms in politics and university would come only in the nineteenth century.

It was into this context that Wesley arrived at Oxford, and it was here that his attempts to reform religion and morals for church and nation began.

Christ Church College

The important years of Wesley's college education are known to us only by his letters because he had not yet taken up diary writing. John's letters home reflected health concerns: a smallpox threat, an unusual bloody nose, and a fascination with George Cheyne's study *Essay of Health and Long Life,* which much later John would abridge and publish. Cheyne's influence on John's health and study of it continued throughout John's life. John's letters expressed no anxiety over academic affairs, but he frequently mentioned money and debt concerns, and his parents responded as they were able.

Miscellaneous other themes arose in John's correspondence. The closeness of his relationship to Samuel, his elder brother, is shown by his ability to share some of his own poetry reflecting interest in a woman. A recurrent interest in the supernatural is shown in the correspondence with his family; while he was at Charterhouse they had informed him of the haunting of the rectory by the apparitions of Old Jeffrey. In turn, he recounted stories of experiences of Oxford men and his own intention to visit a haunted house.

As John graduated and approached the question of ordination, letters from Samuel cautioned delay. Susanna encouraged John to proceed and urged him to be certain of his own conviction of salvation. She also reminded John how she and Samuel were inclined to disagree on many matters. Samuel came around to Susanna's position, and in 1725, John was ordained deacon by the bishop of Oxford. Samuel also urged John not to rely very much on biblical commentaries but to take up the work of comparing biblical texts in Latin, Hebrew, and Greek to advance his understanding.

Architecturally, the ecclesial world John inhabited as a preacher in Oxfordshire was already ancient in his day, with portions of church buildings dating to Norman and Saxon times. When he left Oxford on foot on a Sunday morning to preach, he crossed the Thames just outside the meadows of his former college, Christ Church, with its cathedral and looming Tom Tower. In three miles he passed through Stanton Harcourt where St. Matthew's Church was filled with funerary monuments and tombs of the ancestors of the Harcourt family. The Harcourts lived in the fine Cotswold stone manor house next to the church. He admired the stone tower on their private chapel. A quarter of a century later as a guest of the family, Alexander Pope translated Horace working in the tower, so it became known as Pope's Tower. The footpath continued through the fields for two miles to the churchyard of St. James the Greater. The yard was filled with simple tombstones of the farmers and wood merchants of the region, dating back hundreds of years. Within fifty miles were monuments, pillars, and ancient forts that were abandoned long before the Romans had come. To the south of South Leigh and Stanton Harcourt was the vale of the White Horse dominated by the three-thousand-year-old etching in the green hill of a white chalk running horse. The three-hundred-fifty-meter landmark was maintained and freed of overgrowth once a year by the people of the valley. Many of the nearby rings of stone

Wesley would attribute to Druid worship. He regularly visited the ancient monuments and entered his reflections on long ago people in his diaries and journals. The monuments, like the present great manors and chapels of the Harcourts and others, reminded him of the fleetingness of life.

Wesley's path continued among the gravestones into the church. There in the archway leading to the chancel one can see the powerful, ancient mural (restored in 1933) of the general resurrection painted in the plaster. From every grave a figure is rising as St. Michael is blowing the horn of judgment. The mural divides at the center of the arch. To the left, Satan surrounds the damned and leads them into the serpentlike beast whose mouth is filled with the gnashing teeth of eternal punishment. On the right, Jesus Christ is receiving the saved and guiding them to eternal glory. As Wesley climbed the steps of the simple pulpit, he was aware of the worshipers' eyes on him, and could they see the final judgment? His preaching for the next sixty-five years was in the context of death and judgment, and is peppered with images of heaven and hell with eternal fire and gnashing teeth. On this day in 1727, the sermon was on one of his constant themes: the righteousness of humanity, the Sermon on the Mount, and the love of God. The "gnashing of teeth" text was mentioned in 1790 in a sermon he thought to be the last he would write. Was the mural from St. James in South Leigh still in his mind, or had he drawn his image from another painting as he said those terrible words? "Cast them into outer darkness, there shall be weeping and gnashing of teeth."

After graduation, Wesley pursued study for his master's degree with a thesis on the reasoning powers of animals. A record of his studies in 1727 shortly before taking his degree indicates the breadth of his work.

Monday and Tuesday: Roman and Greek History
Wednesday: Logic and Ethics
Thursday: Hebrew and Arabic
Friday: Metaphysics and Natural Philosophy
Saturday: Poetry and Composition
Sunday: Divinity

Love in the Cotswolds

At Oxford, John had an active social life. He was often in the company of male student friends at the coffee houses, on walks, in sports, and in conversation in college. Occasional trips to London to plays grew more frequent after Charles arrived and developed his own liaisons with the players. As John finished his undergraduate degree, his attention turned toward the Cotswold hills and in particular to the Kirkham family, whose son became a member of Wesley's circle after his return in 1729 from Wroot. Robert's sister, Sally, was to exert a significant pull on John's emotions, but make even more of a contribution to his spiritual life. Their relationship led to conversations and correspondence about religious discipline. John's correspondence with his parents led them to express their views on perfection.

John, as a very young boy, was known for saying he would never marry. He was confirmed that he never could find as good a woman as his father had. He may have met such a woman in Sally Kirkham, whom he encountered in 1725 as he was finishing his studies for ordination. A sister of one of the original members of the Holy Club, she was a daughter of the Stanton rectory in the beautiful Cotswold hills. Sally was bright and vivacious. The circle of friends into which Wesley was drawn loved music, art, dancing, and plays. The general conversation was about culture. Sally, however, had a religious side to her nature, and she probably introduced John to the writing of Thomas à Kempis, which they read and discussed in translation. She had a ready theological wit, and Wesley was neither the first nor the last young theologian to be mentally seduced by the theological banter of the opposite gender. Theological conversation about the love of God encouraged other expressions of love. While discussing Thomas with Sally, John wrote his mother about the theologian. Susanna responded rather disdainfully about his lack of depth. Sally and John, however, found Thomas's writings exciting.

At length John resolved to be ordained, and now supported by both parents in that decision, he had written Susanna about Thomas à Kempis. He had admired the rigor of his version of Christian life, but had resisted Thomas's affirmation of the need for a Christian to be miserable in this life, for had not Solomon promised happiness and peace as flowing from religion? Susanna thought John's interpretation correct. She took the occasion to explain at length about the need to subordinate the inferior to the superior as the way to happiness. Particularly the animal nature of humanity needed to be subordinated to the rational. All is to be rationally subject to the superior through law until it culminates in the grace of Christ that reconciles nature to the omnipotent goodness and rule of God. In divine grace, one would never knowingly offend God, "but still press after greater degrees of Christian perfection,"[8] thereby through virtue, the pleasantness and peace promised are found. His father reinforced this rigorous moral sense when he, while assisting John in securing his ordination, wrote to him: "Love to God, and love to our neighbor, which often in scripture is called charity, is, or ought to be, the principle and rule of all our thoughts, words, and actions, with regard to either. And whatever we do for God or man that flows not from that principle, and is not squared by this rule, is wrong, as wanting a good foundation and a right conduct."[9]

During this time, John's sister Emily was his confidante in the relationship with Sally or Varanese (the name she assumed for their correspondence; Wesley was Cyrus). Emily had lost her lover when the Epworth family broke the engagement. She advised John against long engagements and urged him to get his worldly affairs in order before following love. The romantic relationship between Sally and John also encouraged their dreaming about perfection. A dialogue ensued between them concerning Jeremy Taylor's *Rule and Exercises of Holy Living*, which reinforced in John the desire to journal and to seek to regulate his life toward God by keeping a record. So from 1725 until his death (there are some intermissions and the actual diaries for many years are missing), he kept his diary that would become a basis for his published *Journal*. The diaries are reticent about personal feelings, and their message is hidden in code. The diaries from 1725 to 1735 are not published yet, but Richard Heitzenrater of Duke University is working on a transcript of them. Nehemiah Curnock furnished a summary of some of the first of the nonpublished diaries,[10] and V. H. H. Green presented his paraphrase of their contents in his outstanding *Young Mr. Wesley*.[11]

Wesley rode to Stanton on 20 April 1725, contemplating his actions with Sally. He learned that day that she would marry the schoolmaster, Jack Chapon. The rest of 1725 would drag on, with John attending and dancing at her wedding, and proceeding with ordination studies and his master's degree paper. Soon after that, he withdrew to serve with his father at Epworth and Wroot. Much later his sister Emily wrote, suggesting that if he had not lost the love of Sally, he might never have sought love so desperately in the Holy Club, in Georgia, and among the Moravians. One interpreter gives Chapon credit for being a necessary tool in the unleashing of Wesley's religious revival.[12]

In 1728, John was ordained a priest in the Church of England by Dr. John Potter, bishop of Oxford. John served as curate at Wroot during 1729. He also assisted in preparing his father's massive work, *Job*, and sometimes wrote sermons for him. He read widely, joined a short archaeological expedition, hunted, and hiked. A local girl, Kitty Hargreaves, attracted his attention, and his physical intimacies with her advanced beyond the idealistic, romantic conversation of his relationship with Sally. In his diary he recorded his resolve not to touch a woman's breast again.

Lincoln College called Wesley back from his rural service at Epworth. While there, he had defended his passionate sister Hetty from Samuel's dismissal of her because of a miscarried elopement. John and Samuel were alienated by the sermon on the love of God and the necessity of forgiveness, until Charles's intervention and John's apology led to a reconciliation. From Oxford, though, he found his way back to the charming Cotswolds. Now the widowed Mrs. Pendarves warmed his affections. Mrs. Pendarves (pen name Aspasia) played with John's affections, but she was seeking larger quarry (physically and socially). The name "Aspasia" is derived from the most famous hetaera or "kept woman" of fifth-century Athens who lived with Pericles of political fame. He noticed the similarities of his feelings for Aspasia that he had enjoyed formally for Varanese. He feared he might be again headed for disaster, but he imagined he was healing his wounds rather than opening new ones. Little did Wesley understand how casually she took his affections and his letters. He waited desperately to hear from her while she was on a visit to Ireland. There she was charmed by Dean Swift and then Dr. Patrick Delaney, who would later marry her, giving her the social position through which she became important at court and a friend to royalty. George Handel, after visiting her home in the Cotswolds, remained a lifelong friend, and Edmund Burke regarded her as one of the outstanding women of her day. When she returned to England and tried to resume the correspondence and relationship with Wesley, John refused. His correspondence with his first love, dear Varanese, would linger for ten years, however. Sally Kirkham and Mary Granville (Mrs. Pendarves) added standards to those set by Susanna Wesley that would be impossible for any of John's later loves to fulfill.

Lincoln College (1729–1735)

Samuel had pressed the case for John's fellowship at Lincoln College. The high churchmanship and Tory politics helped in their pursuit of the lectureship reserved usually for men from Lincolnshire. John's seriousness and rigidity were negatives in his consideration for membership in the college that required election by the other fellows. Both John and Samuel persisted in their academic politics, and John's genuine good humor contributed to overcoming early objections. His election took place in 1726, but in 1729 the responsibilities of the college called him away from assisting his father at Wroot. From 1729 to 1735, he served as a tutor at Lincoln. He provided the lectures in the Greek New Testament, served as the college moderator in philosophy, and taught logic. At first, he inherited eight to ten students from a retiring professor, but by the time he left for Georgia, his own students had dwindled to four. He is praised for meeting his students every day, but the fact that his general strictness is recorded may be an indication that this practice of daily sessions with students was a little too much for eighteenth-century Oxford. In a letter to his mother, Wesley adopted a stoic attitude about his declining number of students; he affirmed he had enough, but if he had none, he would seek a church to serve.

Wesley attracted a few students from Lincolnshire. Two of his young followers, John Whitelamb and Westley Hall, came at his encouragement, though they later would break with him. While serving Lincoln, John edited three books: *A Collection of Forms of Prayer for Every Day in the Week* (1733), *A Treatise on Christian Prudence* (extracts from John Norris, 1734), and a translation of Thomas à Kempis's *Imitatio Christi* titled *The Christian Pattern* (1735).[13]

As a tutor in the college, he assigned works in theology and classical works from non-Christian authors who inspired the Enlightenment. From the classics, he taught Cicero's *De Natura Decorum*, Horace's poetry, satires by Juvenal, plays from Terence, and Virgil's *Aeneid*. David Hume took these same titles, which Wesley had taught, with him on his pilgrimage to Paris. One of John's students later taught Edward Gibbon at Magdalen College. The young Gibbon was so disappointed in the instruction that he launched his tirade against Oxford. On the theological side, representative works were John Ellis's *Defense of the Thirty-nine Articles,* Charles Wheatley's *The Church of England: Man's Companion,* and Edward Welchman's *Articuli XXXIX Ecclesiae Anglicanae.* The Christians studied philosophy and used it to express their biblical faith. By contrast, the nonbelieving Enlightenment men took the classics as foundational and regarded biblical faith as superstition. Yet they both relied upon the revival of ancient ideas. Wesley identified with ancient sources and with Christ. Enlightenment thinkers identified with Cicero and used the Platonic texts.

Beyond his hardworking academic schedule, John spent a lot of time reading widely in plays and attending them in London as he could. He knew Shakespeare well and often quoted him from memory. The Wesley brothers' love for the theater threatened their celibate commitments. Charles was involved in a liaison with a London actress, and John admitted to narrowly escaping from a relationship. At the same time, John was regularly preaching in the nearby villages, including his former Cotswold preaching places. Playing tennis, walking, playing cards, dancing, and making trips to the horse races also enlivened his days.

The Holy Club

While John was serving at Wroot and assisting his father at Epworth, Charles deepened his religious life at Christ Church

College. He joined with an Irishman, William Morgan, in founding a religious-study group. When John returned to Oxford in 1729 to take up his tutorial duties at Lincoln College, he assumed the leadership of the small group. The first young men referred to their group as "Our Society." Under John's leadership, they studied both classics and religious texts and began to mold their group discipline under guidelines they regarded as characteristic of primitive Christianity. They practiced weekly observation of Holy Communion, regular prayer life, scriptural study, and disciplined study. In John's case, the discipline extended to accounting for his entire day in a diary and reflecting on his prayer life and spiritual state at regular intervals. Thirty years after the fact, John gave credit to the book *The Country Parson's Advice to His Parishioners* for influencing the club. The book, published first in 1680, reflected aspects of the seventeenth-century London religious societies that had formed within the Church of England for the increase of religious discipline, the study of scriptural religion, and the pursuit of holiness. The rules followed by these earlier societies corresponded closely to the rules adopted by the Holy Club for their community even to the engaging in social service. Samuel Wesley, the boys' father, had participated in the societies and while at Oxford had carried out social ministry to the poor. He had left a record of a sermon to one of the societies and a letter concerning them among his papers. On one of his visits to Oxford, he wrote glowingly to Susanna of his boys' participation in the society. So, their group, though regarded as eccentric during their time at Oxford, had its predecessors within the Church of England.

Others gradually associated with the group. Young faculty members were central to the group, but it included students, especially John's students, who left the fellowship upon graduation. The group reached out from Lincoln College through Charles to others at Christ Church and to another cell at Merton College.

William Morgan took the initiative in leading the group into social service. He started the visitations to prisoners at the two Oxford prisons, Castle and Bocardo. Soon he drew John and Charles into the visits. Their personal involvement with the prisoners expanded to leading Bible study, study of catechism, preaching, and fund-raising for the assistance of the prisoners. They literally freed some who were imprisoned for debt by paying their debts. From the prisons, they expanded their concerns to the poor and eventually to founding a school for children of the poor. They solicited funds from persons with means, including Sir John Phillips, but they also disciplined their own consumption and budget to provide monies for their social work. Morgan's work here was not unique; several organizations in the Church of England sponsored similar social work, including prison visitation and educational projects for prisoners. Samuel Wesley Sr. had engaged in similar projects while he was a student at Oxford. The uniqueness rested in the combination of rigorous social work and intense observances of the disciplines of the religious life on an organized plan. Morgan's social service leadership kept the group from turning inward toward a morbid, religious self-centeredness. But it also multiplied the religious intensity to the point that it first aroused curiosity and then opposition by fellow members of the Church of England in residence at Oxford.

The little group's rigor was perceived as critical of the religious laxness that characterized some of the university. The derisive names used by university critics, the "Holy Club" and "Methodists," came from an earlier approach to medicine by a group of physicians. The Wesley brothers persisted with the written support from both parents. At their father's suggestion, they obtained permission for their work from Bishop Potter of Oxford, who applauded their efforts. Yet the group grew only fitfully. Students graduated and moved out to parishes, some left because of the rigor of the discipline, some simply became distracted, and some fell away because of the growing opposition to the group. John could admit to his father his own discouragement with the group's "ill success." Nonetheless, here were the beginnings of Methodist patterns of religious seriousness, self-examination, and social service.

As opposition grew to the five—John and Charles Wesley, William Morgan, Robert Kirkham (Sally's brother), and John Boyce (son of the mayor of Oxford [1727–1728])—they agreed upon a list of questions for their tormentors. The twenty-two questions were different ways of asking: May we not as Christians serve those who suffer and do all the good we can? Now that they were being taunted as the "Holy Club," the "Godly Club," the "Enthusiasts," and the "Reforming Club," Wesley sought out and received support from Joseph Hoole, the vicar of Haxey; Dr. Potter, the bishop of Oxford; the prison officials; and his father.

The Morgan Case

The group's self-confidence was shaken when young Morgan, who had become sick while serving a church at Holt, died upon his return to his father's home in Dublin. Suspicions against the group deepened, and public criticism grew. Wesley felt the need to defend the group's practices to Richard Morgan, William's father. John's lengthy letter to Richard Morgan is one of the better sources for grasping Wesley's sense of the Holy Club.

John spelled out how influential William (or Will) Morgan had been as a founder of the group and as the originator of its social service. He described their secular and religious studies, and he mentioned their self-discipline in a search for religious patterns fit for the university.

He disabused Mr. Morgan of the notion that Methodist fasting had contributed to young Morgan's death. He said that Morgan had not fasted for months and that the observance of fasting had become deeper since John Clayton joined the group, but that practice followed William's departure for service in Holt. Wesley concluded his letter by agreeing to abandon any disciplines found contrary to law or Scripture, but not to take account that others were now calling them "Methodists" and "Supererogation Men."

Samuel Wesley, John's elder brother, then serving at Westminster School, prepared a poem on William Morgan's death that John published in the *Journal*. Samuel, much appreciated for his poetry, published the elegy in *Poems on Several Occasions*. The poem celebrated Morgan's young life spent in service and preaching to the poor. It honored his steadfast church loyalty and his dedication to good works while capturing the pathos of young death. A few verses demonstrate Morgan's spirit that animated the Wesley group and sum up much of the group's ethic at the time:

> Whose zeal for other men's salvation shown,
> Beyond the reach of Hell secur'd his own.
> Glad'ning, the poor, where'er his steps he turn'd,

Where pin'd the orphan, or the widow mourn'd;
Where prisoners sigh'd beneath guilt's horrid stain,
The worst confinement, and the heaviest chain.
Where death's sad shade th' uninstructed sight
Veil'd with thick darkness in the land of light.
Our Saviour thus fulfill'd his great design.
(If human we may liken to divine)
Heal'd each disease that bodies frail endure,
And preach'd th' unhop'd for gospel to the poor.[14]

Richard Morgan's response indicated his concerns about the reports he had heard of the group.[15] He vindicated the Wesleys, however. He was already a subscriber to Samuel's publication *Job*, and he promised to do whatever he could for them in Ireland.

As Richard Morgan Sr. prepared to send his other son, Richard Jr., into the care of the Wesleys, he wrote John describing for the first time Will's madness and attempts at self-destruction. He feared that the extreme practice of religion might have contributed to it. John's response was that religion had been good for William and that the madness was not related to his religion at all, despite Will's claims that extreme religion had contributed to his downfall. John assured Mr. Morgan that his younger son would not be an appropriate candidate for the Methodist group, who were advanced in their practice. John insisted repeatedly in letters to Mr. Morgan that God required not moderation but wholehearted devotion and service. Even after one reads Wesley's defense, the father's intuitions of the danger of religious extremism to his adolescent son seem appropriate.

Young Richard arrived at Lincoln College with a loaned greyhound and his luggage. John arranged for the return of the hound, and Morgan Sr.'s letter to his namesake did not spare him severe criticism. Young Richard wrote to his father, but perhaps he never sent the letter (which, however, John did read) requesting to leave John's tutoring. John at the time had only three other pupils, and Richard wanted to transfer to another tutor in the college. Richard particularly did not want to be seen as a member of Wesley's group. John corresponded with Morgan Sr. defensively and continued tutoring Richard. After John left for Georgia, Richard joined and became a leader of the Oxford Methodists, and he even considered joining them in Georgia. He ended up practicing law in

Dublin and inheriting his father's bequest. Many years later, John called upon him in Ireland. The lengthy, argumentative correspondence among the three shows the opposition of the Lincoln rector to John's methods as well as John's willingness to challenge bishops and others who preferred to defend a rather torpid approach to religion. The criticism of the Wesleys and their evolving group was severe. The Morgan case could have destroyed the movement at its center, but John's persuasiveness won over both the father and the brother.

Oxford Departure

Shortly before his death, Samuel pleaded with John to take up the ministry at Epworth. John considered it and even took some preliminary steps toward securing the appointment. Brother Samuel insisted John take it up. Partially both Samuels wanted to guarantee Susanna's continuing to live at Epworth. John rejected the arguments of both, assuring his father he could serve others and his own soul best by remaining at Oxford. Shortly thereafter, Samuel Sr. died, and the two younger Wesley boys accompanied Oglethorpe to Georgia. John also interpreted that decision as a mission to others and to save his own soul. A few years later, John assumed the support of his mother, assisted Charles, and aided his sisters, too. The financial means for this support came from a mission that in 1735 none of them could yet imagine.

The mission to Georgia effectively concluded John's relationship with the university. He returned over the course of a few years to preach occasionally, and his fellowship stipend continued until his marriage in 1751. John had tried to live as an academic and as the leader of an academic-religious society. Neither role was successful; both were preparatory. His frustrations with Oxford were most powerfully expressed in his sermon of 1744 at St. Mary's University Church. St. Mary's, the oldest building of the university, dominated the center of High Street. The university sermons were Christian academic rituals with university officials presiding, students and faculty present in their gowns, and had minimal liturgy, prayers, and acts of worship. Often the sermons were difficult to distinguish from religious lectures.

John's final university sermon in 1744 separated him from any further influence on the Anglican university, and alienated him even more than his attempts at reform in the Holy Club had achieved. The sermon was considered so offensive that after 1744, the university found a substitute for his preaching when his turn as a member of the Oxford University clergy came around. This sermon, "Scriptural Christianity," consisted of four parts. It was the last part, the applied Christianity, to which Wesley's fellow academics objected. The first part spoke of the awakening of Christian life in individuals, the second of the faith being communicated from one person to another. The third part imagined the filling of the world with Christianity and the realization of peace internally and externally. Nations would be converted to peace and the eschatological promises of peace fulfilled. In this vision, righteousness and peace are united, and the earth flourishes under peace. There are none who lack necessities, for everyone loves the neighbor and follows the Golden Rule. In the hearts of the inhabitants of the earth can be found only God and love. Then Wesley follows this peaceful vision of the culmination of Christian faith by announcing that he will "close the whole with a plain, practical application."[16]

In this fourth part, John asks where a Christian country can be found and concludes, "We have never yet seen a Christian country upon earth."[17] Furthermore, he denies that Oxford is a Christian city or that the scriptural religion can be found there. He asks whether those teaching the young are doing so with hearts full of God, for if they teach without love, all philosophy and learning fail. After inquiring about their Christian motivation, he asks whether they labor earnestly and with all their might.

Wesley recognizes that not all in the university will be clergy, but insists that all are to be Christians. So he pushes:

> Do ye, brethren, abound in the fruits of the Spirit, in lowliness of mind, in self-denial... in patience, meekness, sobriety, temperance, and in unwearied, restless endeavours to do good in every kind unto all men...? Is this the general character of Fellows of Colleges? I fear it is not. Rather, have not pride and haughtiness of spirit, impatience and peevishness, sloth and indolence, gluttony and sensuality, and even a proverbial uselessness been objected to us?[18]

Then he follows with sharper questions for those called to minister in holy things. He asks for ministers to be directed in zeal by love, so that all words become "sweetness, lowliness, and meekness of wisdom."[19]

Wesley relentlessly raises questions about the waste of time, drunkenness, gambling, diligence, obedience, Sabbath keeping, honoring one's vows, and so on, suggesting that the members of the university trifle with God, and he concludes that Oxford is not a Christian city. If the restoration of scriptural Christianity is not a possible response to the few who advocate it, what will happen? Shall Oxford fall to famine, to pestilence, or to the French, who were threatening invasion in 1744? he asks. With the failure of human help, he prays for the Lord to save, noting that with God all things are possible.

His critique of the university, which understood itself as a church-school in the mid–eighteenth century, was rebuked immediately. The vice-chancellor of the university requested his sermon notes before he, brother Charles, and two others left St. Mary's Church, shunned by others. Benjamin Kennicot, later a distinguished Old Testament scholar, on hearing the sermon as an undergraduate, thought that it would have been praised except for the zeal and use of critical satire in the conclusion of the sermon.[20] But Wesley had indicated in the second part that early churchmen who criticized unrighteousness and worldliness were castigated. The sermon is a whole, and it builds toward the critique. He was turning toward his vocation as an evangelist, and the university's vocation was not evangelical.

William Blackstone, later an authority on English law, heard the sermon and understood that Wesley was to be punished by the university by neglect.[21] Blackstone clearly regarded Wesley's charges of "pride, gluttony, avarice, luxury, sensuality, drunkenness," and uselessness to be overdrawn. Blackstone presented Wesley's critique in more ringing charges than Wesley had, but his tone of offense was clear. The sermon, with its list of particulars, and even Blackstone's refusal to deny that Wesley's charges were characteristic of the university, reveal how far Wesley's piety and discipline and the ministry of the Holy Club were from the general life of the university. His hopes to reform the university and the expected rejection of his hopes were of a piece with the reforming efforts of the Holy Club. His hopes were expressed in his asking if the students of ministry were spending every effort to realize the kingdom of God upon earth. They also corresponded to his entry in the Minutes to the question regarding God's design in raising up preachers called Methodists, to which the answer was: "To reform the nation and, in particular the church, to spread scriptural holiness over the land."[22]

England in the mid–eighteenth century was a confessional state in which Anglicanism was established and enforced by law and accepted by the majority,[23] and Oxford was a university of that Anglican establishment. Wesley had to call it to reform, but in his worldly wisdom, he understood it would not reform itself.

Wesley's critique of Oxford delivered in 1744 reflected the disappointments he felt already in 1735. In fact, after 1735, Oxford would never again be his primary place of residence. Some of his efforts in Oxford in prison visitation, education, and aid to the poor were also ministries of other societies in the Church of England. The ministry he would take up in Georgia of attempting a mission to the Native Americans was also the work of Church of England missionary societies. The uniqueness of the Holy Club resided in its extremism. It attempted to guide every hour in critical service to God in terms perceived as reflecting primitive or radical Christianity. It was a thorough, passionate form of inner-worldly asceticism expressed in Oxford against Oxford hedonism and lukewarm piety.

The society could not grow because its members were fated to leave Oxford to assume the leadership of parish churches upon graduation. At most, it had two generations of students; it declined with Wesley's mission to Georgia. Beyond the Wesleys, its only other prominent member was George Whitefield. Whitefield introduced Wesley, after the mission to Georgia, to evangelical preaching. From the preaching, Wesley organized transformed societies composed of resident laypeople. They continued, in a moderated manner, some of Wesley's learnings from the Methodist society of his Oxford years. Before that could happen, Wesley had to test his relatively extreme religion on the frontier of Georgia. He had not been particularly successful at Oxford in his teaching, in his organization, in his love life, or in his inner religious life. All four were to be tested again in Georgia. He approached his new mission well prepared in academic religion and classics. Even allied with a reforming governor, Oglethorpe, who was well disposed toward the Wesley family, a less naive Englishman might have doubted the responsiveness of the colony and its native neighbors to his skills and learning.

3. Georgia (1735–1737)

John and Charles Wesley were recruited by the Trustees of the Georgia colony to Christianize the colony and to evangelize the native population. Several members of the Holy Club considered accompanying them. Finally, only Benjamin Ingham and Charles Delamotte boarded the *Simmonds* for Georgia with the Wesleys on 14 October 1735. Charles, who had undertaken ordination for the mission, signed on as Governor Oglethorpe's secretary. This bureaucratic responsibility would prevent Charles from having a significant ministry. The needs of Savannah for a minister likewise prevented John from fulfilling his original intention of ministering to the native peoples.

Several factors pushed John Wesley toward Georgia in 1735. None of his love relationships had been fulfilled, and he was not intimately involved with any woman. His father had died, cutting him off from the family hearth at Epworth. In that family, he had been nurtured in thoughts of missionary service by both Samuel and Susanna. The family's study of missionary books had been developed by his own reading. James Oglethorpe, the governor of the colony, was a hero to the family as well as a benefactor. John sincerely wished a mission to the Native Americans, whom he regarded as dwelling in a relative state of primitive innocence. He was looking for a fresh field to establish a primitive Christianity, and both a new colony and, in his opinion, an undeveloped race awaited. Finally, he hoped through new work in a new place to achieve the salvation of his own soul. Oxford, after all, was not going to adopt his version of primitive Christianity, and at the university, the fights were the well-understood old fights. In Oxford, new members joined the circle while others slid away or moved away to the duties of the English pastorate. Oxford was very comfortable and provided opportunities for holiness balanced by temptations for both Charles and himself. Oxford, as well as Epworth, was home, and an ambitious prophet was too easily accommodated, compromised, and even dishonored there.

Even the normal preferments that Oxford could provide to a scholarly cleric were receding from the ascetic, demanding Wesley.

Within three days of sailing, John was leading services and studying German. The German study would enable him to converse with the Moravian refugees sharing the passage, who were being settled in Georgia. Their bishop, David Nitschmann, returned the favor by studying English.

The crossing was tumultuous. They were delayed for a period because of contrary winds. Then the Bay of Biscay was stormy. According to Wesley, he feared death on various occasions and once was covered with water swamping the decks. Throughout the voyage, he and his companions led services, taught, and counseled. Buffeted by storms, the faith of the Moravians was a particularly bold witness to John, who contrasted their religious calm with his own troubled fears. Publishing the *Journal* in 1740, several years after the event, he contrasted the panic of the frightened English with the calm of the faithful Moravians. Despite the scary passage, early in February 1736, they sailed safely into the mouth of the Savannah River. Other Moravians, already in Georgia, welcomed the arrival of the Wesleys. One of their number, August Spangenberg, convinced John that he was still lacking the personal religious assurance that he sought. Moravian diaries in Germany indicate that Wesley's attempt to join the Moravian community was rejected, no doubt for that very lack.

Mission to Native Americans

While still on ship, Wesley enjoyed visits from Native Americans including Chief Tomochichi, who had been presented to the king and queen in London. A return visit by Wesley to Tomochichi's village did not find him at home. Of the two groups, German refugees and Native Americans, Wesley's relationship with the former would deepen and penetrate his own religious formation, while the relations with the Native Americans would decline. He became cynical about them and lost his original mission to "preach to the heathen" within three months.

Wesley's closest approximation to his original mission was the dialogue with five Chickasaw men on 20 July 1736. The conversation was arranged by William Andrews, also from Lincoln College, who translated the talk.[1] The Native Americans under Wesley's questioning affirmed belief in gods and equated salvation with being saved from their enemies. They were fearful that because their enemies were now so numerous, they might not be saved. When Wesley asked them if they would like to learn from the Book that tells about "the beloved one above," they indicated that they could not, now, take the time. "Our enemies are all about us; we have no time now, but to fight. If ever we be at peace we should be glad to know."[2]

The Native Americans said they had understood what Wesley was doing when they watched him preside at the funeral of Rebecca Bovey a week earlier. Then they deferred to their own religious leaders, saying there were things that only the old ones specifically called to religious practice could explain.

Wesley wrote to James Vernon two months later. He credited his companion Ingham with having learned some of the Creek language. He indicated his own desire to learn the language of the Chickasaw. He regarded their trust in providence and gods as good preparation for their evangelization. He also regarded them as humble and teachable, but also as a "despised and almost unheard of nation."[3] He worried about their future, hinting that his departure from them was imminent, and that in any case, there was little time to work with them. He spilled out to Vernon his sense of inadequacy to minister even to Savannah, and he also had all the problems of Frederica on the island of St. Simon.

Wesley drew up a short report for the Georgia Trustees in 1737, which he presented on returning to England. It discussed the land, agricultural potential, its settlements, and the native population. Wesley's failure to significantly engage the Native Americans became part of his rationalization for departing from Savannah. At times, he had intended to proceed on mission to the towns of the native peoples, but affection for a woman called Sophy Hopkey and duties to minister to the colonists kept him within colonized Georgia. His reflections on the Native Americans in his report explained his failure to reach them. His stark criticism of their life, of which he knew something firsthand and quite a bit from conversation with those experienced with Native Americans, contrasts very sharply with his idealized picture of African life before it was disrupted by European encroachment. His discussion of Africa is filled with sweet human sympathy and even a little romanticism toward Africa and the Africans. The native peoples of the New World do not receive the same sympathy. Wesley's comments contributed nothing to increase respect for the Native Americans by the Trustees, whose will was to impose European colonists upon their land. He attributed his report generally to those who had been among the native peoples, especially traders. He wrote that the account was from those who "have no interest in making them better or worse than they are."[4]

He described the Native Americans in Georgia as expelled from other places and basically without religion, laws, or government. He viewed them as practicing whatever occurred to them without regard to laws or morals. They were all, perhaps excepting the Choctaws, "gluttons, drunkards, thieves, dissemblers, liars."[5] Furthermore, he described them as without sexual morality, murderers of children and parents. He reported that the Chickasaws were gluttons, addicted to tobacco, and the most cruel toward their prisoners. The Cherokees farther to the west, inland, received a little better description because they had something approaching government. He saw the Cherokees as less prone to intemperance unless the liquor was free, and he noted avarice among them. He briefly referred to the Yuchis as outstanding in thieving, lying, and cowardice. He believed the Creeks had advisors without authority. He noted that the Native Americans who had the most relations with white men were the worst drunkards and liars among the tribes. Without any interest in learning, particularly in learning about Christianity, they were innocent of friendship or gratitude. With these short caricatures, the account in his journal concluded. The failed missionary seems, in these reports, unusually prejudiced, hostile, and bitter.

With part of his original mission frustrated, John turned his attention to the people of Savannah. Later, he would describe the Savannah meetings as the second founding of the Methodists. Here he tried to apply the strict rules of earlier Anglicanism while calling some into the more rigorous pursuit of holiness.

Politics

Charles was attempting to do ministry in Frederica while employed as secretary to James Oglethorpe, but he was persecuted for his censuring of Oglethorpe for adultery. John ran into this opposition following Charles's departure from Frederica. Mrs. Hawkins, one of the accused adulteresses, set the community against the Wesley brothers. Additionally, the strict Anglicanism of the Prayer Book of 1549, which the Wesleys were attempting to enforce, was neither appreciated nor appropriated by the colonists. Charles's work involved him so deeply as a personal secretary that he could not escape from the shadow of his patron in order to minister. From the early days of tenure, his relationship with his patron was also plagued by his suspicions of Oglethorpe.

With Charles Wesley serving as secretary to the governor and John as minister to Savannah, they were more involved in real politics than they had foreseen. Two of John's letters recorded this development. They provided a preview of John's political activity and writings of his later life.

John wrote a supportive letter to Oglethorpe when Oglethorpe was feeling the criticism of the prime minister, Sir Robert Walpole. He encouraged Oglethorpe to persevere. John framed his letter in terms of Oglethorpe's having been following the designs of Machiavelli or of God. John trusted Oglethorpe to have been doing the latter. The paragraph referencing Machiavelli assumed Oglethorpe's rather detailed knowledge of the Italian political philosopher. It naturally occurs that as Wesley had procured his copy of the *Works of Niccolò Machiavelli* while in Frederica where Oglethorpe resided, the governor may have been Wesley's source. Wesley had been warned that Machiavelli was often misrepresented, and he admitted to a prejudice to favor the work. However, his conclusions were that even if all the teachings of the devils were collected in one place, they would be less dangerous than the advice of Machiavelli to princes. Domitian and Nero, in Wesley's opinion, would appear as children of light when compared to Machiavelli.[6]

Wesley wrote to Archibald Hutcheson, Member of Parliament, in 1736, petitioning that the regulations forbidding Carolina traders from trading with Native Americans in Georgia be enforced. In the letter, he also referred to conversations with the brother of the late governor of Carolina at Oglethorpe's residence. Wesley's motivations, whether to protect the Native Americans or the licensing power of Georgia, were unclear. His family was connected to Hutcheson, and so, he may have been writing on behalf of Oglethorpe's Georgia administration.

On the question of religion and politics, Wesley repented of his former conviction that a Christian priest should preach only the gospel. He noted that there are things a priest should undertake that directly affect "peace and goodwill among men."[7] He indicated that some causes affect the success of ministry even though they do not directly belong to it. With that introduction, he took up his political petition, mentioning to the Member of Parliament the family connections and political connections.

Slaves

An official visit to Carolina introduced John to African slavery. Georgia at that time, expressing the reforming will of Oglethorpe, did not permit slavery. Those contacts would rouse his conscience and provide experiential data for his later campaign against slavery. His written reflections on his subjects at the time focused on evangelization and instruction.

His contacts with African slaves were mainly in Carolina. His instruction of an African woman in the faith led him to believe that with the cooperation of the plantation owners, missionary efforts among the slaves could be fruitful. His record of his conversation over two days with the "young Negro" focused on instructing her as to God the creator who lives above the sky. Her salvation or ability of her soul to live in the sky with God depended upon her being "good." There, she was promised "no one will beat or hurt you."[8] Four days later, he met a young African boy. "This lad, too, I found both very desirous and very capable of instruction."[9]

Sexuality

James Oglethorpe's tenure and life were threatened at Frederica by rumors of mutiny and invasions by Spaniards. At one point on believing false witnesses, he accused Charles of sedition and mutiny, for which Charles could have paid with his life. Charles was able to refute the charge by cross-examining the witness and by providing his own able testimony. But he passed from one danger to another. His formality at service was resented by Oglethorpe and the people. More dangerous were the confusions and charges around Oglethorpe's rumored adultery. On board ship the Wesley's had ministered to both women suspected of adultery with the governor, and both had seemed to be seeking to live a Christian life. But on shore, they were set against each other and violently against the Wesleys. Still both confessed privately to Charles of their indiscretions. Oglethorpe's opposition deprived Charles of access to supplies and enflamed the scorn of the other settlers and soldiers. John Wesley's visit to St. Simon brought filial comfort but another confrontation with Oglethorpe, who protested his innocence. Eventually, Charles recorded his belief in Oglethorpe's innocence of the accusations.

Finally, it fell to John to explain the content of Charles's letter, which Mr. Hawkins, the doctor in Frederica, had revealed to the community. On hearing that all the women were slandered by it, John explained that the charge of adultery, in which Charles had been mistaken, applied only to Mrs. Welch and Mrs. Hawkins. In the uproar that followed, John was verbally attacked, and his brother's flight to England related to charges of his adultery. John appealed to Oglethorpe, who explained that though Charles was indiscreet in his writing, John was not responsible for it. Later that day, Mrs. Welch roundly cursed John. The next day, he responded to an invitation to visit Mrs. Hawkins. Despite John's requiring the invitation-bearing maid to remain in the room, Mrs. Hawkins fell upon him with a pistol and scissors. In restraining her, John was wrestled to the bed with Hawkins astride him. Neither the maid nor the two Hawkins boys could react fast enough, either to dispatch John or to disarm Mrs. Hawkins, as they were importuned by the two parties. The constable and another man also hesitated to act. Finally, Mr. Hawkins himself, with his house filling up, pulled his wife off John Wesley, and she was disarmed.

This commotion led to another hearing before Governor Oglethorpe, who managed to resolve the case without the public trial on assault and felony charges that John had requested. So, the conclusion of the Hawkins' case was that they were forbidden to speak to each other, charges were not filed, and this experiment in Christian counseling came to an end. The incident, of course, ruined any effective ministry John might have pursued at Frederica.

Among the young women, John had taken a special interest in nurturing Sophy Hopkey. She lived with her aunt and uncle, the Caustons. First, John had persuaded her to reject the attentions of a scoundrel, Tom Mellichamp, who had been imprisoned for forgery. His diary indicates he spent considerable time with her thereafter. He was encouraged by her aunt to take Sophy to his house and do with her what he would. The uncle proposed to fix an income on John if he would marry her. John's attentions led to fondling her and kissing her while ostensibly serving as her spiritual advisor. He persuaded her not to return to England and discussed the possibility of marriage with her.

On a trip from Frederica to Savannah in late October of 1736, they slept under the stars with the boat crew nearby. They were often alone discussing marriage or alternative living arrangements for her from her aunt and uncle's home. But John would never propose. He was distracted by a life of celibacy and by a possible vocation of a mission to the Native Americans. According to her aunt, Sophy, at eighteen, was seeking marriage, and John's approach and then sudden withdrawal of intimacy were extremely painful to her. All this confusion was surrounded with their prayer and devotional life and his role as her tutor in Christian living.

His unpublished journal indicates another level of indecision. She was a rather plain, untutored young woman of the colony. John wrote about her virtues as if to convince himself that she was worthy of his love. But his writing also revealed that she was very bland. It was almost as if her humility about herself was appropriate; she was still undeveloped in beauty, learning, refinement, or spirituality. Sophy was no Susanna. He consulted with his friends. He told her he must amend his ways and not assume intimacies, but a few days later, he was kissing her again.

Through these trying events of his heart, John was reading, learning Spanish, studying French with Sophy, visiting the sick and dying, leading prayers, preaching, conducting services, and administering frequent funerals. The other woman with whom he spent the most time was Miss Bovey. His diaries indicate some contact with her almost every day when he was in Savannah. On her announcement that she intended to marry Mr. Burnside, John, in what was becoming almost a pattern of behavior, spoke against Burnside and her relationship with him.

His torment over Sophy continued until he finally told her of his intention never to marry. She responded by indicating she would not be coming to his house for breakfast every morning, studying French, or meeting him alone anymore. His diary notes, as well as the unpublished very personal pages of his journal, indicate a great naïveté. Most of the town understood Sophy to be involved with John, and she spent most mornings and evenings in his home with her guardians' approval. She still indicated a willingness to see him at her aunt's house. However, unknown to John, after this final rejection she opened herself to the courtship of Mr. Williamson. Still, Wesley could not let her go cleanly. With an aching heart and prayer, he had Mr. Delamotte prepare three lots, and John drew "Think of it no more." The lot, adopted from Mennonite practice, finally overruled many of Wesley's confidants, the Caustons, Sophy's wishes, and community expectations. He accepted it as a painful sacrifice of a companion whose equal he might never find again.

On 7 March 1737, he nearly relented to surrender to her, but her uncle's call summoned her back into the house. He recorded: "I was once more 'snatched as a brand out of the fire.'"[10] Two days later, he was asked to publish the bans in Sophy's marriage to Mr. Williamson. Wesley was thrown into pain. Further conversations with her deepened his grief.

Mr. Williamson and Miss Hopkey joined Miss Bovey and Mr. Burnside in going to Purrysburg, where they were married outside John Wesley's jurisdiction. On their return to Savannah, heartache continued to cloud his judgment. He saw Mrs. Burnside privately for lessons and had discussions with Mr. Williamson and with Mr. Causton. Wesley learned through servants later of Sophy's fear that Wesley would disapprove of her marriage and how she kept it secret until the last moment. Sophy's choice was partially a way out from under the Caustons' supervision and home. By 16 May, Wesley recorded that he had five serious religious conversations exhorting her to continue in her strenuous religious pursuits. He also had learned of Mr. Williamson's fear that John was teaching her to be too strict in her religion. His involvement with Mr. Causton deepened.

Wesley's sense of loss turned into bitterness. He could not separate from his pastoral role his anger at Sophy for his suspicions of her lack of honesty. Eventually, he turned her away from Communion for her failure to give notice of intention to participate and for the failure to resolve Wesley's accusations of her dissimulation to him, her pastor. The personal and the professional were blurred in both Sophy's and John's minds. On one occasion, she blamed a miscarriage on John's earlier scolding of her. John thought that he had cleared the denying of Communion to her with her powerful uncle, Mr. Causton. But Causton was deeply offended by the perceived insult to a member of his family.

Mr. Williamson responded by suing Wesley for £1000 and advertising his suit forbidding anyone to assist Wesley in leaving. Mr. Causton responded by demanding a public hearing in the courthouse. Wesley refused the hearing as inappropriate, given the ecclesiastical nature of most of the charges. Sophy's affidavit accusing wrong conduct was contradicted by her friends, the Burnsides, and by Wesley's aide, Mr. Charles Delamotte. So, the stage was set for a trial, but Wesley still denied the appropriateness of a civil court for ecclesiastical affairs. The grand jury, dominated by the magistrate Causton, presented a list of ten complaints, nine of which Wesley judged to be ecclesiastical. He concurred with facing the secular charge of forcing his conversation upon Mrs. Williamson in Savannah. A petition with a dozen of the grand jurors dissenting was sent to Wesley, and he persisted in his own legal defense.

After consulting with friends, Wesley prepared to leave for England. He informed Mr. Causton of his intention and posted an advertisement to that effect. He said the Evening Prayers and then departed after having preached "not as I ought, but as I was able" in Savannah for a year and nine months.[11]

****

He returned to England two years and four months after his departure. The journal describing the events would not be published until summer 1740, after Captain Williams's affidavit against him was proclaimed in Bristol in May.[12] The journal was edited to defend himself, but it was done from a post-Aldersgate experience of faith. So, the conclusion to the published journal is different from the original manuscript journal. It is full of comments on his lack of faith on the return voyage. He could write: "I left my native country in order to teach the Georgian Indians the nature of Christianity. But what have I learned myself in the meantime? Why (what I the least of all suspected), that I who went to America to convert others was never myself converted to God."[13]

Certainly, an inner conviction of evangelical presence would enflame his life that he was yet to discover. But he had displayed an energetic ministry for the God of a Puritan-inspired, high-church Anglicanism. His life was controlled by a remarkable sense of providence that stoked the furnace of his courage. He maintained both his Oxford piety and his relentless Oxford learning in the colony. He did not succumb to the temptations of frontier life. He kept the faith as he knew it through trials and shared it with Jews through learning Spanish, with other Europeans by reading prayers in German, French, and Italian that he labored to learn and improve. If he had been able to persist in his mission, he would have probably learned some Chickasaw, as he intended. His greatest failure was with women. If he had not gotten so close to his spiritual advisees, Mrs. Hawkins's problems would not have engulfed him as they had wounded Charles. If he had not seduced the spirit of Sophy Hopkey or persisted in his inappropriate pastoral supervisory role, he would not have been forced to flee America. He knew neither the ways of women nor his ways with women. This flaw would haunt him the rest of his life.

The greatest friendships and spiritual conversations of the mission had been with the Moravians. Their witness to a vital, personal faith planted seeds that would bear fruit in London. He had also experimented with the Moravian practice of establishing "bands"[14] within the communities of Frederica and Savannah. These small groups of ordinary people, as distinguished from the scholarly club members of Oxford, were to meet for up to three times a week with Wesley for special religious instruction and the deepening of their faith. This commitment to small group organization would propel Wesley into other Moravian societies upon his return to England.

4. Moravians (1738–1739)

John Wesley's ministry in Georgia failed. He fled Savannah and an irregular indictment. The way home was difficult, for he became lost in the Georgia forest and the trip on the North Atlantic was rough. Spiritually, though, a turn had begun. The vital witness of the Moravians on board the ship *Simmonds* and in Georgia led him to seek them out in England. The friendships with the Moravians prepared him for what has been called his conversion, though *conversion* is probably too strong a term for this faithful Church of England priest who was seeking holiness. The Moravians on board the *Simmonds* had presented a calm assurance surpassing his own in the face of death. The talks in Georgia confirmed in Wesley a sense of incompleteness in faith. He believed he was almost a Christian, but he was not yet personally grasped in his emotions. The total commitment that he lacked in his relations with women he also missed in his religious life. Finding this commitment in a Moravian context at Aldersgate led him to seek its historical sources in Germany among the Moravians.

Wesley's second journal is the story of his relationship with the Moravians in England, his Aldersgate experience of 24 May 1738, and the journey to Germany. On 7 February, he met Peter Böhler, and thereafter, he sought conversation with him whenever he could. According to his journal, his preaching and his reports to the Trustees of Georgia were of less importance to him than his conversations with Böhler. By the end of February, he had pledged to speak only of the glory of God, giving up all "levity of behavior," and to be absolutely frank with everyone with whom he talked.[1] Similarly, the following days showed renewed energy in self-disciplining toward holiness. Böhler persuaded John that he really was not a full believer. Wesley's response was to suggest giving up preaching, but Böhler denied that, saying: "Preach faith *till* you have it, and then, *because* you have it, you *will* preach faith."[2]

Regarding salvation by faith alone as a new doctrine, Wesley uneasily began preaching it. Throughout March and April, Wesley preached almost every day, traveling from Manchester to Oxford. John continued to dialogue with Böhler, focusing on whether one could instantaneously be born to a new life of happiness and well-being in Christ.

On 1 May, they founded a society at Fetter Lane in London. In Wesley's mind, it was continuous with his work at Oxford with the club. The Church of England group also contained Moravians, and from it would later come both Moravian and Methodist societies.[3] The society met once a week and was divided into small bands for meetings on Wednesday night. The Sunday evening meetings were love feasts, and the rules of organization required prospective members to go through a trial period and accept the rules of the society.

Wesley was still driven by rules, but Peter Böhler's letter to him confessed God's and Peter's love for John. He assured John that the only way to overcome his sin (which John's rules certainly exposed) was to believe that the blood of Christ could conquer his unbelief and lead him to love and fulfillment in God.[4]

John found that the preaching of faith in Christ alone cost him access to pulpits. He expressed his dismay at the rejection of the doctrine to Charles, who was ill and going through his own soul-searching. In May, John worked himself into a white heat over the new preaching as he was rejected by church after church. He was seeking peace and joy, and knowing discipline and sadness while preaching faith.

Wesley's *Journal* is the key to understanding his religious awakening. Before describing his awakening at Aldersgate, Wesley wrote in his *Journal* his religious biography to show his need of the Aldersgate experience. He summarized his religious home, his less religious school days, renewal and good works at college, the influences of Thomas à Kempis and William Law, the increase of good works, the introduction of mysticism, the meeting on board ship with the Moravians, the time of "beating the air" in Savannah, and the despair on returning to England. Peter Böhler showed him that the faith needed to be focused not just on God, but on Christ in particular, as the source of joy and freedom from sin. Wesley wrote that he resisted this emphasis and asked for witnesses. Böhler produced three witnesses who testified to the truth that faith in Christ had freed them from all guilt and sin.

On 24 May, Wesley reluctantly attended a Moravian society meeting in Aldersgate Street. Upon hearing "Luther's Preface to the Epistle to the Romans" being read: "I felt my heart strangely warmed. I felt I did trust in Christ, Christ alone for salvation, and an assurance was given me that he had taken away *my* sins, even *mine*, and saved *me* from the law of sin and death."[5]

The next two weeks were times of religious peace, but also of temptation. Nevertheless, Wesley was learning to trust and not to fight every question. He preached, prayed, read the New Testament, and sang. By 7 June, he was ready to go to Germany to visit the Moravians: "And I hoped the conversing with these holy men who were themselves living witnesses of the full power of faith, and yet able to bear with those that are weak, would be a means, under God, of so establishing my soul that I might 'go from faith to faith, and from strength to strength.' "[6]

His testimony makes clear that he did not yet feel his spiritual journey had reached its goal. However, an important transition had been made through Aldersgate. The Moravians led Wesley through his reformulation of the faith. As Paul and Martin Luther had become oppressed by their religious striving to fulfill the law of God, so had John Wesley. He came to their type of faith by finally, personally, focusing on Christ, the symbol of forgiveness and assurance through faith rather than upon the transcendent, law-giving God. It is Luther's interpretation of Paul in a Moravian context that permits Wesley to relax a little and to accept acceptance. Still, Wesley is too formed by his previous Protestant discipline to just relax in the love of Christ. Now, the law will follow acceptance rather than replace it. The one thing necessary is faith in the saving work of Christ, but many things follow quickly from the acceptance.

Evangelical Ministry

Peter Böhler's counsel to John to preach faith preceded Aldersgate, but the June sermon on salvation by faith at St. Mary's, Oxford, before he left for Germany is the best example of it. The contrast between seeking holiness through discipline as seen in his letter to Richard Morgan Sr. and the sermon on grace is stark.

"Salvation by Faith" has three parts: "What is faith?" "What is salvation?" and "Answers to Objections."[7] Salvation by faith is not the faith of reason that there is a God, that we are required to be moral, and that there is a state beyond death depending upon our being morally right with God. This reasonable faith is obligatory on the heathen as it is what is known through natural religion. Nor is the faith of salvation what the devil believes. Even the devil knows that Jesus is the Son of God and Savior of the world. The devil also recognizes that Scripture is inspired by God. Nor is the faith of salvation what the disciples knew accurately when Jesus was alive. Faith is the belief in the heart that God has overcome your sin by raising Christ from the dead. Faith is this inward appropriation of Christ's dying for your sin and overcoming it in his resurrection. In the Atonement Christ comes alive in the believer, and his living in us is the sure confidence that sins are forgiven. This sense of heartfelt belief in acceptance Wesley had not received in Epworth, Oxford, or Georgia; this teaching was from his German Moravian brethren.

For Wesley, more than for his brethren friends, sin was completely overcome historically as well as religiously. Sin could not rule in the redeemed. One was really born again. Of one who believes, Wesley said, "At length he comes unto a perfect man, unto the meaning of the stature of the fullness of Christ."[8]

He then responded to the common objections. He argued that it did not encourage pride because it was the result not of one's own effort but of Christ. He argued that it did not encourage immorality, for this faith led to moral works even though no credit derived from them.

He personalized the message, saying his hearers might soon believe it and find their salvation. He expressed his usual critique of Catholicism by saying salvation by faith strikes at the whole of Catholicism. The truthful power of the message, he argued, was what caused the devil to resist and persecute the faithful. The believer is like the little child who overthrows the great adversary, and so his challenge was resented and resisted.

The grounds for resisting the lack of explicit ethics in the Moravians were in the sermon, even though the content was not. But the great contrast with the pre-Georgian, pre-Moravian Wesley was the downplaying of the self-seeking discipline; now it is God who has sought and won the believer. Here was the foundation of Wesley's vocation. It was the inner belief in the Atonement through Christ's sacrifice. This turned him away from the disciplined, educated Oxford don seeking salvation to one preaching salvation, requiring discipline, and promoting education. He was thereafter a preacher of the evangelical revival. But he was one thing more. His friend and member of the Holy Club, George Whitefield, was a powerful preacher of the revival. John Wesley, however, was also an organizer of the revival. In his weaving of the believers together into societies he established a new organization. His Oxford had been organized. It was organized by and for elite Christians. Wesley's new organization was for Atonement-believing Christians who mostly were far from the elite of the society.

The importance of emphasizing the organizing role here is that his ethics need to be understood as developed in practice. They were not the ideal ethics of a speculative thinker, but the practical ethics of a leader of a movement. He was taking care of the movement while articulating the movement's ethics.

Germany

The church that John was leaving England to visit had been reconstituted on a German estate, Berthelsdore, only in 1727. Its defining earlier origins go back to the reforms of John Huss (martyred 6 July 1415). It was composed of the Protestant refugees from Bohemia and Moravia and of German Pietists. Count Nicolaus Ludwig von Zinzendorf was the nominal leader. He had adopted Pietism in Hermann Francke's school in Halle. Zinzendorf focused on Christ in his faith, as had Francke, who also envisaged this personal belief and appropriation of Christ as the way into true joy in the Christian faith. Both the German Pietists and the Protestant refugees from Moravia had experienced persecution as they sought to express their forms of reformation faith. The Pietists who tried to remain Lutheran had evolved small societies, or *ecclesiolae in ecclesia*, to preserve discipline and protect their religion of the heart. Francke had been forceful in founding Christian institutions, particularly orphanages and schools. The movement as a whole was characterized by extensive missionary enterprises. It was a group of these refugees with missionary focus that challenged Wesley's faith aboard the *Simmonds*. August Spangenberg's questions were later followed by those of Böhler, which led to Aldersgate. Spangenberg would, after the death of Zinzendorf in 1760, return to the community at Herrnhut and consolidate the new church. It then evolved away from a few extreme practices that had accompanied its early founding. Zinzendorf had tried to keep the movement within the established churches to renew them, but gradually it had become an independent church. Bethlehem, Pennsylvania, was named by Zinzendorf, and it became the central office of the church in America. The Wesleys were included in this movement from the time of their own awakenings in 1738 until 1740, when two years after John's visit to Germany they separated. It seems probable that though Moravian similarities to the Wesleyan revival are many, its emphasis upon the heart's attachment to Christ gave both movements their zeal.

John's traveling party to Germany included Benjamin Ingham, his assistant from Georgia, John Browne, John Holmes, Richard Viney, Johann Töltschig, Gottlob Hauptmann, and another.[9] They sailed to Rotterdam, then continued to Amsterdam. They were assisted with hospitality by Mennonites and Moravians or their associates. Wesley became very perturbed over German hostels, which refused to accept them, and their exclusion from certain cities unless they had official passes. Such German bureaucratic obfuscation during times of peace seemed entirely inappropriate to John. Their passage was on riverboat where possible and on foot elsewhere.

Wesley and party stayed two weeks with Count Zinzendorf, engaged in conversation with the count and some of the other ninety residents in the community. Wesley spoke directly with them in Latin or English, finding his German too underdeveloped for conversation. While noting some theological differences with the community, he rejoiced over the faith and love of the residents and the obvious joy of living in Christian community.

In Halle, with the assistance of Professor Francke, the son of August Francke (1663–1727), they visited the orphanage, the school, and the other institutions and were impressed by that work. They continued from Leipzig to Dresden. Several times they were denied lodging at inns and questioned by authorities.

On 1 August, they arrived at Herrnhut, the goal of their trip. It was the original center for the refugees from Bohemia and was situated on the Zinzendorf estate near the Bohemian-German border. There, Wesley renewed his acquaintance with a Moravian leader he had known in Georgia. They also were joined by Christian David, the original leader of the Moravians. Wesley visited churches, joined in dialogue, enjoyed Christian David's preaching four times, and experienced their community. Wesley recorded David's final sermon on reconciliation through belief in Christ, in which David taught that reconciliation is not a human work, and human works are not relevant. Righteousness is attributed to one who has faith; one does not do righteousness in one's own power. At the time, Wesley was celebrating their message, and he did not record any disagreement with David. He concluded his visit: "I could gladly have spent my life here; but my Master calling me to labor in another part of his vineyard, on Monday 14, I was constrained to take my leave of this happy place, Martin Dober and a few others of the brethren walking with us about an hour. Oh when shall *This* Christianity cover the earth, as the 'waters cover the sea' "![10]

Wesley used the rest of the *Journal* to recount the testimony of the Brethren at Herrnhut, and to present founding documents of the community, their history, and their community-life rules. The last six pages of the *Journal,*which had been announced as completing the days until his return from Germany, are not in *Journal II,* but form the first entries for *Journal III.* So, *Journal II* ends awkwardly without the German trip finished, concluding with documents and testimony. On the return journey of a little over a month, Wesley learned of Protestant opposition to Herrnhut, and he visited the Brethren work at Jena for a week. They basically retraced their outward journey and arrived in London on 16 September. On 17 September, Wesley resumed preaching, finding occasions for three sermons and a Bible study on that first day back.

The trip of four months reinforced in Wesley the preaching of salvation through personal belief in the atonement of Christ for the world's sins and for his own sins. He could see the joy it produced in individuals, families, and the communities. His own preaching of the salvation through the blood of Christ led to a revival. But soon spoilers disrupted the Fetter Lane Society with criticism of the sacraments and degrees of justifying faith.

Wesley had almost joined the Moravians. His "warm heart" experience had been with them listening to Luther's theology. The trip to Germany awakened doubts about their organization and their leadership. His Christianity from his Calvinized Anglicanism had more of a social ethic than the Moravians expressed as Wesley sought the reform of both church and nation. The split in the Fetter Lane Society was fatefully followed by his joining with Whitefield in the evangelical movement and his increasing distance from the Moravians.

Wesley plunged into nurturing the societies in London and Oxford, visiting the prisons, and preaching several times every week. He found the society at Oxford to need rebuilding. He frequently counseled those moved by his preaching of faith. The engagements in theological disputation also occupied him. He was increasingly unwelcome in many churches.

Uncertainty and Revival

Wesley was preaching belief in the Atonement and personal transformation, but at the same time he was not free of uncertainty. On 4 January 1739, he wrote in his *Journal* a self-accusatory piece: "But that I am not a Christian at this day I as assuredly know as that Jesus is the Christ."[11] He claimed that he knew he did not love God because he did not feel the love. He claimed that he knew from human associations the feeling of love and that he did not have it for God: "I often ask my heart, when I am in company with one that I love, 'Do I take more delight in you or in God?' and cannot but answer *in you*. For in truth I do not delight in God at all. Therefore I am so far from loving God with all my heart that whatever I love at all, I love more than God. So that all the love I have is flat idolatry."[12]

He also admitted in his *Journal* that he did not have joy in the

Holy Spirit or the peace of God. His rigorous self-examination denied himself the title of Christian. He confessed, nay asserted, that he had not the fruits of the Spirit of Christ. All of that was said in a context of belief in the reality of what he denied he had received.

The plain reading of the text indicates that Wesley believed in a message that required feeling, and that he did not have it. Certainly on 24 May 1738, at Aldersgate, he had it. The certainty in belief of Christ's sacrifice for him had allowed him to experience something similar to what Martin Luther had known and to overcome his failed legalism. Elsewhere he could indicate that for ten years he had sought salvation from works only to find it in faith. The *Journal* record witnessed that he was very effective in preaching and organizing on faith even when its confirming signs were denied in his own experience.

He received an invitation to Bristol in March 1739, to assume the work of Whitefield. He had little desire to go, for the work in London was sufficient, but both he and Charles were convinced through their oracular consulting of Scripture that he should go. The members of the Fetter Lane Society, whose permission John needed according to their agreements, decided through lot to permit his going. So John entered a new stage of his vocation that was to be his permanent work.

He included his letter of 1734 to his father in his 1739 *Journal* between the entries for his reception of the invitation to Bristol and his actual departure for Bristol. It was the letter in which he had rejected his father's invitation to succeed him at Epworth. He chose the university life in 1734, and in 1739 he rejected the university as he had before to go to Georgia. This move, again in some degree for the seeking of his own salvation, would lead to the itinerant life and to the rejection of the university reflected in his sermon of 24 August 1744. His reference to his leaving for Bristol is one of beginning "this new period of my life." This reference and the printing of the letter of his rejection of his father's invitation at this point indicate the degree of turmoil that the call to Bristol occasioned.

In Bristol, after soul-searching conversation with Whitefield, he overcame his commitment to "decency and order" and began preaching in the streets and the fields as well as to the meetings of the societies. Soon, according to his numbers, crowds of three to six thousand were assembling for his services. Conversions followed, often accompanied by convulsions. Colleagues and friends complained of the reports of his preaching, and Wesley considered their concerns, prayed about them, often responded to them in his letters—and continued preaching. On Monday, 2 April 1739, he spoke in a brickyard taking as his text:

> The Spirit of the Lord is upon me, because he hath anointed me to preach the gospel to the poor; he hath sent me to heal the brokenhearted, to preach deliverance to the captives, and recovery of sight to the blind, to set at liberty them that are bruised, to proclaim the acceptable year of the Lord. (Luke 4:18-19)

According to Luke, Jesus' use of the text marked the beginning of his ministry. John's choosing of it reflected a changed consciousness of what he was doing. In his commentary on the text, he notes that Jesus was announcing a year of Jubilee when debtors and servants were freed.[13] Two days later, a society was formed for the nurture of eleven of the hearers, with women and men meeting separately after the Moravian practice. The next day he founded two more societies. The combination of the itinerancy of his preaching and the binding of people together in societies was to be the heart of Wesley's lifelong ministry. His novel synthesis combined the Methodist club of Oxford with Moravian evangelical witness and Whitefield's public preaching in a movement still within the Church of England. The reaction to these methods in the 1740s included astonishment, opposition, and violence.

The revival spread from Bristol with John preaching to crowds from one to four thousand, according to his *Journal*. Convulsions, exorcisms, faintings, and loud cries accompanied the revival as Wesley preached that God willed the salvation of all.[14] Within a month the New Room, the first Methodist meetinghouse, was being built.

Whitefield traveled with Wesley, and they shared the opportunities to preach in July 1739, with thousands attending the preaching. Wesley began to experience churches being denied to him. While he was preaching on the Sermon on the Mount at Bowling Green, Bristol, a press gang seized one of the hearers. Wesley protested in the name of traditional English liberties from the Magna Carta. The crowd acquiesced to the seizure.

By September 1739, Wesley recorded speaking to crowds of ten and twenty thousand in London. At that time, he was distinguishing Methodism as the true old Christianity from what was usually called Christianity. He also noted Methodism was "everywhere spoken against."[15] As he closed his third journal, the tempo of the revival picked up in the size of the crowds and also in the ferocity of the opposition. The spiritual opposition was seen both in the form of mobs threatening the evangelists' lives and in spirit-possessed individuals suffering pain, convulsions, and cries of demonic possession.

Wesley found himself defending Whitefield against those, on the one hand, who despised inward religion and those, on the other hand, who denied the effects of his evangelism. In writing on how Whitefield had gone to the coal miners of Kingswood, he recorded:

> And, by the grace of God, their labour was not in vain. The scene is already changed. Kingswood does not now, as a year ago, resound with cursing and blasphemy. It is no more filled with drunkenness and uncleanness, and the idle diversions that naturally lead thereto. It is no longer full of wars and fightings, of clamour and bitterness, of wrath and envyings. Peace and love are there. Great numbers of people are mild, gentle, and easy to be entreated.[16]

The correspondence between Whitefield and Wesley in 1740 shows Wesley's toleration and desire to avoid conflict. Whitefield's letter of 25 September 1740, pushed vigorously the argument that sin persisted until death against Wesley's teaching of Christian perfection. Wesley, on the question of election, wanted to leave it to God to sort out the dispute of opinion. But the disputes would not stay down, and even by the next year, their controversy was in print in England and in America. The disputes extended beyond the doctrine to the funding and care of the schools that they had jointly sponsored in their days of harmony.

The Methodist Societies

While Peter Böhler was engaging the Wesley brothers in theological conversation, he was also organizing religious societies or bands in London and Oxford. The Oxford societies did not develop into a significant movement, but Böhler was very impressed with the results in London. The "bands" represented a synthesis of the preceding English societies and the Herrnhut patterns of organization. Wesley was particularly active in the Fetter Lane Society, and he brought to it his experience from the Holy Club and the bands at Frederica and Savannah. The bands in London were larger than those in Germany, gathering together five or ten persons. Following James 5, members were to confess their faults to one another and to pray for one another. They met once a week and shared their spiritual journeys with the group. Rules were established for regular meetings, a monthly love feast, and group discipline.[17] Böhler's witness, argument, and love prepared Wesley for the deepening of his religious experience; but they also provided him with models of organization that he would put into the service of the evangelical movement. It was in the society of his friend James Hutton in Aldersgate Street that his decisive religious deepening occurred on 24 May 1738.[18] Further exposure to the Moravian band, class, and society system in 1738 in Germany prepared him for the establishment of his own system. His own Methodist society was established with Whitefield's blessing among some of those called by Whitefield's preaching in Bristol. Davies regards the first truly Methodist society as being formed on 11 July 1739, under the name of the United Society in Bristol.[19] By December 1739, the London society at the Foundry was organized.

The Bristol and London societies required no creedal subscription, but only a willingness to "flee from the wrath to come, to be saved from their sins."[20] But discipline followed upon joining. The bands were subdivisions of the larger society and regarded as the centers of the society. A further development was the division of the Bristol society into classes of about a dozen for the purpose of raising money to pay for the cost of the New Room. This ad hoc arrangement developed into a useful subdivision for maintaining discipline and membership, and tickets of membership were provided or withheld from members' classes. The classes and bands continued to coexist, Davies reports, until the 1780s, from which time the bands declined in importance despite the elderly Wesley's urging of their retention. Wesley established two other groups at opposite ends of the religious spectrum. The "select societies" were for those most distinguished in their religious growth and sensitivity, and at the other end were "penitents" who had left the faith, but were rebuilding their piety.[21] These various groups or cells provided much of the dynamism for Methodists. They were invaluable, close-knit communities of support that encouraged and disciplined the members. They were, to the degree possible to a widely itinerant preacher, under Wesley's authority and control. He picked the leaders and, in the earlier days, admitted and excluded people from membership. Though reflecting both German and English precedents to their members in the 1740s, they were clearly John Wesley's groups.

Poetry and Social Holiness

Several of the Wesley children were poets, as was their father. John and Charles published together. In their first volume, they included some of the German hymns John had learned from the Moravians and translated in Georgia. They published more than fifty volumes of poetry in about the same number of years. Seven of the volumes are by John and eight by Charles with seven bearing the names of both brothers. The remainder were extracted from the works of others.[22] Many of these poems appeared as early as 1739 and were later reprinted in the *Arminian Magazine* in 1778 and following years. The preface to the 1739 volume, published by both brothers, has a strong statement of their social convictions within it. In particular, since some of the hymns and poems have a touch of mysticism in them, they were careful to disavow solitary religion and traces of being accepted for "our virtuous habits or tempers."[23] The task is not to build up ourselves but "*He* commands to build up one another." They continued, "'Holy solitaries' is a phrase no more consistent with the Gospel than holy adulterers. The Gospel of Christ knows of no religion, but social; no holiness but social holiness. Faith working by love is the length and breadth and depth and height of Christian perfection."[24]

The words in the preface are remarkable in emphasizing works so soon after the Wesleys' conversion: "And in truth, whosoever loveth his brethren not in words only, but as Christ loved him cannot be zealous but be zealous of good works. He feels in his soul a burning, restless desire of spending and being spent for them."[25]

The German piety of the Moravians informed particularly the brothers' first venture in the joint publication of their poetry. Yet they distanced themselves from their German mentors by their insistence on social holiness. The Methodist movement was committed to the reform of the nation even at the cost of leaving their Moravian brethren behind.

5. Reform (1740s)

The Moravians called John Wesley to appropriate in faith the love of God. He affirmed their solidarity in supporting one another in the church. John split with them in his attempts to reform the Church of England and the nation. His ministry and ethics of ministry were reformist. Both the established church and the nation were failures, but the vision of the kingdom of God and their relatively good social structures called him to active reforming attempts. His ministry is not understandable without grasping his threefold commitment to salvation, solidarity, and reform.

These aspects of his work unfold in the five decades of his mature ministry. In the 1740s, he faced opposition from the church, the local political leadership, and the press, and physical danger from the mob. During the 1750s, the Seven Years' War dominated English life, and Wesley's thought and actions are in the context of world war and domestic rebellion. The 1760s saw the institutionalization of lay preaching and the revolt of Thomas Maxwell. His 1763 "The Reformation of Manners" laid out his program, and he was reconciled with George Whitefield. His social philosophy was articulated out of appreciation of George III, and he confronted the realities of slavery and the American Revolution in the 1770s. In the last years of his life in the decade of the 1780s, the Methodist movement matured, Wesley was accepted, and the origins of the Methodist Church as a world church were established.

Separation from Moravians

The decade of the 1740s began with Wesley moving from the Fetter Lane Society, and the conflicts with both the Moravians and the Calvinists deepened. The ethical consequences of Aldersgate began to distinguish his thought from that of his Moravian brethren. Leon O. Hynson emphasized the importance of the Aldersgate experience for Wesley's ethics: "Before Aldersgate his social ethics grew out of a deep concern to save his own soul. After

Aldersgate, he was motivated by the power of a new affection and gave himself to others out of the love he came to know in Christ."[1]

Wesley published his first *Journal* in 1740, partially to defend his reputation from an affidavit filed against him in Bristol. Captain Williams, a supporter of slavery, had been a member of the anti-Wesley clique at Savannah. He filed the affidavit accusing Wesley of jumping bail in Savannah and of seducing Sophy. Wesley secured letters from Georgia witnessing that no bail had been established. The *Journal* itself was Wesley's summary of his ministry in Georgia and his attempt to explain his relationship with Sophy Hopkey.

Wesley's *Journal* for 1741 includes a letter to the Moravian Church that he began on his return to England in September 1738. In it, after celebrating the faith and love of the Moravians, he expressed his reservations. He thought the role of Count Zinzendorf to be too great. He criticized their levity and waste of time. He objected to their secrecy, cunning, and reserved character. He thought that too often they mixed human wisdom with divine revelation.[2] This letter remained unsent. In his testimony he did not really lose his affection for them until a year later when relations in the society began to separate them.

The disputes with the Moravians led to the Methodists' withdrawal from the Fetter Lane Society in 1740, and to Wesley's divisive letter to Count Zinzendorf.[3] In the letter, he enumerated many problems with the Moravian Church. In the end, he concluded with three great errors that characterized Moravian writing in England. He accused Moravians of advocating universal salvation as distinct from his own teaching of God's wanting the salvation of all. In this he was distancing himself from Calvinists, on the one hand, and Lutheran Moravians, on the other. He also objected to their antinomianism or very minimal use of the law. Here he was closer to Calvinism and farther from Lutheran teaching. Finally, he charged them with a mystical quietism or practice of nonassertion in which they waited for divine action. The Moravian response to Wesley was more irenic, but it held to the impossibility of perfection.[4]

The next month Wesley and Zinzendorf engaged in a combative dialogue in Latin at Gray's Inn Walks, London, on their religious differences. From Wesley's perspective their major difference was the Moravian collapse of sanctification into justification and the consequent neglect of good works and the journey toward perfection. Wesley had not given up the power of the sacraments and human effort to make one better or more sanctified. Zinzendorf regarded humanity as accepted at justification, and that was the end of it; there was no need to seek greater perfection or sanctification. In the split with Zinzendorf, the restless activist side of Methodist ethics became apparent. The early commitments to serve the poor and prisoners would continue, even though on different grounds than before the warming of the heart. The distinctiveness of the Methodists was emerging from the quarrels over the Fetter Lane Society. These distinctive traits rested in rather thoroughgoing free will, antipredestination teaching, which after justification led to the acceptance of commandments. Like Calvin and unlike Luther, there was Christian law for the justified.

The Moravians argued that Christians were not to follow "ordinances." Wesley understood the ordinances set aside by Paul in Colossians to have been Jewish rules, and he regarded Christians as still living under requirements to pray, fast, take Communion, do good works, live ethically, and so forth. On Monday, 20 June 1740, he put it plainly in rejecting the idea that a Christian was not under commandments: "How gross, palpable a contradiction is this to the whole tenor of the New Testament. Every part of which is full of commandments, from St. Matthew to the Revelation!"[5] He continued stressing how many times Christ gave commandments, quoting from Matthew and John. Given a challenge perceived as antinomianism, Wesley responded clearly with a *command ethic of duty.*

Challenges from the Moravians continued urging Wesley to remain still and wait on the Lord. The activism that separated him from the Moravians would also, resting upon convictions of freedom of the will and free grace, lead to the division from George Whitefield. It would take another year and a half, but Wesley and Whitefield were dragged into the conflict by others. Despite their goodwill for each other, the Methodists and the Calvinists divided, leaving many of the evangelical Calvinists in England under the direction of Whitefield's patron, the Countess of Huntingdon. The revival itself gathered momentum through preaching and organization. Conflicts, interruptions, and threats as well as theological disputations were the regular fare of the rapidly moving Mr. Wesley. Wesley had learned and experienced much through Moravian teaching, and he had loved them dearly. The separation was painful, but Wesley's movement was Anglican and Calvinist as well as Moravian, and the division was inevitable. The third journal continued the narration of Wesley's ministry, but its polemical purposes of justifying the separation from the Moravian Brethren are clear from its preface through the documents criticizing Moravian teachings that are inserted in the journal without regard to chronology.

Controversy

In 1741–1743, Wesley continued his preaching itinerancy around England and Wales. Many of his preaching places he had visited before, and he was busy visiting, reviewing, and strengthening the societies. He and Whitefield paid an agreeable visit to the archbishop of Canterbury, who noted their irregularity but did not oppose them. Wesley's reception at his old family church was less gracious. The Reverend Mr. Romney, who had courted his sister and served as curate under his father, prohibited Wesley from preaching at St. Andrew's. So John preached from his father's tomb on the text: "The Kingdom of heaven is not meats and drink, but righteousness, and peace and joy in the Holy Ghost."

In his New Testament commentary and in his published sermon on the text of Romans 14:17, the kingdom of God was the true religion that began on earth in righteousness, peace, and joy. He quoted from his brother's new hymn:

> Everlasting life is won:
> Glory is on earth begun.[6]

Eternal life, Wesley explained, began on earth as the kingdom of heaven to a degree opened in the person's soul. The righteousness of God was the fulfillment of the two great commandments to love God and to love the neighbor, who was every human creature. The love meant doing all the good one could to all. Albert C. Outler named this meaning of love as the "socialization of eudaemonism"[7] or the promotion of all humanity's happiness. This understanding of true religion led Wesley to the call for repentance that is found in the formal text of the printed sermon, "The Kingdom of God is at hand: repent ye, and believe the gospel" (Mark 1:15). This repentance and belief, or faith as personal confidence in the pardon of God, produced righteousness and accepted the salvation from hell. This faith was condemned by Romney as enthusiasm, but for Wesley, it provided the entrance to the kingdom of God.[8] Wesley's opinion was that those who heard him from the tombstone composed the largest congregation ever seen at Epworth. He returned each evening that week (June 6-13) to preach from his father's tomb. Other churches in the region were opened for his preaching in the mornings. On the last Sunday of his week, he preached from the tomb on the Sermon on the Mount for three hours.

On Sunday, 1 August 1742, John buried Susanna, his mother, in Bunhillfield, a Dissenters' burial ground. His journal testified to her good death in the faith. John witnessed that she, as well as her father, grandfather, husband, and three sons, had been a preacher of righteousness. In the *Journal*, he placed two letters after the report of her funeral. One to him described her home schooling of her family in Christian learning. The second described the home worship services she had led, which sometimes attracted two hundred people, while Samuel was away in London.

The growth of the movement and its challenge to religion as usual provoked violent opposition. By deepening or changing the official religion of England, the whole structure of the society was challenged. The violence, though sometimes opposed, was in the early years generally tolerated by the local political authorities. On 12 September 1742, Wesley was hit between the eyes with a rock. After he had wiped the blood away, he was able to continue with his sermon. He commented on how even a little suffering helped the cause of his preaching.

In addition to physical attacks, Wesley found his people being pulled away to the left by the Moravians and to the right by Whitefield and Lady Huntingdon. The correspondence among the three groups (Wesley and his less temperate brother, Charles, the Moravians, and the evangelical Calvinists) was warm and bitter at the same time. A family of faith was breaking up in those years, and the theological fratricide grounded in love and divided by opinion was painful to all. In 1742, Wesley again had to defend himself against Captain Williams's charges that he had jumped bail in Savannah. He published his denial of Williams's charges in an open letter of a London newspaper. At that time, John and Charles were directing their work from London and Bristol and alternating residency between the two when they were not on their evangelical missions around the kingdom. The initiation of the work in Newcastle made clear the need for an expansion in ministry, and few ordained clergy were staying with the Methodist movement.

The points of dispute that led Wesley to publish were often, but not always, about ethics. Wesley responded to three subjects in his 1742 defense[9] against Josiah Tucker, the author of *A Brief History of the Principles of Methodism*. Tucker clearly intended to discredit Methodism by accusing Wesley of belief in justification by faith alone, sinless perfection, and inconsistencies. Wesley affirmed justification by faith to mean that through faith the justificatory actions of God in Jesus Christ are known and accepted. All attempts to justify oneself were rejected. The second charge was against Wesley's ethics. He admitted, and pointed to his sermons and previous writing on the subject, to teaching sinless perfection. He did not mean freedom from sinful acts through ignorance, the escape from temptation, or freedom from participation in the brokenness of society rooted in sin. He meant clearly that one who has been born again can have the mind of Christ. Consequently, one can will to love God with all one's heart, mind, and soul, and to love the neighbor as the self. Wesley claimed this was the scriptural teaching: "This it is to be a perfect man, to be sanctified throughout, created anew in Christ Jesus: Even to have a heart for all—flaming with the love of God, to use Archbishop Usher's words."[10]

This meant for Wesley in principle every thought, word, and action may show forth God's praise. Wesley's critic had thought it enough to accuse Wesley of teaching perfection. Wesley thought it enough to clarify his teaching about perfection. He was between his Moravian and his Calvinist opponents here, or between

Zinzendorf and Whitefield. He did not want to go with Zinzendorf that at justification Christians are perfect in Christ, or with Whitefield that they continue to sin. It may be so for many, but in principle at least, sinless perfection was the way. There may be another solution. Paul in Romans 5–8 allows that Christians continue to sin, though they are saved from domination by sin. Human experience suggests that the overcoming of the power of sin in one's life while still sinning was the most that humans accomplish. The call to love of God and neighbor absolutely can be held as the Christian ethic while admitting that personally and socially Christians sin. It is best to maintain the rigorous ethic Wesley sought; both Zinzendorf and Whitefield relaxed it too much, with Zinzendorf giving up on social reform and Whitefield defending slavery. But the injunctions, if spoken by Jesus in Aramaic and interpreted decades later in Greek, do not need to be taken literally. Ethical rigor is one thing; claims for perfection another. Wesley tried to remain loving of his neighbor in his response to Tucker's critique. His success in the attempt needs to be honored while recognizing Wesley's failure in other situations. His third defense against inconsistencies was to show that the texts Tucker was discussing were really the opinions of Count Zinzendorf and Christian David that did not agree. Wesley used the occasion to state his own judgments on the meaning and implications of justification.

When, in 1743, Wesley published a pamphlet on the character of a Methodist, he hastened to say that Methodists were not distinguishable from other Christians by opinion or behavior. That is, they were not exceptionable in either. He wanted to distinguish Methodists by their fervor in loving God and neighbor. Furthermore, by following these two loves, the Methodist keeps all the commandments of God: "His one invariable Rule is this, *Whatever ye do in Word or Deed, do it all in the Name of the Lord Jesus, giving Thanks to God and the Father by him.*"[11]

Wesley wanted to see the fruits of faith as the distinguishing marks of Methodists. Probably, the words of enthusiasm and rigor in the classical virtues of Christianity express the intention of his pamphlet. The prayer that life is to be lived on earth as it is in heaven reflected the passion Wesley knew. All the moral imperatives were to be fulfilled while one was seeking to do all the possible good for the neighbor. It was the love of God itself that animates the moral rigor Wesley breathes into his exhortations.

He hastened to conclude that Methodists do not want to be distinguished from other Christians. The principles of Methodism are common, he argued, to all Christians. He wanted to be distinguished from the unbelieving world in heart and life, as were all who have Christ's mind. The essay ended in an ecumenical spirit: "Is thy heart right, as my heart is with thine? I ask no further questions. If it be give me thy hand. For opinions or terms, let us not destroy the work of God. Dost thou love and fear God? It is enough. I give thee the right hand of fellowship."[12]

Wesley analyzed the various physical reactions to the evangelical preaching. The convulsions, fainting, and other expressions led to criticisms of the Methodists by church people desiring a less enthusiastic expression of religion. For Wesley, the physical reactions were expressions within the combat of the spiritual world between Christ and Satan. Some of this spiritual struggle reached him in material ways.

John was accosted on the first day of 1743 by an anti-Methodist drunken traveler on the road between Doncaster and Epworth. At Epworth itself the next day, he was denied Communion by the Reverend Mr. Romney, whom his father had trained in the ministry. He preached again from his father's tomb in St. Andrew's churchyard.

Nonetheless, Wesley kept seeing the beneficent responses of people to the preaching and societies. He understood the need for follow-up, and he resolved not to preach where he could not return or organize those seeking salvation. Reading his sermons in the twenty-first century, one finds it hard to understand the reactions they caused. They do not seem overly emotional or designed to provoke physical manifestations. Of course, the perspective from twenty-first-century America is that of one conditioned by two centuries of evangelical preaching. It was the event of the time, and it provoked spiritual conflicts in individuals who experienced the revival and in those who opposed it from the perspective of either formal religion or no religion. He responded to the critics in his major publication of 1743, "An Earnest Appeal to Men of Reason and Religion."

An Earnest Appeal

The pamphlet was a justifying defense of the movement that was attracting detractors from the ranks of both skeptics and church people. It was a positive statement of Methodism's position and a refutation of the criticisms. John hoped to convince some that there was a religion of love reflecting the goodness of the God who inspired it. It came from the love of God and was a response of love to God and to every soul whom God had created. *Love* was the first word of this religion because it was of the nature of God.

The second word was *faith,* which was the straight way to communion with God. Wesley explained faith in several paragraphs. Fundamentally, it was the additional sense given by God for the experiencing of God. It was "the demonstrative evidence of things not seen." Here he was Lockean in epistemology with his own addition. Everything known is from sensory experience, and as other senses cannot reveal the spiritual world of the loving God, faith was the sense that opened that world to humanity. In particular, faith communicated the love of God to the human heart. From this love, perceived by faith, came happiness, virtue, joy, righteousness, and peace.

Wesley was responding to charges brought against Methodism in various pamphlets by the clergy of Newcastle, Bishop Gibson of London, the archbishop of York, and the bishop of Lichfield and Coventry. Although he was enthusiastic, or at least crowds responded to him enthusiastically, he needed to appear reasonable to the learned of the eighteenth century. So, he defined enthusiasm as participation in religious illusion and argued he was simply teaching the truth according to Scripture, the Church of England, and reason. He also had to defend his preaching outside churches and his increasing use of lay leadership. He argued that preaching needed to take place where the people were. Also, John reminded his critics of the pivotal role of nonordained leadership in the church, including Jesus and John Calvin.

The document was, as the title states, an appeal. Particularly, it was an appeal to the religious believer of the eighteenth century influenced by rationalism. It was a gentle piece; it did not attack the religion of others but argued that rational reading of Scripture and Anglican tradition will lead to the plain meanings associated with Methodism. The original appeal was brief and quite straight-forward; later revisions of "Appeals" would lengthen it and make it more complex.

In summary of its ethics, it was a clear statement of the ethics of Christianity as love for the neighbor, meaning the active pursuit of the good of every living person. This love was practiced in the church by the fulfillment of all of the Ten Commandments. On refuting the charge that Methodists were leaving the church, he wrote on ethics: "Do we leave the *practice* of the Church, the standard whereof are the Ten Commandments—which are so essentially inwrought in her constitution (as little as you may apprehend it) that whosoever breaks one of the least of these is no member of the Church of England?"[13]

The seriousness of the appeal to the understanding of the churchmen is inspired in part by the threats to Wesley's life that were incited by official church displeasure with his new ministry. These attacks continued in 1743. He suffered a blow to the head at St. Ives in September. In October, he was subject to a dangerous mob action at Wednesbury that threatened his death. Some of his protectors were beaten. Justices refused to protect him even when the mob carried him to their houses. Wesley alternatively prayed, reasoned, and tried to flee. He received several blows before the mob was stilled. A few days later, Wesley was blamed for the riots by the justices, who had failed to intervene.

Another appeal for toleration was made to the mayor of Newcastle. The mayor had forbidden Wesley to preach anymore at Sand Hill. Wesley in his letter respectfully acquiesced, but also suggested the rioting was the fault of the gentleman who had paid men to raise the tumult. Except for the gentleman's intervention, Wesley assured the mayor he would have quieted the crowd and had a respectful audience. He also argued that he had come at the bequest of the Countess of Huntingdon to preach to the sinful coal miners of Newcastle who attended no church. He indicated that many were willing to testify to the effects of his mission in that more were sober, fewer were cursing, and the violating of the Sabbath had lessened.[14]

Letter to the King

Persecution of the Methodists plagued Wesley in 1744. At the first Conference in June, they discussed the fundamental theological points that separated them from the Moravians and Whitefield despite their affection for them. The war with France affected them deeply. Methodist workers were subject to impressment under George II as vagabonds without employment. In one instance in 1745, Wesley was seized but then released. Methodists were able to carry their evangelism among the army quartered in Germany. Wesley's correspondence encouraged John Haime in the ministry to the army. Haime had seen the fury of war at Dettingen where George II led the English to victory over the French, marking the last time an English monarch would lead the army into battle.

The war with France had stirred rumors of French support for the return of the Stuart Pretender to England. Wesley felt the need to clear himself and his movement from accusations of Jacobite and Roman Catholic prejudices. On 5 March, he wrote a rather humble letter to the king disassociating himself from papists and Dissenters. He pledged loyalty to the king and his house and proclaimed Methodist goals to be the promotion of "justice, mercy and truth, the glory of God, and peace and goodwill among men."[15] He indicated that as much as loyalty to Scripture permitted, they would follow the king, and that conscience demanded reverence for "the higher powers." He closed with promise of prayers for the king. John Wesley's enthusiasm for George II would never rise as high as it would for the reverent but embattled George III, but the Stuart return in 1745 engaged his monarchical support. The letter is clear refutation of interpreters who suggested latent Jacobite tendencies on John's part. His mother, Susanna, and his brother, Samuel, were Jacobite supporters, but on this issue John was his father's son and a loyal supporter of the Hanoverian house. On the advice of Charles, he laid the letter aside rather than send it.

As discussed earlier, on 24 August 1744, Wesley preached his last sermon to official Oxford at St. Mary's on High Street. Thereafter, the university found substitutes rather than allow him to preach.[16] He, of course, remained a fellow of Lincoln College and received a stipend from the college until he married in 1751 and resigned his fellowship.

A couple of days before Christmas, John felt ill and experienced heavy nose bleeding. The next day, he was exhausted until at evening prayers, he experienced the presence of God. The next day, Christmas, he again felt this unique closeness to God: "So that God was before me all the day long; I sought and found him in every place, and could truly say when I lay down at night, 'now I have *lived* a day.' "[17]

If 1744 was the year for receiving blows, 1745 seemed to be Wesley's year for being repeatedly pelted with stones and mud. More seriously, even, his opponents circulated charges of his alliance with the Pretender. When the Scots arose in 1745 and Bonnie Prince Charlie returned to wage war for the Crown, Wesley hurried to the north country where his preaching missions had been successful in Newcastle, and among the surrounding coal miners, Wesley preached and encouraged the English to resist the invasion. During the rebellion, he wrote to the Honorable James West, offering to raise a company of two hundred armed men and to support them from Methodist contributions. Charles's success would have increased French influence and Catholic influence, and Wesley dreaded both prospects. In his letter to the mayor of Newcastle of 26 October 1745, he offered to preach to the defenders of the city. He worried about the lack of public morals displayed by the defenders. He assured the mayor of the steadfastness of those affected by the evangelical message by describing the bravery of his assistants John Haime, William Clements, and John Evans at the Battle of Fontenoy on 11 May 1745. Wesley joined in the public prayers of thanksgiving for the victory over the Scottish supporters of the Pretender at the Battle of Culloden in 1746. A lover of peace and one who, in the spirit of the Sermon on the Mount, urged active peacemaking, he was realistic about the defeat of the usurpers when war came. There is no record in this case of his appropriation of just war criteria being used to judge the wrong of the unnecessary English slaughter of the Highlanders after the battle.

Social Action

The unity between church organization and social welfare work was very clear in Wesley's "Plain Account of the Methodists" (1749).

His description of his society's organization into classes, bands, select bands, and penitent bands was followed by the responsibilities of the society's offices and the practical relief work of the society. Throughout "A Plain Account," the reader saw Wesley's prudential adjustment of the growing society's organization and rules to meet practical needs.

Wesley found that he could not administer the poor relief funds of the society, so stewards were appointed to distribute the funds "as everyone had need." The system was satisfactory, even though the need often left him in debt. He mentioned being £100 in debt in 1749. The stewards were not able to visit all the sick, so a category of visitors was created and the city divided into zones; two visitors took responsibility for each zone.

Soon, however, it became clear that more medical help was needed for the poor. This need led to Wesley's establishing a medical clinic with the aid of an apothecary and a surgeon. Wesley himself maintained the dispensary, practicing medicine for many years until the expense became too heavy. He also established a poor house for a community of widows and other poor who could not care for themselves. Methodist preachers ate with the group when they were in town: "For I myself, as well as the other preachers who are in town, diet with the poor on the same food and at the same table. And we rejoice herein as a comfortable earnest of our eating bread together in our Father's Kingdom."[18]

For a while, he supported another school in his home in addition to the Kingswood School, which still exists. It was for the children of the very poor with expenses defrayed by contributions.[19] His description of the achievement of the pupils in behavior, religious temperament, as well as learning in reading, writing, and arithmetic was revealing of his deep compassion and his conviction regarding learning and self-improvement.

The final action of social amelioration mentioned in "A Plain Account" was the establishment of a revolving loan fund to save the poor from the pawnbroker. His review of the accounts of his stewards led him to conclude that 250 people had been assisted in one year. He pleaded that more people would join in supporting the fund. Then he concluded his account by indicating that he used the society's funds for these services, and that for his own needs, he drew upon them the same way the poor found relief. He concluded with the veiled criticism of the religious establishment that this was the original way all church revenues were used. He urged that all church funds continue to be used for the poor by the authorities or that they face God's judgment. His combined efforts at provision of funds for clothing and food, education of children, establishment of housing, founding of a health clinic, and creation of a small loan fund were a relatively complete model for any church. Other services were developed later, but by 1749, a thorough program was in place. Other elements were needed for a complete program of social relief in a cruel age, but then and now, the assumption of these tasks by Christians would lead to further discoveries of need and policies.

The motifs of doing all the good one could, to all one could, characterized his public life in the closing years of the 1740s. He was not the first to develop loan funds for the poor and for persons beginning businesses. But when small loan funds without interest were combined with the discipline and social solidarity of the Methodist classes, they were very effective. All of the relief services were characterized by generosity and religious conviction that motivated the recipients.

The closing of the medical clinics due to the high cost did not lead to giving up the work on health. He never abandoned his holistic approach of recommending walking as exercise, temperance in food, abstinence from strong liquor as opposed to wine or weak beer, regular sleep, and cleanliness.

The publication of *Primitive Physic* in 1746 went further in recommending almost three hundred folk medicines for specific ailments.[20] In his *Physic* he followed the writings of the respected medical doctor George Cheyne, plus his own readings and experience, and testimonies he trusted. By contributing the volume, he continued a family tradition shared by Grandfather and Great-grandfather Wesley.

These practical solutions of medicines, remedies, loans, and schools were, for him, all expressions of the basic ethic of loving the neighbor. His concerns in this period moved beyond the immediate physical needs, however, to counseling his followers and others on politics. He did not hesitate to recommend candidates whom he regarded as loyal to the king. Even his preachers were allowed to defend the king and the king's policies in their preaching. The king was the head of the church in its practical administration, and he served at God's pleasure. Also, the king's bench was the one level of justice that shielded the Methodists from their persecutors. But beyond this strong monarchical bent, which was consistent with his hierarchical leanings in church government, John pleaded for honesty in voting. He spoke and wrote about the dignity of not selling one's vote or accepting food or drink from candidates for office. At this time, he still had a vote in the university's choice of members of Parliament. In these issues, he was a high churchman and a king's supporter, as his father had been.

In 1746, John published the first volume of his *Sermons on Several Occasions*. By 1750, he had added two more volumes for a total of almost forty published sermons in the three volumes. Many of his sermons, including some published in the books, also circulated in the form of pamphlets and single-sermon publications. He intended the sermons, along with his *Notes upon the New Testament*, to become the guideposts of the meaning of the Methodist movement. The first sermons on faith, real Christianity, challenge to conventional religion, scriptural Christianity, justification, righteousness, and the series on the spirit set out his distinctive theological interests. The presentation of his theology in the sermonic form is a reminder of his vocation as an itinerant, evangelical preacher. Similarly, his ethics are best captured in their rigorous personal demands in his thirteen sermons on the Sermon on the Mount written in this form in 1748–1750 though drawing upon more than one hundred previous occasions of preaching. His second sermon in 1725 had been on the Sermon on the Mount, as was one of the sermons from his father's tomb in 1742.

The School in Kingswood

The school at Kingswood was Wesley's creation, and when he could give energy to it, the school revived. Unfortunately for the school, his vocation as an evangelical, itinerant preacher came first, and he could seldom attend to it. His visits to the school often involved him in setting it right again. The first two schoolmasters employed by Wesley were the worst. After embezzling school funds, they were arrested for highway robbery. Robert Ramsey was executed, and Gwillam Snowde, perhaps due to Wesley's pleading, was deported.

The plan for the school, which he published in 1749, reads as a hybrid of Susanna Wesley's methods and John Wesley's Oxford learning.[21] It had the rigorous, ascetic schedule of Susanna and the study of works influential in John's life. He intended his students to be better prepared than those from Oxford. The school would accept only boarders who would not leave for any vacation until they had completed the program. They came between six and twelve years of age. John thought of it as a school he would have planned for his own children if he had any, and it served as a school for children of his preachers.

The plan was in eight years to learn Latin, Greek, Hebrew, and French, and to become proficient in English. Other major subjects included arithmetic, history, geography, rhetoric, logic, ethics, music, geometry, algebra, and physics. The reading list reflected Wesley's journey from his *Lessons for Children* to favorite works *The Manners of Ancient Christians, Primitive Christianity, The Pilgrim's Progress, Imitation of Christ, The Life of Mr. Haliburton, Christian Perfection, Serious Call, Iliad,* and Genesis. The children were up at 4:00 A.M. (Wesley's rising hour), and their day was planned with no time for playing. The plan included Wesley's Friday fast until three in the afternoon. At eight o'clock, the children went to bed. The whole plan would, if evangelical conversion occurred, come as close to producing more John Wesleys as any educational plan could have. The days were so strictly planned that even the grace-filled moments of the Epworth parsonage seem to be excluded. An interesting omission is that given Wesley's experience while at Oxford with works of social service, no inclusion of volunteer activity was envisioned. Of course, that was only the plan as written by Wesley; his *Journal* indicates that the practice often differed. The boys did not bend that easily, and the salaries never seemed to attract outstanding masters. The school caused Wesley much anguish in addition to his caper with thirty-four-year-old Sarah Ryan, the housemistress of the school, which in his fifty-fifth year drove his wife away.

An Amour

Wesley had been persuaded at Conference in 1748 that his ascetic thoughts toward marriage had been extreme. So, he moved
away from his "Thoughts on Marriage" toward a more moderate
stance. Yet he never overcame his personal asceticism. The love of
God and the love for the threatened souls of his listeners meant he
would never abandon his vocation. Since his conversion to the
encompassing love of God in 1738, he had never been romantically
minded. Women were attracted to him, but a lifestyle of 7,500
miles of annual travel on horseback and eighteen or so sermons a
week did not permit time for romance. Umphrey Lee has summarized his travels for 1747.[22] In January, he was preaching around
Bristol, and in February, he was in Lincolnshire. He traveled
through Yorkshire and the Midlands from March through May. In
June, he alternated among London, Bristol, and Plymouth. He
preached at his regular places in Cornwall in July. In August, he
itinerated through Wales and Ireland, returning to Wales in
September. He spent the last three months of the year in and
around London. His vocation and the love of God for the damned
souls of his neighbors obscured the need for love of a woman until
1748.

He would not have fallen in love then, either, but he became desperately ill. In fact, his three most important loves originated in his
being nursed back to health by a woman. While he was convalesc-
ing, he almost promised to marry Grace Murray, a widowed
worker in the Methodist movement. Wesley assumed he had won
her hand, but as before, in the long ago case of Sophy Hopkey, he
dithered. She toured with him, but he left her at Cheshire. There,
she became engaged to one of Wesley's preachers, John Bennet.
During the winter, however, she vacillated and came to John
Wesley in the spring at Bristol.

On a preaching tour of Ireland with her, John and Grace fell
more deeply in love. They pledged their marriage with the Prayer
Book and a witness, but John, still procrastinating, indicated (1) his
brother Charles must agree, (2) John Bennet must concur, and
(3) the Methodist societies must support the marriage. All of this
ambiguity forced a debate among twentieth-century Methodist

historians as to whether or not John and Grace were legally married.[23] Grace indicated she would not wait more than a year for the conditions to be met, so regardless of the niceties of eighteenth-century law, neither she nor John regarded themselves as married or even completely committed.

While John was agonizing and writing a long paper on Grace's spiritual journey and his considerations of her for marriage, Grace heard gossip about John and Molly Francis. John seemed to have been dimly aware of a crisis brewing in his engagement. But he had preaching obligations to meet, and he did not secure his fiancée to himself.

Charles tempestuously threw himself into the fray. He misled Grace and took her to John Bennet, whom he persuaded to proceed with his marriage. Grace and Bennet were married. Charles confronted his brother John with sharp accusations for violating Bennet's engagement, for planning to marry beneath himself, and for threatening to break up the Methodist movement. Neither George Whitefield nor John Nelson, who were comforting John, could prevent Charles from leveling his accusations.

Though John formally forgave Grace, John Bennet, and Charles, he would see Grace only once more, years later, in London after Bennet had died. Bennet had left the Wesley connection for Calvinism shortly after his marriage. Charles was never as close to John after the intervention as he had been. Eventually, Charles, recently married, would give up the itinerancy, live in London, and chide John for moving too far from the Church of England.

Wesley wrote up his version of this relationship. It has been known for most of a century by students of Wesley, though its publication has not been wide and it has not been part of Methodist folklore. Clearly, both John Wesley and John Bennet believed Grace was engaged to them. Grace herself seemed to intend to marry whichever one would accomplish it, as she vacillated back and forth.

It is, of course, difficult to read her intentions because we have only John's version of her thoughts.[24] She was both a house servant and an assistant in the evangelical vocation to John Wesley. The power was his, and she was awed by it. John certainly saw in her a traveling companion and coworker, qualities he pursued in the future Mrs. Wesley until the travel proved too much. Also of note was that she had been brought to heightened religious consciousness first by the preaching of George Whitefield and then by Wesley himself. On her exposure to Wesley's preaching, she was struck down and overtaken by groans. Later, she was assisted home by two women. Her conversion brought tension into her relations with her husband who was lost at sea a few years after her conversion. She then moved to Newcastle to her mother's home, at the advice of John Wesley.

There began the meetings that culminated in the flowering and losing of love. As a widow, she had more married experience than Wesley, but in both spiritual and practical matters, he was the charismatic leader of the society. Basically, she did what he advised. Some of the time she was living in his house with others and sometimes with her mother in Newcastle. Their trips together caused dissension and gossip within the society. John had advised her against a relationship with John Brydon and had sent her on a journey away from him. Later when John Brydon married and then became less religiously serious, Grace blamed herself. When John Wesley had lost her, he confessed his knowledge that Grace had loved him for ten years. The record shows Wesley advising her to return to Newcastle in October of 1742. If the ten years were taken as an exact figure, it would push her love for him back to the time of her conversion when her husband was still living. It is probable that her conversion and subsequent spiritual development synthesized love for God and for God's messenger.

Sexual expression between the two remains a matter of conjecture. Wesley never confessed to it. George Whitefield told John Bennet, however, that he regarded Grace as Wesley's wife. Wesley's account of their relationship was that others regarded her as his mistress. One of his preachers, according to John's record, accused John of wishing his whore to be put aside out of Newcastle. Wesley, while presenting these judgments of others, did not contradict them. It stretches the modern mind to assume John, once he had renounced celibacy as a clerical necessity, had not been intimate with her on their long journeys and repeated pledges of troth to each other. Yet John Wesley was an extremely disciplined man. Nevertheless in this case with Grace, the entire situation was one of neither perfection nor righteousness. Wesley had particularly his brother to blame for telling her that John would not have anything to do with her. After hearing that, she accepted John Bennet's proposal. Wesley was broken by the betrayal of his lover, his preacher, and Charles. In his sorrow, he wrote a long poem while traveling from Leeds to Newcastle. Often kept from human love by love for the divine, in his sorrow he returned to divine love. Wesley resumed his vocation, publishing that same year the sermons on the Sermon on the Mount.

6. Sermon on the Mount
(1748–1750)

The importance of the Sermon on the Mount to Wesley's ethics is established by the fact that he had preached on it at least one hundred times by the time he published his sermons on the Sermon. Moreover, the sermons on the Sermon occupied one-third of the *Standard Sermons*, which he had the Conference adopt as one of the two norms for Methodist doctrine and preaching. The Sermon on the Mount was for Wesley the standard of pure religion and had been presented by God. It showed the way of salvation and, therefore, was for Wesley what contemporary interpreters could call the way of orthopraxis or the way of right conduct for those choosing the way of salvation in Christ.

The ethic of the Christian person is for Wesley grounded in Scripture. Scriptural ethics are absolute. There is no error in scriptural moral instruction, and it has the authority of God behind it. The issue is in the interpretation of Scripture. The interpretation is not to find an author's perspective but to find the divine perspective by using all of Scripture to interpret Scripture according to its plain teaching. The tradition of church interpretation is consulted, as are contemporary eighteenth-century interpretations, but the central task is to find God's will. The clearest, detailed statement of the divine will is for Wesley in the Sermon on the Mount.

Wesley's evolving understanding of Christian ethics has been surveyed in the previous chapters. It can be summarized as the seeking of God's human holiness in the years before Aldersgate, the priority of faith directing one toward action after awakening in 1738, and the maturing position of "faith working by love." This third position is presented clearly in "The Wedding Garment" sermon of 1790 and throughout his most extensive presentation of Christian ethics in the discourses of 1748–1750 on the Sermon on the Mount. The thirteen discourses resemble sermons, but they are essays or sermonic essays on the Sermon on the Mount.

110

Wedding Garment

Half of the short sermon of eight pages is given to the question of "What is the wedding garment of Matthew 22:12?"[1] Wesley sets aside various interpretations almost as if he were clearing away the alternative interpretations in an academic lecture. Then he pounces: of course, the wedding garment necessary for salvation is holiness. Both the holiness of Christ and the "personal holiness" save humanity from being cast into hellfire. Wesley then engages in a couple of paragraphs of Roman Catholic bashing. He regards its reliance on prayers to saints as idolatry, and he dismisses its persecution of heretics as contrary to all true religion. He also condemns Protestant persecution and the burdening of believers with matters of a trifling nature. One could be honest, modest, and of benefit to the world and still be far from holiness. This holiness that expresses love is given in detail in his discourses or sermonic essays on the Sermon on the Mount.

The wedding garment, necessary for salvation, is the "new creation [of] the renewal of the soul in the image of God."[2] This is the keeping of the commandments of God, particularly "Thou shalt love the Lord thy God with all thy heart, and thy neighbor as thyself." In a word, holiness is the having of "the mind that was in Christ," and the "walking as Christ walked."[3] Wesley then continues that this has been his position for sixty years without any change. This claim of sixty years reaches back to pre-Aldersgate experience and to his early preaching at Oxford of everything depending on the love of God and neighbor.[4] Both at Oxford and now nearing the end of his life, supposing this might be the last sermon he would write, he opposed Christianity's sometimes drift toward antinomianism.

The conclusion of the sermon, which Wesley knew would be printed in his magazine the *Arminian*, summarizes his ethic.

> The sum of all is this: the God of love is willing to save all the souls that he has made. This he has proclaimed to them in his Word, together with the terms of salvation revealed by the Son of his love, who gave his own life that they that believe in him might have everlasting life. And for these he has prepared a kingdom from the foundation of the world. But he will not force them

to accept of it. He leaves them in the hands of their own counsel. He saith: "Behold, I set before you life and death, blessing and cursing; choose life, that ye may live." Choose holiness by my grace, which is the way, the only way, to everlasting life. He cries aloud, "Be holy, and be happy; happy in this world, and happy in the world to come." "Holiness becometh his house for ever!" This is the wedding garment of all that are called to "the marriage of the Lamb." Clothed in this they will not be found naked: "they have washed their robes and made them white in the blood of the Lamb." But as to all those who appear in the last day without the wedding garment, the Judge will say: "Cast them into outer darkness; there shall be weeping and gnashing of teeth."

Madeley, March 16, 1790[5]

The detailed filling out of this summary is presented in Wesley's sermons on the Sermon on the Mount, written from 1748 to 1750. For Wesley, Matthew had written the chronologically First Gospel. Mark, Luke, and John had, in his opinion, supplemented Matthew by reporting material he had omitted and presenting the message in terms of their time, place, and religious context. Consequently, the Sermon on the Mount's uniqueness to Matthew stemmed from the fact that the others saw no need to repeat what was already presented by the Gospel of Matthew.

Sermon on the Mount

Although it is a common principle of interpretation of the early twenty-first century that the Sermon on the Mount is an original construction of the author of Matthew, Wesley believed it was God's speech. Wesley was not worried about the author's sources or how many authentic words of Jesus were preserved in Matthew 5–7. For him it was God's teaching through Jesus on a mountain expounding the evangelical way of life. Everything needful for the way of life was present in the Sermon. In fact, the Sermon contained all that was necessary to prevent authentic Christianity from becoming corrupted, according to Wesley. Probably this is the definitive source for Wesley's understanding of God's given ethic. The sermons of 1748–1750 are midlife sermons for Wesley. Once he had written and published them, he never felt the need to rework them, though he continued to preach on the Sermon on the

Mount, as he had from his youth. For Wesley, the Sermon on the Mount was intended for all time and for everyone who would accept it.

According to Wesley, in the fifth chapter of Matthew the authentic summary of religion is given, and the mistakes of people are countered. In the sixth chapter, rules for our intentions, which guide actions, are presented, and the seventh chapter cautions against religious mistakes and applies the whole sermon.

Discourse I: Humility

"Blessed are the poor in spirit: for theirs is the kingdom of heaven" is interpreted as the humble acceptance of forgiveness by God of the sin that alienated humanity. It is the antidote to pride from the basic message of salvation preached by Wesley. So it is the beginning of the Christian journey. It is not particularly related to material poverty, but one who took any pride in riches would not be saved. "And this is the true, genuine, Christian humility, which flows from a sense of the love of God, reconciled to us in Christ Jesus."[6]

The second beatitude, "Blessed are they that mourn," is developed as the sorrowful state of those who, having known reconciliation, fall into sadness, wanting the assurance of God's presence that they once knew. The premise is that these Christian mourners will receive again joy in the presence of Christ. A secondary meaning is that the assured Christian mourns out of sympathy for the fallen, suffering world. Wesley closes this first sermon on the Beatitudes promising blessing to those who after conversion have mourned the absent God and to those who, sensing the lostness of unbelievers, mourn their condition. Because all live on the precipice of hell, he calls forth mourning first for oneself when God seems absent, and then for the neighbor's danger when one is safe.

The sermon placed the humility and mourning of the Beatitudes squarely in an evangelical-sermonic context. They are recognizably still virtues, but as habits, clearly dependent upon Wesley's summary of the evangelical message. In his *Explanatory Notes upon the New Testament* published half a decade later, he changed the translation from *blessed* to *happiness*. The change revealed the degree to which his eschatology was a present one. Real happiness was granted to the believer in this history.

Discourse II: Righteousness

The second sermon exposits briefly the blessings of the meek and those who hunger and thirst for righteousness, and then interprets the blessing of the merciful in terms of Paul's writing on love. The blessing to the meek is to those who inherit the earth when God's fulfillment is realized and to the meek for whom God provides all they need from the earth. Meekness is a blessing that is to increase in Christians, producing patience within a person, resignation before God's will, and gentleness toward all people. This meekness prohibits all anger toward people while permitting anger at sin. Humanity cannot continue in anger toward others and still commune with God. Wesley reads this beatitude to imply the need to take initiative. One must seek out reconciliation with the enemy. The meek inherit the earth in the sense that God provides them what they need. With what they receive they are content, so they have inherited the earth.

With the hindrances of pride, thoughtlessness, and anger removed, Wesley understood Matthew to present the gift of thirst and hunger for righteousness as an attitude of loving God and neighbor. The pursuit of righteousness for Wesley is presented here as a higher righteousness of fellowship with God and of being purified. Significantly, before the higher righteousness search begins the religion of the world has been fulfilled in first "doing no harm," "relieving the poor," and using the means of grace, entrusted to the church.[7]

Discourse III: Peacemaking

The sermon on Matthew 5:8-12 concludes the Beatitudes and the interpretation of the blessings on the pure in heart, the peacemakers, and the persecuted for righteousness. The sermon begins with the reference to the double love commandments and their dependence on God's love. Twenty pages later, it ends with the injunction to holiness. These Beatitudes, interpreted through love with the direction of holiness, are for Wesley the essentials of Jesus' religion.

The blessedness for the pure in heart is the apprehension of God and a close personal relationship with God. Wesley says one who is pure in heart talks with God as one does with a friend.

Wesley does not forbid divorce in this sermon, but he forbids remarriage to all except those who divorced because of their spouse's adultery. His interpretation here followed that of some Anglican bishops, but was less stringent on remarriage than some others.

His position on oaths was similarly a middle position. He interpreted the injunction not to take an oath as ruling out false oaths and everyday oaths, but not oaths taken before a magistrate. In fact, he attempted to show that both Jesus and Paul had done so.

He concludes his writing on what he labeled the religion of the heart with a beautiful paragraph:

> But the great lesson which our blessed Lord inculcates here, and which he illustrates by this example, is that God is in all things, and that we are to see the Creator in the glass of every creature; that we should use and look upon nothing as separate from God, which indeed is a kind of practical atheism; but with a true magnificence of thought survey heaven and earth and all that is therein as contained by God in the hollow of his hand, who by his intimate presence holds them all in being, who pervades and actuates the whole created frame, and is in a true sense the soul of the universe.[8]

"Blessed are the peacemakers" is interpreted primarily in terms of doing all the good one can for others. It is the full exertion of powers so that goodwill increases, and peace is preserved or restored. Self-love is seen as the enemy of peacemaking, and the seeking of the common good as essential to the meaning of the beatitude.

The process of peacemaking, Wesley recognizes, leads to persecution. Persecution is the inevitable fruit of serious religion. All Christians should expect persecution for their pursuit of righteousness. Particularly, they are persecuted for being peacemakers.

The Christian is not to seek persecution, but to expect it. Wesley realizes that in his day it will not ordinarily be persecution unto death but harassment and slander. He returns to the theme of meekness and to the need to love all, including enemies. The sermon is full of the direct application of the stringent teachings of Jesus.

Another version of Wesley's economic ethics appears. Owe no one anything, provide for your family, and then lend or give away any surplus to the needy. The sermon concludes with Wesley's call to perfection in the name of this "genuine religion of Jesus Christ."

Discourse IV: Social Religion

The sermon on Matthew 5:13-16 encourages listeners to seek to be the salt of the earth and the light of the world so that others may appreciate good works and glorify the Father. The sermon explicitly refers to the character of the believer who is being transformed into the likeness of God. Wesley's contribution in the sermon is to demonstrate that Christian life is a public life of doing good. He is impatient with the world-denying, individualistic interpretations of these texts.

His outline of the sermon is to show, first, that "Christianity is essentially a social religion, and that to turn it into a solitary one is to destroy it."[9] Second, he argues that it is impossible to turn Christianity into a concealed religion, and finally, he provides practical application. So the sermon celebrates good works and opposes the quietistic inward tendencies of the Moravians.

He is not opposed to seasons of "religious retirement," but periods of retreat for prayer and renewal cannot usefully become dominant. The nature of Christianity is to be social; Christians are to act as salt and light in influencing others. The virtues of Christianity require interaction with others. He reflects upon his decision in the move to Lincoln College to decide to deal with many acquaintances without becoming intimate friends with them.

Peacemaking, like meekness, requires interaction with other people. He interprets it as a virtue requiring social interaction. "Another necessary branch of true Christianity is peacemaking, or doing of good."[10]

It is not only that the virtues of Jesus' teaching require public interaction; it is also that by social witness, others are called to appreciate God and drawn toward the light. "Love cannot be hid any more than light, and least of all when it shines forth in action when ye exercise yourselves in the labor of love in beneficence of every kind."[11] Wesley, of course, is clear that good works are pursued not for salvation or for their intrinsic value, but for glorifying God. "Let the light which is in your heart shine in all good works, both works of piety and works of mercy."[12]

Discourse V: Moral Law

His discourse on Matthew 5:17-20 emphasizes Wesley's moralism. Following Matthew, he insists that Jesus is not an innovator in religious morality. All of the moral law of Moses is to be kept without fail, and Christians are under the authority of Jesus himself to be more righteous than the scribes and the Pharisees.

Wesley teaches that Jesus set aside all the ceremonial law taught by Moses for the ritual and sacrifice of the temple. This is peculiar teaching, for Jesus honored the temple, and there is no record of Jesus' abolishing the ritual or law regarding the temple. In Wesley's day, the temple was long gone, but it was not so in Jesus' day. If Jesus had destroyed all the temple ordinances, he would have been the very radical religious innovator that Wesley deplored. Wesley is in a particular bind: he wants to keep some of the moral law, particularly the Ten Commandments, and he knows that much of Leviticus, Deuteronomy, and so forth has no relevance to England. He believes it is from God through Moses. Only Jesus could set it aside, but unfortunately for his argument, there is very little evidence that he did. From a modern perspective it is absurd to believe that Moses legislated for a temple that was not built until centuries after his death in a city he never saw. Similarly, much of the moral law attributed to Moses in Deuteronomy is specifically for a land and a situation of the seventh century B.C. of which Moses could have known nothing. But even given Wesley's presuppositions about the authorship of scripture, his division by Jesus of the law into moral and irrelevant temple law is peculiar—even if common in his day.

The moral law of the Old Testament is for Wesley binding on all of humanity "not depending either on time or place, or any other circumstances liable to change."[13] He does not say in the sermon exactly which laws he regards as binding moral laws, but the moral rigor of the sermon is clear without the specifics. He urges the giving of alms, the study of Scripture, the act of fasting, frequent Communion, and frequent prayer. The relevance of the sermon is saved by his neglect of detailing any of the laws he regards as eternal and by the warmth of his conclusion. All of this law that is also gospel to Wesley is for the love of God and humanity. He urges a religion of the heart that is willing to be meek and to suffer for righteousness. A thirst for God is a sign of the Christian who seriously seeks to live life to achieve "everlasting glory, or everlasting burning."[14]

Discourse VI: Lord's Prayer

Wesley's discourse on Matthew 6:1-15 deals with two subjects: almsgiving and the Lord's Prayer. Though Matthew gives no indication that he is commenting on anything more than alms, Wesley expands alms to mean all good works of charity. They are not to be undertaken for human praise. They are to be done without expectation of human or earthly reward. For Wesley, the more important consideration is that they be done. His voice rings authentically when he urges feeding the hungry, visiting the sick and those in prison, instructing the uneducated, reproving the sinner, encouraging the do-gooder and all other works of mercy. The practices he lists are exactly what he has been doing. He is not extreme in urging that good works be kept secret. Their motive is God's glory, but sometimes they need to be seen to move people toward God.

His comments on the text of Matthew on prayer are similar. It is of extreme urgency that the prayers be offered. Matthew seems concerned about secrecy. Wesley's interpretation urges they be given in the congregation or in private. Whereas Matthew condemns much speaking and vain repetitions, Wesley thinks some repetition is justified, and he does not want to limit the prayer's length as much as he is concerned that it is meaningful. The meaning of the petitions is mostly to the hearer, for God, as Matthew said, knows what one needs before one prays. Wesley's paraphrase of the Lord's Prayer, with which he closes his commentary on the prayer, is six times as long as the prayer in Matthew.

Wesley's commentary on the prayer has many dimensions worthy of exploration. For a study in ethics it is of particular importance. It is almost a summary of the Christian life for Wesley. It includes everything we should pray for. It contains all we should desire because we should not desire anything we cannot pray for. It includes duties to God and other humans.

Wesley interprets the prayer from the perspective of a rich Christology and a fully developed doctrine of the Trinity, moving beyond Matthew's version by including other biblical texts and postbiblical theological developments. In particular, the Gospel of John's theology of love provides a framework for understanding the Father reference. The early petitions—"Hallowed be thy name," "Thy kingdom come," "Thy will be done in earth, as it is in heaven"—are to be taken in an activist sense. Wesley notes that many would hear "only an expression of, or petition for, resignation; for a readiness to suffer the will of God."[15] But this for Wesley is not the point: "We pray, not so much for a passive, as for an active, conformity to the will of God, in saying, 'Thy will be done in earth, as it is in heaven.'"[16] The angels do it willingly, perfectly, continually, and so are those to act who pray the prayer. As the angels do it solely because it is God's will, so are all humans to enact God's will on earth.

Wesley uses the translation "trespasses" to mean the debts we owe to God. It contains the obligation for the one praying to forgive the wrongs done to oneself as a response to the forgiveness of God. Temptation will come, but with God's help it will be overcome and the prayer prays for relief from temptation. He uses the closing doxology of kingdom, power, and glory from the Authorized Version. Throughout the interpretation of the prayer, a warm confidence of love for God prevails. The most noteworthy theme for ethical reflection is the urgency of doing what one prays for to realize the will of God.

Discourse VII: Fasting and Charity

In 6:16-18 the Gospel of Matthew enjoins those who fast to fast for God and not to let others know they are fasting. The injunction is clearly parallel to those for prayer and almsgiving—keep it secret. The secrecy is not so important to Wesley. He takes the text and interprets it through his practice of fasting but not to extremes. He also uses it as an opportunity for arguing again that faith and good works belong together. Religion is meant to be not inner or outer but both.

He discusses fasting in the Old and New Testaments and in church history. He notes the Anglican Church's days for stated fasting. The origins of fasting he attributes to deep emotions of sorrow or repentance wherein one forgot to eat. Others may fast to reduce the lure of sensuality or to be a means of self-punishment on the occasion of sin. It is also followed to assist in prayer.

Wesley returns to his strong command ethic regarding fasting. Because the conditions for almsgiving, prayer, and fasting were all given by Jesus, in the sermon the obligation to undertake them was implied, as was the promised reward by the one who saw the practices in secret.

Wesley did not refer to his practice of fasting in the sermon. All through these sermons he speaks of matters relating to his experience without referring to himself.

The conclusion of the discourse returns to one of his themes. Just as fasting needed to be for God and not for self and related to prayer, the fast needed charitable actions. Quoting from Isaiah 58:6-11, Wesley trumpets that the proper fast is to free the oppressed, to feed the hungry, and to care for the poor.

Discourse VIII: Anti-Wealth

At its best, Wesley's spirituality is of one piece. This is strikingly true in his discourse eight on the Matthean text of laying up treasures in heaven and not on earth: "For where your treasure is, there will be your heart also." He fears for the Christian who sets out to become rich and who squanders life and eternal life by pursuing riches.

Here at the beginning of the capitalist era he attacks greed as a spiritual sin. It really is not possible to pursue mammon and God at the same time. So many investigations into the relationship of Christian ethics and business go bankrupt right at the beginning point. The pursuit of riches and the pursuit of Jesus Christ are antithetical. Wesley knew this and often taught it. Part of the inspiration for his polemics against the covetousness of wealth comes from this text of Matthew 6:19-23.

It begins with singleness of purpose of a life. If the life is focused on God, one is given understanding, holiness, and happiness. To turn away from God for money produces darkness with ignorance, sin, and misery.[17] He makes an interesting comparison of the Christians of Europe to the pagans of Africa and America. Generally, one morality does not seem better than the other. But on this moral question of the pursuit of wealth the "heathen" have the moral edge. Basically, the native peoples of Africa and America do much better in refraining from the amassing of wealth. The Christians of Europe had lost the moral reluctance to pile up riches. What Max Weber would find distinctive about Protestant Europeans in his twentieth-century works, Wesley found deplorable in the Europeans of the eighteenth century. Rather than exhibit what Weber would characterize as the essence of the "Spirit of Capitalism," Wesley here denounces it.

Wesley notes that most Christians pay no attention to the commandment not to pile up riches: "It might as well be still hid in its original Greek for any notice they take of it."[18] He said then and it seems true today: "There is no one instance of spiritual infatuation in the world which is more amazing than this."[19] Christians pursuing riches and at the expense of the whole world, what could be more ridiculous?

For the sake of being clear on what is forbidden, he spells out what is not forbidden. In his economic ethic the Christian is to be free of debt, to provide sufficiently for one's family, and to provide the resources for children and widows of the household. This last provision providing some inheritance is to provide for necessities, not luxuries, and assumes diligent labor on the part of the heirs, as they are able. There is no provision for encouraging luxury or idleness. Allowance is also granted for the resources needed for carrying on one's worldly business.

The laying up of wealth beyond the necessities mentioned above is, for Wesley, "absolutely forbidden."[20] He allows that beyond one's own pursuit, providence might have made one rich. If so, then one must give abundantly to the needy with all one's power. The dangers of riches are great. With God salvation is possible, but riches are a seductive trap. Wesley piles up argument upon argument in trying to persuade Christians not to violate the commandment against pursuing wealth. He quotes William Law on how riches cause great hurt to those who possess them.

He also accuses the rich who find it so hard to enter the kingdom of God of "robbing the poor, the hungry, the naked, wronging the widow and the fatherless, and making themselves accountable for all the want, affliction, and distress which they do not remove."[21] This robbery of the poor is in addition to robbing God continually and falling under God's curse.

Wesley does not end with the curses. He concludes by charging those who have the means to help the poor, to be merciful as one has the power, to defend the oppressed, to heal the sick, and to care for the prisoner. Following Matthew 25, his last sentence of this bitingly strong sermon is: "Come, ye blessed of my Father, receive the Kingdom prepared for you from the foundation of the world."

Discourse IX: Anti-Mammon

The sermon on Matthew 6:24-34 continues the previous theses about the dangers of the pursuit of wealth. Now, however, it is framed between the emphases "Ye cannot serve God and mammon" and "Take therefore no thought for the morrow." Mammon is understood to mean, following Milton, a Syrian god who symbolized the god of money, or it may come from the Greek work reflecting Aramaic usage signifying riches.[22]

The serving of God is a total commitment, and the striving for money becomes a controlling commitment. For Wesley, the two cannot coexist. Serving mammon means trusting in riches, loving the world, conforming to the ways of the world, and obeying the world. A Christian may practice prudent business abhorring sloth, but the commitment to achieving wealth must be abandoned or love of God is lost. Care for families, children, and necessary business is encouraged. Scrupulous businesspeople could find some comfort in Wesley's words approving the "long and serious thought, not without much and earnest care,"[23] which such business might entail.

But close to the conclusion of the sermon he returns to the theme of "Therefore take no thought for the morrow." What one really needs will be provided. The overanxious care for necessities leads to service to the devil and a headlong rush into hell. Contrary to the calculating, prudent, bourgeois existence into which Wesley saw many of his Methodists drifting, he preached, live these moments. The past was gone, the future is unknown, and for you it may not come, so "Live thou today."[24] Improve the present; it is all you have. The present is to be lived in the gracious, freeing presence of Christ. In the closing three pages of the sermon freedom in Christ only in the present seems to push out the methodical review of the past and planning for the future associated with Methodism. In current terms this is Christian existentialism within the trinitarian faith and a modest insertion regarding the fear of hell. The sermon is one of a very few to be printed with a formal trinitarian blessing as a conclusion.[25] It may have captured the immediate celebration of the "now" within the symbols of the faith.

Discourse X: The Golden Rule

Wesley understands Jesus in Matthew 7 to be turning away from the interior intentions of pure religion toward things that could hinder this religion. The last four sermons of this concluding part are considerably shorter than the preceding nine. The first subject is the temptation to misjudge others. Wesley interprets the injunction against judging not as refraining from an opinion, but as judging that lacks love. This could be a judgment against the innocent or the imposition of more guilt than is appropriate or condemning one without sufficient evidence. Wesley is not urging lack of discernment, for in the next section he interprets: "Give not that which is holy unto the dogs," as advice not to speak of the depth of Christian faith to those regarded as unable to hear it. He is interpreting Jesus as both making judgments and protecting pure religion as appropriate. Wesley, who had been subject to much harassment, stoning, assault, and insult from disorderly mobs, could not be accused of timidity. He expected hatred for trying to save their souls or, in his own words, for attempting "to pluck them as brands out of the burning."[26] Still, prudence in witness and judgment in love were recommended as having Jesus' authority.

Wesley then turns to Matthew's "Ask, and it shall be given you; seek, and ye shall find; knock, and it shall be opened unto you," which expresses Wesley's evangelical confidence. One is to pursue God diligently and ask for what one needs. This is all to be in the context of a life of charity. Even here, when Wesley is exhorting to prayer, it is controlled by charity or love. In fact, prayer without love may, according to Wesley, bring a curse upon oneself.

He plunges into the conclusion of the sermon on the text: "Therefore all things whatsoever ye would that men should do to you, do ye even so to them: for this is the law and the prophets." Wesley names it the "golden rule of mercy as well as justice,"[27] and can even say, "And this rightly understood, comprises the whole of the religion which our Lord came to establish upon earth."[28] For a minute in Wesley's reductionism he sounds like an Enlightenment moralist. Here a rule of compassionate equity is all of religion, and it has the Lord's authority. How many good people or people attempting to be good or at least fair have seized on this Golden Rule as all they needed of Christian faith? Not Wesley—he crashes on to his evangelical conclusion. None of us can fulfill this rule without the love of God. Belief in Jesus Christ is the way to the love of God. Matthew's it "is the law and the prophets" makes it seem that the rule must be love. The text does not say so. Wesley says it is, and the expression "It is the law and the prophets" is used elsewhere of the double commandment. It is so close to "Love your neighbor as yourself" that it is almost indistinguishable, but its use in the double love commandment sequence ties the commandment closer to the divine will than Matthew's presentation of it would demand, and there is no suggestion of the evangelical conclusion that Wesley's hermeneutic places upon it. Still Wesley's relating it to fair and compassionate judgment is suggestive for all morality.

Discourse XI: Hell

The sermon on "narrow is the way, which leadeth unto life" is the shortest of the series and the one with the most references to hell. Matthew does not mention hell here, but Wesley assumes "destruction" to be hell. Several of the other sermons mention hell as the penalty for missing the way of life. But this short sermon hits the theme very hard. The other major theme is also not exactly in the text, that is, the plea to "strive to enter" in "at the strait gate." The word *strive* is from the Lukan parallel text, but Wesley grasps the term to urge the vigor that he exhorts his listeners to practice.

The narrow way is the way of "universal holiness" of doing good to all and suffering evil for Christ's sake. Very few are to be found traveling the way of life, and as the vast majority turn into the broad way to hell, their very numbers and examples tempt believers off the narrow path to life. The sermon is a relatively straightforward interpretation of the text by one concerned about hell and believing in the urgent quest for the correct way of life. The way to hell is broad and pursued by most; the way to heaven is narrow, and it requires a disciplined life that can stand against the hell-bound masses.

Discourse XII: Prophecy

The twelfth sermon continues the themes of the previous one on the narrow way. The text, Matthew 7:15-20, deals with false prophecy and its lack of productivity. Prophecy following the Puritans is faith telling, not prediction.[29] It is describing the ways of God with humans. True prophetic speaking produces love of God and love of neighbor; if it does not, it is false. False religious leadership is commonplace, and many are misled.

The false prophets are the wolves in sheep's clothing that lead many to hell. Wesley's condemnation of the false teacher promises that hell will come forward to claim the slayers of human souls. The false teachers are deceivers, and they promise love, ease, and understanding for those they mislead. Wesley urges his hearers and readers to be patient with those they suspect of false teaching. Beyond the criterion of love he urges tests of the "plain passages" of Scripture. Beyond these tests the false religious teacher will be known by failure. The false message will produce no solid growth among Christians.

Discourse XIII: Authority and Love

Wesley hurries to close his writing on the Sermon on the Mount. The discourses become shorter; the writing indicates he is closing the work. The reader wonders whether Wesley is preparing to run off to a preaching opportunity.

He restates the authority the Sermon has behind it of a divine teacher. Throughout his commentary on Matthew 7:21-27, he uses the whole of Scripture to interpret these verses on the necessity of following what Jesus has taught in the Sermon. As the whole Scripture has divine authority underlying it, Wesley can use any of it to interpret any other part of Scripture. First he shows that religion leading to other than the love of God and neighbor in holiness is inadequate. If one follows Jesus' way truly loving God and the neighbor fully, the foundation is strong or built upon the rock. Both total faith and good works are urged as the meaning of following Jesus. The contrast between building on the rock or on sand is as stark as the contrast he presents of heaven and hell.

The reader of this last sermon finds no new themes, but the constantly presented themes are urged here with vigor. He concludes:

> In a word: let thy religion be the religion of the heart.... Be serious. Let the whole stream of thy thoughts, words, and actions flow from the deepest conviction that thou standest on the edge of the great gulf, thou and all the children of men, just ready to drop in, either into everlasting glory or everlasting burning.... Be thou a lover of God and of all mankind. In this spirit do and suffer all things. Thus show thy faith by thy works: thus do the will of thy Father which is in heaven. And as sure as thou now walkest with God on earth, thou shalt also reign with him in glory.[30]

The Sermon on the Mount was, for Wesley, the guide to practical Christian living.[31] It had more social implications than either Wesley's Moravian mentors or Lutheran forerunners in the faith would admit. Calvinist ethics were more inclined to rely on the Ten Commandments while Wesley, trusting more in the transforming power of love, stressed the Sermon on the Mount. The love ethic has been criticized for its lack of specificity, but for all followers of Calvin, it contained the Ten Commandments, and for John Wesley, the love ethic was expressed very specifically in the Sermon.

7. Marriage and War (1750s)

Marriage

Wesley buried the pain from his 3 October 1749, loss of Grace Murray in his poetry and his work. Having finally resolved to marry, he met a well-off Huguenot widow, Mrs. Mary Vazeille. Their date of meeting is unknown, but Charles Wesley had met her in July 1749; he regarded her as a woman of sorrowful spirit. Most of Wesley's biographers consider the marriage a mistake and Mrs. Wesley a quarrelsome, cold woman. Mr. Wesley provided her with much to quarrel about.

The *Journal* covering the fateful February of 1751, published in 1756, did not mention the marriage. By the time he edited the *Journal* for publication, Wesley expunged the marriage from the public record. In fact, unpublished manuscript pages of his *Journal* indicate that the marriage was unhappy by December 1751, and that Mrs. Wesley was extremely jealous. What misery this quick alliance brought to both of them.

Wesley had slipped on the ice on London Bridge on Sunday, 10 February 1751, spraining his ankle. Mary Vazeille nursed him toward recovery for a week at her home on Threadneedle Street. At the end of the week, on 17 or 18 February, they were married. Actually, he recorded that his time was spent during recovery in reading, conversation, prayer, and "writing an *Hebrew Grammar*, and *Lessons for Children*." On Sunday, the seventeenth, he again preached, and on 4 March, he left for Bristol.

An interpreter of Wesley cannot help noting on the first Sunday after his marriage he preached at Spitalfields where many who had wandered from the movement evidenced a willingness to return. He wrote about the service:

> How is it that we are so ready
> to despair of one another. For
> want of the "love" that "hopeth all things."[1]

Was he already despairing of his marriage? The reference to 1 Corinthians 13:7 is in the middle of the chapter indicating that without love we are nothing and that love can endure all things and still hope. It promises that love never fails, but was his already failing? The whole text of 1 Corinthians 13 is now a favorite text for weddings, and even then it was a central context for determining the meaning of love and for Wesley's philosophy of love. All three of Wesley's most important love affairs were with women who nursed him to recovery from illness. It seems that he realized his folly in marrying even before his ankle healed. Only that month had he resolved that he could serve more usefully if he were married. Apparently, he had not considered either the mutuality of marriage or the hatred that the lack of personal compatibility can produce.

Mrs. Wesley was autonomous, thanks to a widow's settlement of £10,000 and an annual income of £300 guaranteed by the marriage agreement to her and her four children. Whitefield had thought it a good match—but then he also showed little success in marriage. The Wesley family could not accommodate her, and in general the Methodists took John's side in the ensuing struggles.[2]

As required by the statutes of Oxford University, upon marriage Wesley resigned his Lincoln College fellowship. The resignation reduced his income, which was already stretched thin by an agreement with Charles. Charles's marriage had been arranged with John guaranteeing him an income from his writing of almost £100 annually. John was closer to poverty than before the Wesley marriages.

The poverty was an emotional poverty, too. Wesley's March 1751 letters to his wife were affectionate, but they were not the passionate Wesley we know from his correspondence to other women. He seemed to be adjusting to an uncomfortable fact while refusing to violate his clear judgment that married Methodist preachers must carry on with the same travel schedule and number of services as before their marriages. In fact, he had said they were to work as if they were not married. Mary's Huguenot tradition was the other major Christian group that had a tradition of field preaching under persecution. Though Wesley cajoled her to more practice of religious acts, she had religious convictions, and she was willing to endure hardship on the road with him. But Wesley was troubled by her grumbling on the road. She had reason to grumble.

Accommodations were uncertain, the roads were rough, and rioters threatened her. Wesley remembered the uncomplaining Grace
Murray when he and Mary (Molly) retraced his Ireland itinerary.
The clash of their personalities and the rigor of the itinerant preaching circuit gradually led her to abandon the travel. His tolerance of
discomfort and her complaining nature clashed on the road. His
dominating, patriarchal manner also gave offense to this mature,
independent widow. His long absences and his affectionate relations with other women contributed understandably to her jealousy. Wesley was a prime example of Henry Fielding's observation
in *Tom Jones* of how affections engendered in religious sympathy
may warm the relations between the genders. On one occasion, it
was reported, Molly resorted to battery. John's friend said he saw
Molly dragging the diminutive John around the room by his hair.
On releasing him, supposedly she had a handful of his white hair.

The marital disputes and Mary's broadcasting the news of the
discord troubled John deeply. The editors of the definitive
Bicentennial Edition of the Works of John Wesley suggested that the
distress of the marriage was implicated in his serious medical dis-
orders of 1753. His *Journal* suggests he became ill in the church
where he was thought to have been married. They then suggested:
"If, as has been conjectured John Wesley was married in
Manning's Church, his disorder was very comprehensible; for his
matrimonial difficulties were creating personal problems in his
milieu and straining his own robust constitution."[3]

Wesley became ill in October 1753, but he continued preaching
as his strength would allow. By 26 November, he was so ill that he
wrote his epitaph:

Here lieth

The body of John Wesley

A Brand plucked out of the burning

Who died of a consumption in the fifty-first year of his age

Not leaving, after his debts are paid, ten pounds

behind him

Praying

God be merciful to me, an unprofitable servant!

He ordered that this, if any inscription, should be placed on his
tombstone.[4]

Here at his own misperceived end, he returned to the phrase from his salvation from burning. His parents' actions and his self-identification merge in this text of salvation from Amos and Zechariah, "A brand plucked out of the burning." It is the text he used for sinners who repented. Immediately after salvation, he dealt with faithfulness in use of money, and then, he pleaded for the forgiveness denied the unprofitable servant in the Gospel of Matthew. Trusting in his salvation, still he pleaded for mercy to be saved from "outer darkness" and "gnashing of teeth."

Whitefield wrote him on 3 December 1753, commending him to Jesus and triumphant love. Whitefield hoped to visit him within the week if Wesley lived. He hoped to find Wesley still in the land of the living, but if not, he paid his last living respects: "My heart is too big, tears trickle down too fast, and you I fear, are too weak for me to enlarge. Underneath you may there be Christ's everlasting arms."[5]

Though estranged by doctrinal emphasis, the boyhood companions from the Holy Club were at midlife joined in love. Wesley recovered after four months' absence from preaching and outlived Whitefield. Only a month earlier, Wesley had scolded his brother Charles for not acting in concert with him. He had accused Charles of being as disconnected from him for the last ten years as Mr. Whitefield. The same letter had indicated the discord between Charles and his family and Mrs. Mary Wesley. He used his time of recuperation to prepare his *Notes upon the New Testament.*

He had appointed thrice married Mrs. Sarah Ryan to be headmistress of Kingswood School. Thus, the woman of ill reputation presided at meals at Kingswood, which was an affront to Mrs. Wesley as well as others. To Wesley, her repentance was genuine, and he regarded her as a sensitive, religious person. Wesley wrote her an affectionate, deeply personal letter on 20 January 1758, after having been with her at Kingswood on 4 January. Mrs. Wesley found the letter unsealed in his coat pocket and, after scolding him, left him. Several sentences in the letter could drive a jealous woman to leave an unsatisfying marriage. He had written about Sarah's feelings of trial and resentment and her possible wish that "things should be otherwise."

> I never saw you so much moved as you appeared to be that evening. Your soul was then greatly troubled, and a variety of

conflicting passions, love, sorrow, desire, with a kind of despair, were easy to read in your countenance.... The conversing with you, either by speaking or writing, is an unspeakable blessing to me. I cannot think of you without thinking of God. Others often lead me to Him; but it is, as it were, going around about; you bring me straight into his presence.[6]

Mary certainly had clear evidence that John wrote more passionately to Sarah than to herself. She also had circumstantial evidence of a love affair between Wesley and Sarah. In other circumstances, she wildly accused him of making his brother's wife, Sally, his mistress and of having other affairs. This was all too much to bear, and she left him.

He wrote again to Sarah Ryan, informing her that his wife had left, vowing never to return. He recorded in his *Journal* that he would not seek her return. More surprisingly, he wrote he did not know why she left. He described to Sarah that Molly had found his letter to her while he was preaching, and that it had broken her heart. Her temper, as Wesley described it, was one he had not seen for years. His letter mentioned Sarah's letters to him, but these were lost or perhaps destroyed by Mrs. Wesley. The rest of his letter to Sarah can be read as a pursuit of clues to her tangled emotions or as spiritual advice to a follower who needs to be confronted about pride. We cannot be sure, but again Wesley seemed to be toying with her emotions. He made Sarah dependent upon him, won her emotionally, allowed their relationship to sever the disagreeable Molly from his side, but the correspondence revealed his ambivalence.

Wesley's commitment to an ethic of love needed more structures of justice. These women, particularly Sophy, Grace, and Sarah, needed protection from the lovable Wesley. If he wanted to be their spiritual advisor, he needed not to manipulate their sentiments of affection toward himself. However, he was in over his head. He lacked understanding of what he was doing.

Marriage Deteriorates

Mrs. Wesley returned from her first departure after a few days. She would leave several more times. There was a kind letter from him to her in 1758, thanking her for entertaining his sister. Still, he provided advice to her and insisted on his right of choosing his own company. He complained that they had been squabbling about his rights to converse with whom he would for seven years. The letters of 1759 were more nagging, particularly about her taking his papers. He called upon her to repent. During most of these months he was away, sometimes riding fifty or sixty miles per day, and often preaching three times each day. He was dependent on her rerouting of his London correspondence, and he resented her reading it first. His affectionate letters to other women in the Methodist connection continued. In October 1759, he complained about her taking his papers, her suspicious nature, her lack of hospitality to his family, her slander, her false accusations, and her generally bad temper; and he instructed her on reforming her character.

In the spring of 1760, he reminded her of her obligations to obey him according to the marriage vow and wrote: "Consequently every act of disobedience is an act of rebellion against God and the King as well as against your affectionate husband."[7]

From Ireland where he traveled for six months in 1760, he wrote to her anticipating that she would be with him at Conference in Bristol:

> My desire is to live peaceably with all men; with you in particular.... And there is nothing which I should rejoice in more than the having you always with me; provided only that I could keep you in a good humour, and that you must not speak against me behind my back. I still love you for your indefatigable industry, for your exact frugality, and for your uncommon neatness and cleanliness—your patience, skill, and tenderness in assisting the sick.... If it please God we meet again, let us meet for good.[8]

The *Journal* for 23 January 1771, indicated Mrs. Wesley left for Newcastle vowing "Never to return." Return she did, however, and they were together at least for part of the summer of 1772. The extant correspondence would suggest they may have met occasionally after that.[9]

His letter to her of 9 December 1771, responded to her accusing letter to him. In it, he rejected the story that she ever beat him or pulled his hair. He dismissed it as a silly tale; still, it was repeated in many biographies of him. He indicated that he had not known another with such an unhappy temper or biting tongue. He considered the accusations of jealousy against her just. He rejected her charges that he tried to separate her from her wealth. He accused her of taking his papers and quoting bits of them out of context, and he returned again to charges of her misplaced jealousy. He doubted that she had any affection for him. However, his claim that his affections were focused solely on her is clearly repudiated by his letters to other women.

He admitted to shaking her twice: once at Snowfields and later at the Foundry. He denied that he ever struck her. The second page of the letter entered into their financial disputes. She wanted £50.00 per year, but as she still had an estate of £5000 and he was in debt, he denied it to her. He told her she could return whenever she wanted to or shut the gate of reconciliation forever.[10]

The second letter from York on 15 July 1774, rehearsed the same charges of jealousy, temper, pilfering of his papers and letters, and financial quarrels.[11] It noted that a few weeks after they married, she had her first temper outbreak at Kingswood. He admitted his inability to restore good relations, even though he tried to in his own way to the best of his ability. At the end of the letter, he instructed her to be humble and not to infringe upon his liberties. He promised to govern her gently and to show that he loved her as Christ loved the church.

Finally, in the last known letter to Molly in 1777, he indicated that given their ages, they would probably not meet again on earth, he accused her of besmirching his reputation, doing much harm to true religion, and he bid her farewell.[12]

Mary Wesley died on 8 October 1781. His entry published in his *Journal* could not be shorter: "Friday 11, I came to London and was informed that my wife died on Monday. This evening she was buried, though I was not informed of it till a day or two after."[13]

New Testament Notes

During his recovery at Bristol Hot-Wells in 1753, Wesley undertook to finish his translation of the New Testament and to combine his reflections on it with his translation of passages from

Bengelius's *Gnomon Novi Testamenti*.[14] He also used work from Heylin, Guyse, and Doddridge without assigning credit when the opinions were theirs. He intended this work to be a resource not for scholars but for those who read only English. In fact, he urged its use upon his unlearned preachers as a standard for their preaching.

Wesley combined a willingness to risk his judgment about the best choice of text to follow with his own translation. He attempted to avoid controversy, recognizing that all Christians have a common gentle master whose words should not be made into weapons. As to the Scripture itself, it was God speaking to people. Scripture, according to Wesley, contained the utmost depth, but it also provided ease of understanding. God spoke as God to God's messengers, but to understand them accurately, Wesley wanted their emphasis, affections, and tempers to be examined.[15]

The notes on the Sermon on the Mount support Wesley's earlier preaching of so many sermons on the Sermon. His translation of the beatitude blessings as happy reflected his spirit of finding happiness in the good news of the New Testament. He did not let difficult passages stand as a stumbling block to his confidence that Christian faith, active in love, was the way to happiness. His belief that listeners to his sermons could be persuaded of the truth of the New Testament message of love led him away from his Calvinist evangelical allies. Just before his work on the *Notes upon the New Testament*, he had published against the Calvinist doctrine of predestination. In his New Testament work, he drew upon Calvinist authors, but he excised their work if it defended predestination. The divisions emerging in the 1750s between the Methodists and the Calvinists would lead to a more sustained debate in the 1760s and 1770s. Some of his preachers left the Methodist convention to identify with the Calvinists. Some Calvinists became Methodists. Presbyterian chapels were often open to Wesley's preaching when Church of England churches were denied him. In the 1750s, the relationship among evangelical Calvinists and Methodists was fluid, like the relationship between Wesley and Whitefield.

The combination of Arminian and Calvinist threads in Methodism was very unstable. Almost from their earliest showing of evangelical leadership, Whitefield and Wesley had sparred over the issue of predestination. Often John provoked the controversy, but sometimes Whitefield started it. Whitefield's association with Lady Huntingdon had allowed an outlet for the Calvinists. John's relationship with the Huntingdon people was usually strained, but there were periods of cooperation. Charles managed to associate more easily with the Calvinists in the Huntingdon branch. The most divisive issues were predestination and perfection. John addressed both in the 1750s. The dispute over predestination, or as Wesley later put it in his reflections on the history of Methodism, between universal and particular redemption, had divided the Methodists as early as 1741.

His pamphlet of 1752, "Predestination Calmly Considered," began with a statement of his appreciation for the religious origins of the conviction that the grace of God was irresistible.[16] Although he conceded that for some people it was irresistible, he denied that it was irresistible for all people. He thought those who experienced it would regard it as irresistible and come to believe they were unconditionally predestined to life. Wesley argued that belief in the Decree of Election necessitated belief in the Decree of Reprobation. To believe that only some were decreed by God for salvation implied that others were decreed by God for damnation. Those who wanted election without reprobation ascribed to God were inconsistent, according to Wesley.[17]

Most of Wesley's argument was scriptural. He could not find unconditional election in Scripture. He found people saved or damned depending on their faithful or unfaithful response to Christ. The damned could not believe God's promise of salvation in Christ, for then they would be saved. Wesley believed that he knew from Scripture that God loved and would save all humanity.

Two of his arguments were from his ethics. First, the justice of God cannot be reconciled to God's damning some from all eternity to the fires of hell. Second, the belief in predestination encouraged the dismissal of moral standards. One could, assuming one's salvation was eventually assured, raise hell now, postponing belief and righteousness until later. Or on the other hand, if one believed one's soul was damned, there was no motivation to seek salvation and the life of holiness. Wesley also knew of the antinomianism of grace that had led those close to him to trust in irresistible grace and to fail to resist sin.

Wesley believed if the Decree of Reprobation were true, Scripture would be false. He opposed it because he believed it was destructive. The same love that drove him from one end of England to the other to save souls forced him to oppose the teaching. The strongest condemnation of the doctrine was near the end of the essay: the doctrine of absolute predestination naturally leads to the chambers of death.[18]

He then closed with a plea to Christian unity in opposition to the devil and to daily growth in "Grace and in the knowledge of our Lord Jesus Christ." His publication the very next year explained more fully what this growth in Christ would look like.

Genuine Christianity

Wesley's "A Plain Account of Genuine Christianity" echoed his farewell sermon at St. Mary's Church in Oxford.[19] He pushed the question: Can true Christians be distinguished from others? He thinks that they can, and even that their testimony may be trusted because they confessed to what had happened to them.

The marks of a Christian are abasement before the glory of God, dependence on and confidence in God, love of neighbor as universal social, not self, love, patience, humility, truthfulness, social responsibility, and happiness in God. These desirable characteristics mark the real Christian, not particular opinions or manners of worship.

Christian doctrine "describes this character...in the most lively and affecting manner."[20] It also promises that the character can be realized within the Christian. It is both a promise and a command to realize this character. God will put God's laws into the innermost being of the Christian. Christianity informs one that all of the above is achieved through faith. Faith is the power of God, which enlivens the spirit to see into the spiritual world.[21] In particular, it is to know for oneself that one is reconciled to God through Christ. This personal knowledge is for Wesley more persuasive than the traditional sources of knowledge. His inner conviction is given now; it is not a question of historical probability regarding seventeen-hundred-year-old events. It is new and enlivening now. Wesley concludes by saying if the character appeals, ask the plain

Christian about its source. As the formerly blind who now see are the best witnesses to the recovery of sight, so Christians freed from their old sin are the best witnesses of new life.

One could see in this pamphlet the suggestion of a character ethic in Wesley. But the character is one of religiously transformed people or new beings empowered by the source of life. The character produced by the Christian life is also what is commanded. The whole character is surrounded by divine love and obligated to love. These discussions of character are not the usual model of discourse in Wesley, and when they appear, they are connected to prescriptive discourse. Very little here is reminiscent of an Aristotelian ethic other than a few terms used by both Aristotle and Wesley in different systems of ethical discourse. Wesley bore witness to this character as it was recorded in the New Testament. These marks of character were New Testament marks. In reality, he knew the bitterness of a failed marriage and of Christians continually making war upon each other. War was never far from his mind.

War

Historians of war observe that the wars Wesley knew were relatively moderate. The preceding century had seen the fury of religious wars in Europe. The nineteenth century was to see the horror of the ideological wars of the French Revolution and the even more brutal American Civil War. To some degree the wars of the eighteenth century in Europe were wars directed by monarchs who wanted to preserve both their armies and their navies. They would rather secure modest victory through maneuver than risk catastrophic loss through major battle. To a surprising degree, they observed rules of war and, generally, in Europe avoided warring directly upon civilians. Objectives were often kept moderate by both the monarchs and the generals. Yet Wesley's critique of war was not moderate. Wesley correctly saw that war was the worst expression of human sin. Its sources were not to his mind unique, but revealed convincingly that "the very foundations of all things, civil and religious, are utterly out of course in the Christian as well as the heathen world."[22]

Eric Robson made an empirical point connecting the wars of the first half of the eighteenth century to marriage or its failure. Of course, beneath the dynastic quarrels lurked international power rivalries. "The names of the three chief wars of the first half of the century, the wars of Spanish, Polish and Austrian Succession, suggest that war only occurred when matrimonial arrangements had failed or become inextricably confused."[23]

For Wesley, confusion in the family and resentment there derived from the same human condition as discord among the nation's sin. His sixty-five-page pamphlet was directed against the optimistic view of human sin of the deists and the philosophers. Titled "The Dignity of Human Nature," it demonstrated how little dignity human nature exhibited. From its most intimate relations to its international relations, it expressed brokenness founded in sin.

In "The Dignity of Human Nature," Wesley was as realistic as Reinhold Niebuhr in his World War II work *The Nature and Destiny of Man*.[24] Their opponents in both cases were the optimists, Christians and secular, of their own day. Niebuhr as a Christian liberal castigated the liberal notions of human progress; Wesley as a Christian rationalist attacked the progressive optimism of rationalism. Christianity requires realism, or there is no need for its scheme of salvation. For both Wesley and Niebuhr, realism about human existence and nature was required by their empiricism.

Wesley's reflections about war were ignited by the outbreak of the French and Indian War of 1754. Following the diplomatic revolution of 1756 in which the Austrian-English alliance was replaced by the Prussian-English combination against France, Austria, Russia, and Sweden, the war was transmuted into the first world war, called the Seven Years' War. The war raged in Europe, the Atlantic, the Caribbean, the Indian Ocean, the Pacific Ocean, India, the Philippines, and the New World.

John raised money to clothe the French prisoners of war, and he wrote to *Lloyd's Evening Post* on 26 October 1759, to protest the lack of care for them. His preachers were subject to impressment for military service. In 1759, a press-gang at Stockton seized his traveling companions, Joseph Jones and William Alwood. The crowd rioted, stoned the gang, and broke the lieutenant's head. His companions were released. Evangelism went forward among the

English armies on the Continent and in America, and Wesley often preached to troops in England and Ireland.

He shared fears of the French plans to invade England and Ireland. In 1756, he wrote to a member of Parliament volunteering to raise two hundred volunteers at Methodist expense to be armed from munitions in the Tower of London and serve as a home guard. His earlier discussions of combining with Whitefield had suggested five hundred men, but when faced with carrying it forward himself, he volunteered to support two hundred. The plan was not accepted. This effort, along with his earlier militant response to Prince Charles's invasion, refutes all attempts to interpret John Wesley as a pacifist.[25] He understood the need for Christians to participate in defense although he hated war and expected Methodists to be active peacemakers.

He analyzed, or rather repeated, causes of war he had learned from another writer. Among them are ambition of rulers, corruption of statesmen, religious differences, and questions of taste. A war might be to take the dominions of another, as in the Seven Years' War. Sometimes wars are fought because one prince is perceived as too strong and sometimes because a prince is weak. Sometimes wars arise out of covetousness or a desire to rationalize borders. Sometimes wars are to take the lands of non-European peoples. Whatever the cause, Wesley went on, the consequences are death to thousands in violation of reason and humanity. He quoted an eyewitness to the deaths of thousands to illustrate his argument against war. As long as war continued, all of the human claims of virtue and human reason were falsified. Even heathens knew, he said, that if there were to be a time of reason, war would have no place.[26]

Wesley described the intolerable ignorance among the English he knew. Elsewhere, he had described the pathos of the majority of the world living under idolatry or the despotism of Islam. Now he revealed not only how ignorant the Highlanders and the Irish were, but also how little knowledge there was in England. Wesley knew that in a so-called age of Enlightenment most English would die without knowing how to read.

The essay as a whole was an attack on the humanistic optimism of the Enlightenment. Regarding war, he followed the melancholy ruminations of a Mr. Cowley, but in so doing, he presented a worthy, realistic list of reasons why nations resorted to war. Behind his analysis was his great sadness that Christians slaughtered each other. It was not only that their religion failed to restrain them. He knew full well that often their religious judgments were the very reason for their rapacious killing. Compared to Kenneth Waltz's contemporary explanation of the reasons for war as failures in the three areas of human nature, state, and international order,[27] Wesley covered the causes of war in the first area as rooted in the miserable nature of humanity. He also covered the second origin of war, that of the faults of the nation-state contributing to war. The third, that the international system itself was disordered, was very evident in the Seven Years' War, and he spoke of the very foundations of humanity being disordered. Still the third alternative described by Kenneth Waltz as the cause of war, that of international anarchy, probably was not emphasized by Wesley. However, at such a time as 1756–1763, to suggest international disorder as anything but a given fact of life might have seemed gratuitous. Wesley had no dreams of international order or utopia before Christ's coming. In his reflections on war, sin, and optimistic humanism, his ethics were as realistic as Reinhold Niebuhr's Christian realism.

Following the analysis of Mr. Brerewood, Wesley divided the world into thirty approximately equal parts. He regarded nineteen of these as heathen, six as Islamic, and five as Christian. In the decade of the 1750s, he was utterly realistic about the failure of religion and morals in all thirty areas. From the sources he read, he found little of human nobility in any of the world's nations. At this point his criticisms of the lack of religion and morality were as harshly directed against Asians and Africans of whom he had a little firsthand knowledge as against Native Americans. Later, under the influence of more romantic writers in Africa, he would present a more sentimental picture of pacific Africans. His compassion for Africans in this decade was expressed in his baptism of Africans and noting of their religious sensibilities. He dreamed of the conversion of the continent and their consequent improvement. The active engagement in the abolition of slavery movement was a development of the 1770s. In these pages from "The Dignity of

Human Nature," and "The Doctrine of Original Sin," all were cursed by the sin of Adam. True Christianity was for him light, but the historical practices of Christians did not lift them above the deplorable condition of the others. In Christians' warring on one another their alienation from God was proved. His realism about human nature reinforced his Calvinist inheritance that Christians need moral instruction as well as acceptance of grace.

Ten Commandments

Wesley based his explicit moral teaching more on the Sermon on the Mount than he did on the Ten Commandments. He insisted on the observance of the Ten Commandments as the morality of the church, but he wrote little about their meaning. He corrected this by publishing in 1759 *A Short Exposition of the Ten Commandments*,[28] extracted from Bishop Hopkins. He praised the bishop's work so fully that it is a reasonable assumption that he approved of what he had extracted, edited, and published. The bishop's writing certainly was a strong antidote to the antinomianism Wesley figured to be lurking in his Moravian and Calvinist opponents.

Wesley made four points in his preface.[29] (1) Salvation required the particular holiness that was faith working in love. (2) That holiness was required by the Ten Commandments given by God, in person, to Moses and delivered to the church. (3) Previous writers had not adequately explained how faith was the foundation of love written in law on the heart. (4) Bishop Hopkins, Wesley declared, showed with true exactness both the literal and the spiritual meaning of every commandment based on faith in Christ. Love was the end of every commandment. Without faith expressed in love, he said religion was a dead carcass.

The bishop wrote about love as Wesley claimed, but he balanced it with the fear of God. He read all of the Church of England morality into Moses' Ten Commandments. For example, out of the injunction to honor your father and mother, he gathered pages of injunctions on government in the family, the church, and the Commonwealth. The three pages of explanation of the bishop's perspective on the duties of masters and servants are—from the perspective of the twenty-first century—seen as less than eternal, and full of the class bias of the elite bishop. Of course, all exposition of the Ten Commandments will reflect time, place, and context. One can correct this, however, by being clear about what is binding law.[30] The bishop tended toward an Anglican legalism, and he imposed it upon Moses. The publication of the extracts failed to fulfill Wesley's intention that every law would be seen to express love, which enlivened vital faith. His own notes on the New Testament revealed a less harsh and more lively spirit than the bishop's sometimes heavy moralism.

Conclusion to Decade

Wesley's travels in 1758 and 1759 took him again to Ireland, Wales, and Scotland as well as his usual itinerary in England. The riotous opposition during the two closing years of the decade was less than previously. At the conference in Limerick, Ireland, he had fourteen preachers present. Often most of the crowd attending his preaching in Ireland was Roman Catholic. On an occasion where he found himself preaching on the grounds of a former camp of Oliver Cromwell, he exalted in the better purpose to which the ground was now put.

In late 1759, he had a number of the gentry in the congregation at his field preaching. He reflected that it would be well if a few of the rich were saved, but he sincerely hoped it would be because of the ministry of others. He personally preferred to "preach the gospel to the poor" as he had undertaken to do for some quarter of a century.

He concluded the decade with writings on perfection in love and human sin.[31] His arguments, in his perspective, were based on Scripture and sound reason, and he had little use for the elaborations of mystics like Jacob Bohme or others who added to the plain sense of Christian faith. He produced his long work on sin as a challenge to the teaching of Dr. John Taylor, who had a national reputation as a learned cleric. When Taylor declined to respond, Wesley addressed him in a long letter asking for a reply. Taylor had excused himself from public reply with a disinclination to make it into a personal matter between Wesley and Taylor. Wesley's response was that it was not a personal matter but a matter of extreme urgency that the doctrine of sin be understood rightly. For if the power of sin were minimized, then all of the church's thought about justification and sanctification was mistaken. The church's thought about salvation correlated to its estimate of the situation of human alienation. The question was essential.

As the war continued, Wesley preached to soldiers at Canterbury and to prisoners of war near Bristol. He continued to raise money for clothes and to plead for better treatment of the French prisoners. He reflected several times during the two years on how he really was a field preacher. He admitted he liked comfortable preaching rooms and handsome pulpits, but the poor would not come to those places. It was his fate to seek to save the poor where they could be found, and that required prison visits and field preaching. While there was no doubt that Wesley's passion was to save souls from burning eternally in hell, his religion was not escapist. It called the converted to a dual citizenship in heaven and to a society on earth. In his itinerary at the close of the decade, he recorded both concerns. He was vitally concerned about response to his preaching and to the health of his Methodist societies. He knew that many who responded to his preaching would fall away. The way to change the folk was through binding them, in solidarity, to other serious Christians. The social solidarity required the awakening through preaching. The continued nurturing toward sanctification required the societal solidarity.

As the new year turned toward the 1760s, Wesley's movement was maturing, mob violence was lessening, and some of the societies were flourishing. His marriage was in tatters; the hated war of Christians killing Christians continued. At the beginning of the next decade, George II died, and George III was crowned. With a king he approved of as well as necessarily honored as king, Wesley turned to writing social-political philosophy and commenting on political policy.

8. Maturation (1760s–1770s)

During the decades of the 1760s and 1770s, John Wesley wrote important essays on social ethics, in particular on economic ethics, political liberty, and slavery. The writings on economic ethics conclude this chapter while those on liberty in the political order and slavery, because of their importance, are discussed separately in the following two chapters. All of these writings reflect his personal maturity as well as the maturation of the Methodist movement. By this time he was leading seventy itinerant preachers, controlled many chapels, and was a notable public intellectual. His writings were intended not just to voice opinion but to lead. So, there is a sense of responsibility about these writings by an evangelical preacher who was also governing a growing society within the Church of England.

Beyond reflecting Wesley's mature leadership role, these essays reveal the New World, imperial role of England and its wars with France. Wesley never visited France, he did not like the French language, and he feared French Catholicism. Only a few years earlier, the revolution of Bonnie Prince Charlie had been put down after it threatened English stability. Wesley's loyalties were to the Hanoverian dynasty, and he was particularly appreciative of George III, who ascended the throne in 1760. Hanoverian troops, under the command of the Hanoverian Duke of Cumberland, had been crucial in the defeat and slaughter of the French-encouraged Highlanders and the Catholic threat at the Battle of Culloden in 1746. John's only meeting with a French general, however, was quite amicable. He also exerted a great deal of effort in ministering to French prisoners of war and raising funds for the improvement of their conditions in prison camps within England.

John encountered the war personally on his six-month itinerancy in Ireland. At Carrickfergus, he shared a house with the occupying French General Cavignac. The occupation of the town after a short battle was brief because the French fleet was only seeking provisions. Five days after leaving Carrickfergus, a battle ensued in which the French fleet was defeated with the loss of three hundred men, including the naval commander Thurot. John recorded that his conversation with the general had been on general topics as well as religion. The general, Wesley reported, agreed with him on the meaning of true religion.

Theological-Ethical Writings

Despite the emergence of Wesley as a social philosopher in this period of political engagement with a king whom he appreciated, his other writings continued to be significant. He took up the issues of Christian perfection and predestination again and published his mature conclusions on these subjects. On both perfection and predestination, he held to the positions he had learned from Susanna. Even on the issues of women preaching and leadership in ministry, the influence of his late mother can be seen. The influence of his father is evident in his writings on the Old Testament, and Samuel's minor roles in history receive notice in Wesley's *History of England*. Their combined contribution is certainly felt in his dogged holding on to inclusion in the Church of England and his passionate political opinions. Wesley's writings on science appear to have their origins in his Oxford student days and his master's thesis on the reasoning powers of animals.

All of these factors—imperial England, George III, war, theological reflections, broad intellectual writings, leadership of a movement of reform within the Church of England—provide the wider context for understanding what Wesley was about when he directed his social philosophy or Christian social ethics out of love. The motivation and the norms were from the reality of God's love as grace and the double love commandments as norms. Much of the language discussing society was taken from social thought of his day as he perceived it through his understanding of English history.

Perfection

Wesley had pursued and preached Christian perfection from the days of the Holy Club at Oxford. His mother had taught him Christian perfection from childhood, drawn from both the Puritan

145

and Anglo-Catholic traditions of Christian perfection. John L. Peters's study provided the detailed background of the idea of Christian perfection that was in the English air of Wesley's day.[1] Wesley himself attributed his early emphasis on perfection to Jeremy Taylor, Thomas à Kempis, and William Law. Perhaps the greatest influence should be attributed to the popular *Treatise on Christian Perfection* by William Law. Law's urging of utter seriousness in the Christian life contributed to Wesley's deepening religious devotion of 1725. To Law, Christian perfection was the radical turning away from the spirit of worldliness to the spirit of Christ. First Corinthians 13, in its demand for total love over all else, expressed the thesis of his last chapter, "An Exhortation to Christian Perfection." He was further inspired by reading in early church fathers and scriptural studies, particularly in the First Epistle of John, to deepen his understanding of Christian perfection. In Wesley's mind, the meanings of the present reality of eternal law, the injunctions to be holy, the promises of overcoming sin, the demands for total love, and even the experiences of the assurance of faith meant that the converted could live Christian perfection. There is a lot of language in the Bible and the tradition, especially the mystical tradition, that encouraged the view that sin can be totally overcome. This is true if, as Wesley often did, sin is understood as the voluntary defying of God.

Though Wesley apparently believed that perfection was instantly given as grace as the Moravians taught, he also held to the view that it could be acquired gradually. He rejected Calvinist claims that perfection was possible only after death or Catholic teaching that implied perfection was achieved in purgatory, and he urged that it was available in life. According to John Peters and Henry D. Rack, there obviously were strains of both Catholic and Protestant insight in his synthesis.[2]

Wesley often feared that his Methodist preachers would drop the emphasis on perfection and that omission would lead to the decline of the movement. But in the 1760s, a revival in the emphasis on perfection occurred. Hundreds testified to knowing the perfection of Christian love. These cases gave Wesley material to reflect upon, but the extreme manifestations of enthusiasm for perfection led to other problems.

The enthusiasm and wild preaching of George Bell in London led Wesley to investigate and meet with Bell and others who were preaching a perfection that was too extravagant for Wesley. George Bell was associated with Wesley's dear friend Thomas Maxwell, who was also censured by Wesley. This led to several preachers leaving the Methodist connection and to disruption in the London societies. The preaching of perfection in London had led to severe criticism of the Methodists as Bell and Maxwell had pushed Wesley's favorite emphasis to the point of heresy.

George Bell had disturbed many by prophesying the end of the world for 28 February 1763. Bell was arrested and placed in prison to await its end. Wesley preached on the absurdity of such predictions, but many remained uneasy and some fled London. While appreciating some of their strengths he listed, Wesley resisted their pride, prophesying, and what he called enthusiasm. The extremes of some of these preachers led to the need, in Wesley's opinion, of more discipline and authority. That discipline was achieved in 1763 when the preachers' conference laid down more standards of discipline for the preachers and set Wesley's four volumes of sermons and his *Notes upon the New Testament* as doctrinal guides for those permitted to preach in Methodist preaching houses. The same conference appointed William Grimshaw to succeed the Wesleys with their special privileges in relationship to Methodist property. His death soon after the conference left the question of succession unsettled.

In the same year, Wesley published his twenty-three-page tract "A Discourse on Sin in Believers." It was directed against all those who would insist that there was not sin in the justified Christian. For Wesley, the flesh was corrupt and exerted a power of sin in the redeemed. Sin did not reign in the Christian, but it still contested with Christ, who reigned. Count Zinzendorf had mistakenly introduced the new notion of sin-free Christians, as Wesley made a strong argument for tradition: "But whatever doctrine is *new* must be wrong. For the *Old* Religion is the only true one."[3] He also used Scripture and reason in his argument, and he made one reference to experience. Wesley painted a portrait of the Christian still struggling without referring directly to his distinctive emphasis on Christian perfection.

Wesley's emphasis on *perfection* was one of his more unique contributions to theology, but it was not entirely successful. It focused the meaning of total love of God and love of neighbor as the self. It was intended as a guard against enthusiastic Christians falling into a disregard of ethics because they had been justified. It marked his movement as one of sanctification as well as justification by grace. But it encouraged an overenthusiasm that he had to restrain as in his writing on the sin of believers. The reading of Paul in that essay as still plagued by sin had been absent from his earlier sermonic publication on sanctification in 1741. Wesley had explained that he published his thoughts then in response to Dr. Gibson's suggestion. But the sermon had few of his later reservations and qualifications. He had written: "It remains, then, that Christians are saved in this world from all sin, from all unrighteousness; that they are now in such a sense perfect as not to commit sin, and to be freed from evil thoughts and evil tempers."[4]

In this early publication, he seemed to mean that Christians did not sin either consciously or unconsciously, though he admitted they made mistakes and some of those mistakes could violate God's law. He arrived at his position by selective use of scripture, and later, he defended it by witnessing to the reality of people who claimed perfection in the sense of freedom from sin.

In correspondence, he often said that the meaning of perfection was the love commandment: "Love God with all your heart, mind, and soul and your neighbor as yourself." This insistence on love as the heart of vital religion is a valid reading of Christian life. There is little reason to suggest that it means perfection. He sometimes suggested that he did not insist on the term *perfection* as he meant love. These texts indicate that he would have been well advised to drop the term. Perfection was not just from the New Testament; it also picked up and exaggerated the Enlightenment, optimistic themes that Wesley, usually, wisely kept suppressed. Perfection is a difficult claim for ethics because many ethical issues require the loss of value to secure other value, and perfection implies a total achievement not possible in human life in time and space.

His more mature "The Scripture Way of Salvation" in 1765 avoided asserting that the sanctified were totally sinless and secure. Here sanctification and justification were works of faith. Salvation included both and was a present blessing: "There is a real as well as a relative change."[5] But love may not drive out sin completely. Because one felt it was overcome did not necessarily mean all sin was gone forever. What was perfection here? He said it was the perfect love that drove out "pride, self-will, anger, unbelief." So, in 1765, sanctification depended upon the belief that produced love. In this mature reflection, he conceded sin may cleave to the believer, even though it had been defeated. He retained the moral rigor, he refused to concede, and he cleansed his doctrine from any tendencies to pride that its enthusiastic exponents sometimes exhibited. Wesley wanted to use "saved from sin" in two ways. One was saved from the domination of sin by faith; in short, sin's destructive consequences were annulled spiritually by grace. He also wanted to say it was overcome, but as his thought matured, he saw that it may not be overcome totally in fact. But he could not admit to living easily with sin as some Christians did or saying it did not matter as others did. While for some it was overcome immediately, and for others gradually, for all real Christians its power was broken by grace received in faith that exhibited love. Love, of course, produced good works; and they effectively were part of the ongoing overcoming of sin.

All of this could have been said without reference to perfection, Calvinist critics would not have been silenced by the omission, but their target would have been more difficult to hit. Without the term *perfection* some of the eschatological enthusiasm for a totally sinless state might not have been encouraged. Love, of course, has perfectionist trajectories; but they do not have to be exaggerated to encourage moral Christian life in the security of God's grace. Perfection as the total love of God and neighbor still includes the need for forgiveness by God's grace. He wrote: "What is perfection? The word has various senses: here it means perfect love. It is love excluding sin, love filling the heart, taking up the whole capacity of the soul. It is love 'rejoicing ever more, praying without ceasing, in everything giving thanks' [cf. 1 Thess. 5:16-18]."[6]

The "Scripture Way of Salvation" was a balanced essay. It took account of the persistence of sin, yet spoke of the power of love and the place of works of mercy in the Christian life. It provided for the work of the power of atonement in the interior life of the Christian's psyche while still acknowledging the reality of sin.

Calvinist accusations that Wesley was leading people to disillusionment and that he was inconsistent caused some consternation among his preachers at the Bristol Conference of 1758. He warned the preachers to exercise care in how they spoke about perfection. As a response he published "Thoughts on Christian Perfection," one of his clearest statements on the issue.

Again, he made it clear that *perfection* was "The loving God with all our heart, mind, soul, and strength." He noted that there were defects and mistakes, and while he would rather not call them sins, if others wanted to do so, they might. He would not use the term *sinless perfection*. But he believed that there were those in this life for whom love was so real that they did not voluntarily sin.[7] He stated that if he did not believe that some had received this grace, he would stop preaching it and hold with others that sin had to remain until one died.

In 1762, he tried to clarify the concept again with his "Cautions and Directions Given to the Greatest Professors in the Methodist Societies."[8] In it, he mentioned some of the extremes among Methodists. There were those who believed they would not die and they could not err. Others visited believers to persuade them that they, too, were perfect. Some believed they possessed special spirits and could not sin or fall. Wesley leveled several warnings against those tempted by this enthusiasm. He urged them to guard against pride and its daughter, enthusiasm. Antinomianism, especially in its Moravian form, was dangerous. He cautioned: stay mindful of sins of omission and remain active, seek God and avoid schism, think not of separating from one another because of opinions, and avoid giving offense that would cause others to secede from you.

Neither the secession of Maxwell nor Wesley's publications silenced the critics. Wesley's claims that he had always preached the same message are not as persuasive as his goodwill in trying to hold his followers in one camp. The teaching of *perfection* could not hold them together. His emphasis on its meaning *love* with both of its trajectories toward absolute devotion to God and radical responsibility toward the neighbor's good, in all probability, would have held more within the Methodist Society.

Wesley, of course, would disagree with the above. He pulled

together, in an edited compendium, many of his writings on perfection and called it *A Plain Account of Christian Perfection*. One can read in it the very shifts in emphasis that he is trying to deny. As the worst exaggerations of perfection were not his, he would respond: "But this doctrine has been much abused." So has that of justification by faith. But that is no reason for giving up either this or any other scriptural decline. "When you wash your child," as one speaks, "throw away the water; but do not throw away the child."[9]

Wesley observed the qualitative difference that assurance of grace made in believers. He never claimed perfection for himself. He admitted that many had fallen away from perfection, but he could not give up the knowledge that humanity was to grow toward perfection. He trusted in a coming Kingdom, and he knew that people were capable of loving acts. As an exponent of Christian ethics, he refused to surrender the high moral calling of his interpretation of the New Testament. Such a scrupulous emphasis on the perfection of overcoming sin represents his reading of certain New Testament texts. A biblical realist reading of the same texts and other texts can relax the demand somewhat. The rigorous morality can be emphasized, but the love for the neighbor may force us to utilize ambiguous elements like the local police force and judiciary for the neighbor's protection. So, even love may cause us to use sinful instruments for good. It is probably wiser to confess with Paul that the power of sin, even when we overcome its control, still exerts influence, and that we will in history live by forgiveness as well as a will to radically love God and neighbor.

Wesley's minimalist interpretation of perfection corresponds to William Law's religious seriousness and the possibility of acting in love without consciously defying any known law of God. Albert Outler's suggestions that Wesley never intended the term *perfection* to mean faultlessness reinforces the appropriateness of the minimalist interpretation. Even a contemporary realist, Reinhold Niebuhr, would insist that Jesus' commandment of love and the Sermon on the Mount constructed by Matthew had perfectionist as well as realist trajectories. Wesley's minimalist position, with the recognition that even this achievement of loving action may be a temporary reality and a fall into moral ambiguity may follow, seems true to experience and respectful of the need for moral rigor. It was not acceptable to his Calvinist critics with whom he also disagreed on predestination and politics.

Predestination

Although his *History of England* indicated some reservations about the Bill of Rights and the constitutional settlement with King William, it showed little sympathy for the Presbyterians or the Jacobites. The small book Wesley published for Joseph Galloway on the American Revolution saw the Revolution centered in Presbyterian and Congregationalist conspiracies while the Church of England, Methodist Societies, and Quakers opposed the Revolution.[10] Many of Wesley's most severe Calvinist critics in England were also supporters of the American cause and changes in England. So, some political fights were correlated with the Wesleyan-Calvinist theological struggle over free will and predestination.

It is not patronizing to say that some of John's best friends were Calvinist predestinarians. The Presbyterian evangelicals and the Methodist evangelicals were mixed together in the early societies. George Whitefield would never surrender his friendship with John Wesley. Charles Wesley maintained a close relationship to Lady Huntingdon. When she founded a seminary for her chapels, she appointed John's best theologian and second behind himself in authority, John Fletcher, to direct it. She entertained the first Conference of Methodist preachers in her home at 12 Downing Street in London and advised and supported John at least until after Whitefield's death in 1770.

Though Whitefield and John disagreed over predestination, they had been friends since the Holy Club days, and their correspondence kept returning to their hopes for full reconciliation. John's memorial sermon for George did not move far enough in the Calvinist direction for Whitefield's predestination followers. Also, after the removal of Whitefield from the scene, Lady Huntingdon led her chapels to distance themselves farther from the Wesleyan movement.

Another underlying force to the seriousness of the dispute was that Wesleyan preachers and members, upon being persuaded of the truth of predestination, would leave the Wesleyan connection, which John was trying to unify against several centrifugal forces. John would observe that their adherence to Calvinism had not increased their growth in holiness; in fact, he stressed their falling away from Christian discipline. The bitterness of the battle, which occupied him from the 1770s until his death in 1791, producing a flood of Wesleyan attacks during the American Revolution, should not obscure his respect for and dependence on John Calvin. John Wesley never outgrew the influence of his Calvinist parents, and Methodist ethics and Calvinist ethics are of a similar rigorous, somewhat ascetic-political cast. But as Calvinists needed to set aside the optimistic tones of *perfection,* Wesleyans had to reject the determinism of *predestination.*

Wesley knew that the force of God upon human decision was often so powerful that it seemed irresistible. He knew that within the religious experience, one could believe it was from a force beyond one's own volitional choice. Early in his ministry, to agree with Calvinists, he conceded that some were chosen this way. Later, he omitted that concession in his writing.

In 1774, he quarreled with Jonathan Edwards in "Thoughts upon Necessity." To Wesley, Edwards's argument that people under necessity still did what they did, making it their voluntary action, missed the point.

> For their will on your supposition is irresistibly impelled. So they cannot help willing this or that. If so, they are no more blameable for that *will* than for the actions which followed it. There is no blame if they are under a necessity of willing. There can be no moral Good or Evil unless they have *Liberty* as well as *Will,* which is an entirely different thing. And the not adverting to this seems to be the direct occasion of Mr. Edwards' whole mistake.[11]

Wesley thought that the teaching of necessity—whether in Edwards, the Westminster Confession, ancient heathens, modern deists, or Christians—destroyed freedom in humanity and reduced human dignity. It left no room for divine judgment or the justice of the Divine Judge. Liberty to Wesley was necessary for all discussion of reward and punishment. Here the importance of ethics to Wesley's whole understanding of theology appears.

Without freedom, the whole story of divine justice, judgment, atonement, and forgiveness was rendered unnecessary. The "horrible decrees" before creation would have determined everything, making a mockery of the divine-human drama of Scripture and of the evangelical revival. Wesley argued from Scripture that the God of power and love cured evil that human conscience could reveal but not cure. But God would not force happiness on humanity or force it to be miserable. Humanity had real choices to make.[12]

Two years later, he reviewed the Calvinist confessions of Paris (1559), Dort (1618), and Westminster (1646), and confessed that he could not find unconditional election in Scripture and that he could not believe it.[13] He assembled pages of scriptural references that to him indicated real human choices.

A short piece in 1777 distinguished between God's work in creation and divine work in governing and judging humanity. In creation, he thought God worked by decree in all that God created, but that judgment presupposed human freedom. In God's governing function, humanity was created to be free. God's justice presupposed, for Wesley, that humanity had free agency. "The judge of the earth will do right. He will punish no man for doing any thing which he could not possibly avoid."[14]

The Methodists were willing to compromise a little under pressure from Lady Huntingdon, and they qualified the Conference minutes of 1760, which implied sanctification through work. But John Fletcher rose to defend the 1760 statement, and the debate spread to include several Calvinist divines as well as the more able Methodist apologists. Augustus Toplady, a young vicar and author of "Rock of Ages," was probably the best informed of the Calvinists, but the debate with him degenerated from logic, Scripture, and analysis of religious experience to mudslinging. Toplady published a translation of Zanchi Girolamo's *De Praedestinatione* with a title of *More Work for Mr. Wesley*. Wesley, rising to the bait, extracted it into a twelve-page tract and published it under the title "Doctrine of Absolute Predestination Stated and Summarized" by his own publisher in 1770. Toplady responded, and the Methodist Nathan Walker responded with a long attack on predestination. He even defended Wesley's doggerel, which had offended Toplady. Wesley joined in with the others. Attacking

Toplady, he appended to his translation of the predestination text: "One in twenty (suppose) of mankind are elected; nineteen in twenty are reprobated. The elect shall be saved, do what they will; the reprobate shall be damned, do what they can. Reader believe this or be damned. Witness my hand, A____ T____."[15] When Toplady wanted to pursue the debate over the insult, Wesley refused. "Mr. Augustus Toplady I know well, but I do not fight with chimney sweepers. He is too dirty a writer for me to meddle with. I should only foul my fingers."[16]

Beneath the debate, including definitions and logic, were the Methodist fears of Calvinism becoming antinomian and failing to encourage holiness. As Calvinism evolved, it was as much tempted by moral legalism as Methodism; probably, Wesley's fears here were not warranted. Calvinism feared that Methodism was drifting into works righteousness; probably, there was a temptation here. In fact, both movements, as they became churches in the United States, strayed toward works righteousness. Because of the stress on freedom, the Methodists were more inclined toward the Pelagian side (freedom and moralism) of the Pelagian-Augustinian dialectic that is essential to any Western orthodox church. The Calvinists moved toward the Augustinian side (determinism) of the dialectic. The Calvinists were more inclined to revolution (despite Calvin) in both the 1640s and the 1770s than the broader church Arminians, be they Church of England or Methodists.

Wesley had wanted to publish his own magazine for years. The critical pressures from Calvinist magazines encouraged him, also, to publish his replies in a magazine format. When he finally undertook the project, he named his magazine after the most famous anti-predestination thinker, Arminius.

Wesley published the *Arminian* beginning on 1 January 1778. It included the story of several lives: Arminius, Luther, Bishop Bedell, Peter Jaco, and others. It contained poetry, portraits, letters, and several anti-Calvinist essays. Its purpose was to proclaim "the universal love of God and His willingness to save all men from all sin" by publishing the best essays on the subject. Its message and policies were set directly against the Calvinist magazines, the *Gospel* and the *Spiritual,* which had featured many attacks on Wesley.

The first few issues in 1778 ran a long, continued biography of Jacob Arminius, whom Wesley credited with articulating universal salvation, free grace, and free will. The account of the Calvinist Synod of Dort, which suppressed Arminius's doctrine, was even longer. Another running account was a biography of Martin Luther. By the fifth issue, Wesley was publishing an account of John Calvin's persecution of Sebastien Castellio and Michael Servetus. Letters of the Wesley family were strongly represented as well as poetry and hymns, all with a free-grace-for-all, anti-Calvinist flavor to them. An early letter of Susanna shares her rejecting double predestination. Probably, the theme is captured best by the title of a hymn in the first number "Salvation Depends not on Absolute Decrees."[17]

The strong ethical emphasis in Wesley seen in both theological controversies over perfection and predestination and in the essays on economy, liberty, and slavery reflects the humanism and Enlightenment strains in his thought. The terms *humanist* and *Enlightenment* should probably not be used alone to describe Wesley. The fuller, more accurate way is to speak of him as a Christian humanist or a representative of the profoundly Christian Enlightenment. His mature writings reflect this Oxford-trained Christian scholar of the Age of Reason. To present analyses of all of his writings of the 1760s–1770s would distract from clarifying his ethics, but some analysis on three of these areas—the writings on nature, history, and the Old Testament—points to the breadth of his scholarly concerns.

Scholarly Research

Natural Philosophy

Wesley's love for nature and interest in science drove him to frequent reading of published works in natural science, and to investigate reported curiosities from earthquake sites to newly displayed animals. Unfortunately, his master's degree paper on the reasoning capacity of animals is not extant. He published three volumes on natural science in the 1760s. *A Survey of the Wisdom of God in the Creation or a Compendium of Natural Philosophy* (1763) was a work of extracting, but it was also more. Its title page quoted

Milton to reveal its purpose: "These are thy glorious Works, Parent of Good, Almighty! Thine this universal Frame, Thus wondrous fair! Thyself how wondrous then!"[18]

He wanted to publish a descriptive survey of what was known about nature without mathematics or much casual speculation. To accomplish his purpose, he translated from the Latin the work of John Francis Buddeus, professor of philosophy in Jena, Germany. To this, he added notes from John Ray, William Derham, and Oliver Goldsmith while he edited, added, and deleted from Buddeus. He also added the more recent discoveries from Chamber's *Dictionary*, descriptions of uncommon natural phenomena, and illustrations from art expressing the human spirit. He admitted to the limited understanding of causes and restricted his work largely to facts that were plain to human senses. From all this, he expected to increase the awareness of the greatness of God and the ignorance of humanity. He regarded the boasted discoveries of so *enlightened* an age as amounting to little. He hoped to humble human pride and to display the amazing power of God.

John's concern for the health of the poor met his interest in science. His early work, *The Primitive Physic*, had been a collection of folklore prescriptions for various ailments. Its support came from testimonies that certain folk remedies worked. It revealed his reliance on testimony and a sometime credulity in belief in what the folk tradition contained. He did not rely simply on folklore, however. He experimented on himself and others in the use of electrical shock treatments for a variety of maladies. Beyond his experiments and practiced therapies with electricity, he read widely on the fundamental properties of electricity.

Wesley's fundamental concerns about the relationship of theology and science, the reasoning capacity of animals, the value of folk remedies in medicine, and the application of technology (including electricity to health) are still with us in the twenty-first century. Although some contemporary conclusions differ from his insights, his boldness is stimulating today. For Wesley, history and nature were parts of God's universe. History and nature interacted, and he did not separate them radically. In all probability, postmodern theology will need to reunite the history and nature that theology, more modern than Wesley, had separated.

History of England

Wesley faulted most English historians for presenting too much detail and lacking the judgment necessary to judiciously interpret it. He also regretted that God, the governor of history, seemed to be omitted from the general histories of England. He set out to omit unnecessary details from the substance of English history by extracting from standard history texts. He attempted to avoid bias, and he hoped that it would appear so to the unprejudiced lovers of naked truth. Finally, in his preface, he wrote he wanted to show that God was the ruler of all things in nature and history. He acknowledged that his was to be a "Christian History of what is still called, (tho' by a strong figure) a Christian Country."[19] The text of the volumes, though, did not present many providential or judgmental interventions by God, leaving the impression of a pretty secularized history. Many of the early kingdoms in Britain rise and fall with no trace of God's hand being revealed in the history. Probably, his sources, as he had complained, really left him no alternative.

The fourth volume, particularly from Queen Anne through George II, describes the times of Wesley himself. It shows the highly politically charged times of his family and his ministry. Wesley is best understood as an influential intellectual with one foot among the poor and the other close to royal politics. His ancestors had suffered in their ministry even more than he would from the church-politics turmoil. The political role of his father, Samuel, never reached his estimate of his political abilities, but through the Church Convention in London, he was in touch with power brokers.

In the history of England that Wesley extracted and edited, he disclosed in a footnote that his father had written the defense of the Tory spokesman Rev. Henry Sacheverell. The trial of Sacheverell in 1710 before Parliament led to riots, the burning of dissenting meetinghouses, and prepared the ground for Queen Anne's calling for a new election. In the conclusion of the trial, Sacheverell was found guilty of libel against the Dissenters, a high crime and misdemeanor, and banned from preaching for three years; and two of his intolerant sermons were burned by the hangman. His history told of the intrigue by which the Tories were able to turn the Whig ministers out of the cabinet and eventually to cause the downfall of the Duke of Marlborough, who had been so victorious against the French in Belgium. Wesley's ethic came through in the conclusion to chapter 2 of book 4, in commenting on the financial reward to the duke of his campaigns and plunder: "In the whole, he had received about five hundred and twenty-three thousand pounds of the public money which he never accounted for and probably he had received four millions by plunder and presents. Poor again, if he lost his own soul."[20]

On another occasion, Wesley revealed that his father had requested Archbishop Sharp to ask the queen about any thoughts she had concerning resigning in favor of the Stuart pretender. Wesley recorded her negative response to the archbishop's question.

The history itself was written in the traditional manner. It moved chapter by chapter from the reign of one monarch to another. It focused on wars and international diplomacy. The emphasis on palace, court, and parliamentary intrigue dominated the volumes to the detriment of social, cultural, or intellectual history. It revealed realist political assumptions that one would as likely subscribe to Thucydides or the rejected Machiavelli as to Wesley. For example: "Treaties between nations are seldom observed any longer than interest or fear obliges; and among nations that take every advantage, political faith is a term without meaning."[21] Or, "From these campaigns, succeeding generals will take their lessons of devastation, and improve upon the arts of increasing human calamity."[22]

The volumes are helpful to persons interested in knowing how Wesley thought of the history of his own time from his birth to 1760. They must be supplemented, however, for his *Journal*, in more than one place, reveals his repugnance at British imperialism and the subordinating of the world's people to British commerce. The history, on the other hand, reports with some enthusiasm of the British supremacy after the Seven Years' War: "It must be confessed, that the efforts of England at this time, over every part of the globe, were amazing; and the experience of her operations greater than had ever been disbursed by any nation before."[23]

The selections of the history recorded are, of course, Wesley's, and sometimes the omissions seem peculiar to the reader. He is very interested, for example, in the conquest of Canada in the mid-1750s, and he presents quite a bit of detail on General Braddock's defeat near Fort Duquesne (now Pittsburgh). But the American reader from Pittsburgh can only smile at his omitting the story of George Washington's role in the assassination of Coulon de Jumonville and the surrender at Fort Necessity near Pittsburgh. Wesley noted his choice: "They [the French] had fought with General Lawrence to the North and Colonel Washington to the South, and come off victorious. It is unnecessary, however, to transmit these trifling details to posterity."[24]

Wesley's political commentary actually was more inclined to risk the judgments of God's providential governing of history than was his *A Concise History of England*. The subject matter of the Old Testament dictated that God's providence be examined in more detail there than in his reflections in *A Concise History of England*.

Old Testament

A decade after publishing his notes on the New Testament, Wesley undertook to publish *Explanatory Notes upon the Old Testament*.[25] The work is 2,713 pages long, despite his repeated announcements that his goal was to keep the work as short as possible. The notes take up about half the text of each page, the remainder being the Authorized Version of the text being commented upon. He started his work by extracting from the notes of Matthew Henry's exposition, while leaving out all of his predestinarian judgments. Gradually, he shifted over, by his own testimony, to following first Matthew Pool's notes, then adding Henry's comments, and then his own findings. He admits to lacking facility in Hebrew (though he had good knowledge of Greek). One assumes that in his discussion of Hebrew words, he is following Henry and Pool in terms of his own theology whereby *Elohim*, the council of the gods in Genesis 1, is interpreted as the Christian Trinity. He also occasionally includes extracts from other authors. All of this is woven together without any guidance about whether one is reading Wesley, Henry, Pool, or others. In the end, Wesley took what he wanted from the others, so it is his work and his name is on the title page as author. Such an approach is, of course, totally unacceptable to modern scholarship.

As much as possible, he sought to render and interpret passages plainly and literally. Obviously, he was embarrassed at the increasing length of the work, which was being paid for by subscribers to the *Notes*. Fearing the rising costs and the number of volumes to be produced, he promised to include *A Print of Mr. Wesley* gratis with each volume for a frontispiece. He also indicated that the money was of no concern to him. "What is money to me? Dung and Dross. I love it as I do the mire in the streets." As published in the 1765 edition, it had only three volumes, but these may have been sent out in many more numbers (Wesley mentions fourteen) to subscribers.

In his recommendations about reading the Bible, he suggested a chapter of each of the testaments in the morning and the night in an effort to balance law and gospel. It should also be read with prayer and meditation. The grand doctrines of sin, faith, new birth, inward and outward holiness needed to be kept in view as it was read. The undertaking was enormous, and one can feel sympathy for the sixty-two-year-old preacher in Edinburgh writing: "In the meantime I myself have far the worst of it: the great burden falls upon me. A burden which, if I had seen before all the world would not have persuaded me to take up. I am employed day and night and I must go on, whither I will or no less the printer should stand still."[26]

The Old Testament notes did not achieve the influence of the New Testament notes and were never held up as a standard of doctrine. Wesley was more of a New Testament preacher, and his preachers correspondingly followed suit. Tellingly, in the 1780s the Conference lowered the price by half because they still had half of the huge work in stock.

These massive productions of Christian humanist scholarship were secondary to Wesley's itinerant preaching and the resultant societal organizational work that accompanied the evangelization. The issues of ordination of his preachers kept arising at Conference, and issues of doctrine, polity, and finances were continual. Many of the solutions to these controversies are relatively insignificant today. The issues around women preaching, however, remain under debate in the twenty-first century.

Women Preaching

Sarah Crosby met with classes in 1761, as many other women had done. On meeting about two hundred in a class where she had expected thirty, she resorted to public speaking. She found a sense of God's presence, so she led a hymn and prayed with them as well as witnessed to them. She followed this up with another public service and found it successful. She wrote to Wesley, requesting his advice on this new development. He responded: "Hitherto, I think you have not gone too far. You could not well do less." He cautioned her to warn her listeners that the Methodists do not allow women preachers. He advised her that she could preface her remarks by delivering some of his *Notes upon the New Testament* or by reading a published sermon to them, as other women had done. The Methodist Conference did not grant women the right to preach, but Sarah continued to do so until her death. L. Tyerman listed Hannah Harrison, Miss Bosanquet, Miss Horral, Miss Newman, Mary Barrett, and others "as women who preached," and concluded, "To say the least, Wesley connived at it."[27] Dr. Samuel Johnson, poet, lexicographer, and staunch churchman who was a friend of the Wesley family, had a much more crude response to these developments: "Sir, a woman preaching is like a dog walking on his hind legs. It is not well done, but you are surprised to find it done at all."[28] The opposition to women preaching was fierce. Wesley's letter to Sarah Crosby in 1769 advised her how to disguise the fact that she was preaching by avoiding announcing texts, referring to her gathering as a prayer meeting, and interspersing remarks with prayers.

Sarah Crosby had lived for a time with Sarah Ryan, and her correspondence with John also raised Molly Wesley's wrath. Wesley's business manager and friend, Ebenezer Blackwell, was also concerned in the case. She was only the first of the Methodist women preachers documented by Leslie White as conducting effective evangelistic missions with Wesley's blessing.[29] They were commonly referred to as preachers and sometimes listed in the official Methodist records as preachers. Probably, the most famous of the women preachers was Elizabeth Evans, reflected in George Eliot's *Adam Bede*.[30] She progressed through rejection of finery, private devotion, love of ordinary village people to sensing a call to preach. After riding in the cart with a woman to her execution, she received, in her estimation, divine sanction to preach, regardless of whatever men would say. When asked if the

Methodist society sanctioned women to preach, she said, "It does not forbid them."[31]

John Wesley explicitly encouraged several of the women preachers, and they were able to avoid official suppression until after his death. He authorized the preaching of his dear friend Sarah Mallet: "We give the right hand of fellowship to Sarah Mallet, and have no objection to her being a preacher in our connection, so long as she preaches the Methodist doctrines, and attends to our discipline."[32] The authorization was conveyed by Joseph Harper on behalf of both Wesley and the Conference meeting in Manchester in 1787.[33] She continued to receive affectionate, advisory correspondence from Wesley until the last letter by another hand was delivered a few days before his death.

Wesley knew that neither the Scripture nor tradition that he was familiar with sanctioned women preaching. He listened to their testimonies of religious call and learned of the results of their speaking. At first, he treated their calls as exceptions to the general rule against their preaching. Experience softened his resistance, and with the authorization of 1787, he removed all of his reservations except prudence. In this case, experience outweighed his reading of Scripture and tradition in favor of more equality in an important church polity, ethical issue.

The later suppression of women ministers by Methodists, and the failure to ordain until the twentieth century, caused John Wesley's prophetic leadership on the issue to be obscured. Of his major social-ethical issues beyond the life of his societies, the one least neglected has been that of economic ethics. On this subject, at least, some of his teaching has been remembered, in part, while subject to mistreatment by popular and scholarly interpretation.

Economic Ethics

In 1760, Wesley published *Sermons on Several Occasions,* including as the last sermon, "The Use of Money." Wesley preached regularly on the theme of money, and he often used the text Luke 16:9: "I say unto you, Make unto yourselves friends of the mammon of unrighteousness, that when ye fail, they may receive you into the everlasting happiness. Luke 16:9." John saw the need for the wise understanding and control of money. The Christian was not to serve money, for that idolatry prevented one from serving God. But one was to deal calculatingly with money. Wesley lived frugally but not meanly. His commitment was to labor intensely for God. To that degree, he was an exponent of the work ethic, but his commitment to work had nothing to do with the Weber-Tawney thesis concerning the relationship of salvation to work. He worked from a prescriptive ethic of love for the good of others.

He noted that money had been rejected by poets, orators, and philosophers and even regarded as the source of evil. Not so, said Wesley: "The love of money, we know, is the root of evil; but not the thing itself."[34] Wesley knew that his world was controlled by business oligarchies and large landowners, and that he preferred to minister to the lesser classes and to the poor; but he did not reject economy. He taught how business might be used for good. Nevertheless, Wesley had no toleration for the accumulation of surplus capital. His sermon has three parts. It had been given without notes several times, and one can see, even in the written text, how easy it would be to deliver a version of it orally without manuscript or written outline. His outline was: "Gain all you can," "Save all you can," and "Give all you can."[35]

The gaining all you can was qualified. One was not to work so that one's health was endangered. Likewise, the Christian should abandon any occupation involving cheating, fraud, or corruption. One ought not ruin the business of the other as one conducts business "without hurting our neighbor." One could not gain ethically by anything that hurt the neighbor's health. He came down with fury on those who would destroy the neighbor by preparing or selling distilled spirits. They were cursed and damned to "the nethermost hell." Next in line for criticism were all those in the medical profession who misused their profession to prolong the suffering of patients for the sake of monetary gain. Also, the critique was directed toward those who hurt the soul by providing sinful entertainments or enticing anyone to intemperance in food, drink, or entertainment. Honest industry urged one to gain all one could while loving the neighbor. Business was to be pursued vigorously. Common sense and study were to be used to improve the way one worked.

Second, one should save as much as possible. Idle expenses were to be avoided. Waste was to be shunned. Luxury in living was regarded as wasteful. Expensive homes and furniture gratified pride and were not to be sought, nor was fine clothing. One should not waste money needlessly on children. One's household was to be taken care of and not encouraged to be wasteful, and one was to exercise care in leaving money to one's heirs so that it was not a further temptation to them.

Finally, the goal of the process was to give the money away. One was to act as a responsible steward toward one's family and toward the poor. What one had was from God and was to be shared according to God's will. Neither covetousness nor waste was a part of the Christian life: "Employ whatever God has entrusted you with in doing good, all possible good, in every possible kind and degree, to the household of faith, to all men. This is no small part of the wisdom of the just."[36]

This sermon was Wesley's personal economic ethic. He presented a picture of the activist pursuit of economic well-being. Compared to resignation in economic questions, it was modern, rational, and aggressive. Still, it was generous to a fault as well as prudent. Its strictures against waste, conspicuous consumption, and harmful vocations were solid ethical insights toward a more just economy than Wesley or succeeding generations have known.

As the decade neared its end, six friends within the society in London decided upon a new approach to meet the needs of the poor. They covenanted together to contribute a penny a week to form a common fund from which they could meet the needs of the poor outside the society. A dispute arose as their class leader disapproved of the new charity. The intention of the half dozen was to provide assistance on a regular basis to strangers who had no parish or friends to help. The dispute was referred to Wesley in 1777; he judged their intentions and plans worthy and contributed immediately while promising regular support through his own subscription to their scheme. By 1790, he had written up the formal rules for the Strangers Friend Society, which had become a regularized part of Methodist philanthropy.

John Turner's title "Wesley's Pragmatic Theology" can also be applied to his social work.[37] Wesley was committed to aiding the poor out of love, and he was very pragmatic in his choice of means. By the time he approved the Strangers Friend Society work, he had gone through most of the possibilities for alleviating the suffering of the poor. His love for the poor was the meeting of their real needs and a deep compassion for them as individuals and as eternal souls. He had been visiting them since the Holy Club days of 1729. The club's work involved teaching, visiting prisons, providing goods and clothes, paying debts to release prisoners, evangelizing, and organizing themselves for their ministry.

For fifty years, the inheritors of the Holy Club's enthusiastic discipline had visited and ministered to the poor. In that half-century, England and its people had become wealthier. The trade of the island was expanding, the population was growing, industrialization was beginning, and new economic policies were promising better lives for the English. But some were suffering more as urbanization and the forcing of population off the countryside increased poverty. The Methodist strategies together provided a rich pattern for combating poverty, but neither their financial resources nor their numbers were sufficient to accomplish much beyond their immediate circles. Though the Methodists came from all classes, the majority were women, and most of the men worked as artisans.

The cities and towns alike were overcrowded. Housing was inadequate, and below the level of the wealthy artisans, the poor lived in hovels or shacks. There was no sanitation, and water supplies were frequently the bearers of disease. Medical treatment was rare and steeped in superstition. Streets were unpaved, and transportation between towns was on roads that in rain turned into quagmires.

In describing urban conditions that led to the transportation of criminals away from England, first to America, and then to Australia, Robert Hughes summarized the conditions of London.[38] The population of London was mostly illiterate. The poorest lived as long as they could, sometimes reduced to picking up animal feces for fuel or food. Those who worked had some guild protections from the Tudor era, but occupational hazards were fundamentally unregulated. The sawyers of timber went blind, as did the tailors. Metal workers fell to lead poisoning. Glassblowers suffered from silicosis while hairdressers knew lung diseases from the mineral-based powder with which they worked. Workers alternated between fourteen-hour workdays and unemployment with no support. Children suffered long work hours with beatings for discipline, and the medical profession testified that such conditions were acceptable to society and the children's well-being.

With the arrival of the Dutch in the Glorious Revolution, gin made from corn and flavored with juniper berry became the opiate of the masses. It was cheap and available. "Drunk for a penny, and dead drunk for two pence" became the escape for many of the mob. Fear of the mob as a criminal class arose, and the elite responded by increasing the sanctions against crime. The mob only occasionally could be given political direction, but it could on occasions produce fearful riots. Police were neither effective nor organized, but children could be hanged for stealing a handkerchief, and public hangings were utilized as an ineffective means of deterrence and public spectacle.

The Methodist message of universal salvation for all free human beings who would trust it was expected to transform human beings. The Methodist literature is full of testimonies of people who found freedom and strength in their acceptance. Then the converted person was ideally brought into a society that supported one and with which one would join the work. If the society had been able to reform the Church of England to engage its resources, a major effort for the poor might have been launched. But by 1779, it was clear to all that the established church would not follow the lead of the Methodists. The potential for Methodism to influence the nation as a whole rested in its opportunity for carrying the energies of England's church with it. Methodism was fundamentally a religious movement. It had social consequences, but the potential for the religion influencing the society depended first on its religious results. The settlement of 1688 had provided religious toleration for all but Catholics. The Dissenters, perhaps 6 percent of the eighteenth-century population, were denied access to political office, university, and preferments. They also paid special taxes, but toleration was spreading from the rationalism of John Locke's toleration and the exhaustion from partially religious wars. Yet the Dissenters were defeated political-religious parties that had overthrown king and church, and they suffered under the renewed restoration of Anglicanism. Catholicism or old English religion was found largely in rural estates, London, and Lancaster. Though subject to more pressures than Protestant dissent, it was generally not persecuted except in times of Jacobite rebellion.

Perhaps 90 percent of the population gave allegiance to the Church of England, the established religion of the realm. The clergy provided leadership in education, morals, and charity. The bishops had seats in the House of Lords and, as ecclesiastical lords, had secular-political responsibilities as well. The church was the civil religion participating in both the benefits and the legitimization of society and state. To strike at Anglicanism was to strike at England. England of the eighteenth century was seldom inclined to reform. The revolutions of the seventeenth century being seen as quite sufficient, Anglicanism was not about to reform its practices.

The role of the ecclesiastical courts in enforcing church attendance, discipline, and public morals declined in the century. As church coercion faded, voluntary church societies arose to persuade the society toward Christian practice. The Society for Promoting Christian Knowledge (1698), the Society for the Propagation of the Gospel (1701), and the Societies for the Reformation of Manners (1690–1730) promoted literature, missionary service, and social reform.[39] All initiated work that became part of the ministry of the Wesley revival.

About 15,000 men served as priests in 10,000 parishes. Most of them were professionals fulfilling an expected role. A sense of divine call to office was not an Anglican expectation as in the traditions of dissent or the evangelical revival. Some of the clergy led a life of luxury and neglected their duties, but most carried out their assigned roles. In rural England, many of the clergy also farmed to support themselves and their families. The available records of attendance indicate that church attendance declined during the eighteenth century along with the celebration of Communion. Henry Rack believes the general pattern to have been the observance of Communion three or four times a year in country churches.[40] Preaching was the central form of church service at this time, with central pulpits taking the focus away from the altars. Of course, church life, daily spirituality, ecclesiastical patterns, and concerns varied from parish to parish, so it is hard to obtain a general picture of the religious life of a whole nation in the absence of much of the relevant data.

There probably is no better observer of the religious life of this period than Wesley, who traveled as broadly as anyone in intimate contact with the religious life of England. The religious aspirations and needs of the English people in prayer and conflict come alive in his journals and letters. Certain tendencies toward less sacramentalism, more rationalism, and more moralism were characteristic of the eighteenth century compared to the seventeenth. But these were also resisted. Newtonian science needed to be reconciled to faith, and Lockean rationalism needed to be related to deeper sources of faith. However, it was not all a fight between deism and orthodoxy. Various trends contended before the evangelical revival, and then combined in new ways within Wesley himself and within his followers and theological opponents.

Within Methodism's immediate circle of influence, education followed upon the basic religious message. Basic religious instruction in class meetings, the founding of schools, the production of cheap editions of literature, the distribution of inexpensive tracts, the establishment of Sunday schools all promoted education.

On the financial side, loan funds were created to help people escape debt, to buy tools, and to start income-producing enterprises. Wesley also created centers of employment to counter the displacement economic change was causing.

A third major area of intervention was the provision of free medical clinics, free medicines, and the publication of folk medicine remedies. Wesley kept up his study of medicine and recommended therapies as well as prayed for the health of the sick.

Summarizing Wesley's work on behalf of the poor, we have the gospel message of love restoring dignity and hope, a community of solidarity, a commitment to a message and effort for national change, and the interventions in terms of education, capital formation, and health care. These efforts were characteristic. But in the recession of 1773, Wesley was moved to make recommendations for national economic policy. They paralleled his efforts to campaign against slavery as a national issue of economics and liberty. In "Thoughts on the Present Scarcity of Provisions," he raised questions about why starvation and unemployment were allowed to haunt Britain.[41] Why was food so expensive? His answers were that the national debt was too high, drawing off capital investment resources. The wealthy were living too luxuriously and not returning enough to the workers or for investment. Needless military fortifications and heavy expenditures for military pensions were increasing governmental expenses and the national debt. Finally, the transportation system of horse-drawn vehicles was used inefficiently. Too many horses were consuming too much grain, keeping the prices high. Exports of highly bred horses to France was responsible for driving other animals off the market as well as overconsumption of grain. In addition, the hated distillery industry was drawing down too much on grain supplies, pushing the prices up.

It has been the fashion to praise Wesley's intentions but to dismiss his economics. A recent book suggests that the recommendations were more suited to a mercantile society than a capitalist world.[42] Wesley's tract preceded Adam Smith's capitalist publication by three years, and his world was a mixture of capitalism and mercantilism or an age of transition. A current reappraisal of Wesley's program to lower taxes by cutting unnecessary military pensions, thereby reducing the national debt, could regard it as compassionate new liberalism. The increase of taxes on the unnecessary aspects (luxury travel in private coaches) of the transportation system may be a national policy choice if applied prudently. Measures to reduce the price of grain for the nation's food supply have characteristically been one of the strengths and human blessings of the United States economy. Finding the right price for the farmer is not an easy measure, however. Many societies, liberal and Communist, have been forced to act to regulate and sometimes to attempt to suppress the liquor traffic for both economic and moral reasons. Wesley's concerns here do not appear outdated either. Some of the criticisms of Wesley's economic recommendations from Manfred Marquardt may be due to the conviction that Wesley was not socialist enough.[43] He certainly was no socialist, and his economics were largely Christian pragmatic (i.e., let us see what will work to improve the condition of the least). Certainly, the collapse of liberation theology has freed contemporary interpreters from seeing his social theology as a forerunner of liberation theology except for interpretations of his abolitionism in these terms. However, abolitionism could only be seen as liberation theology anachronistically and is as well interpreted as the ethical fruit of Christian realism or liberalism. In Wesley's case, it was evangelical-Anglican theology with both realist and liberal themes.

The closing Conference of the decade in 1779 noted that membership in the London Society had declined. The next decade still had to resolve the anomaly of a society looking more and more like a church, and it continued the contention with Calvinism. But the political-social issues of the late 1760s–1770s remain to be considered to complete the analysis of Wesley as the mature leader of the movement and teacher of Christian social ethics.

9. Liberty

John Wesley contributed several essays to Christian political philosophy from 1768 to 1782. The 120 pages on politics are divided about equally between reflections on liberty during the rebellion of John Wilkes and the revolution of the American colonies. He published "Thoughts upon Slavery" in the middle of this period in 1774.

Wesley sought to clarify the meaning of liberty and attempted to disassociate both the Wilkes mob and the American revolutionary from the idea of liberty. His concept of liberty was closer to that of Samuel Johnson, upon whom he drew in his own writings, or Edmund Burke than that of John Locke. He believed that the out-working of the Glorious Revolution of 1688 had provided Englishmen with more liberty than they had ever known before, and that the American colonists also were free. Liberty meant the capacity to direct one's life and to be free from coercion in matters of religion or property. Religious liberty was given by God in the assumption of each person being responsible to God for the care of his or her soul. Self-direction of the use of one's property and life was, of course, limited by the sovereign's imposition of taxes and law. But in Wesley's judgment those were relatively insignificant limitations in England. Englishmen enjoyed greater liberty than people in other countries; Wesley felt it was to be protected, not risked through visionary assertions of liberty leading to mob rule or revolution. He was particularly scornful throughout this whole period of Englishmen who considered they were enslaved by their sovereign. To Wesley, the lack of personal freedom of the African slave was not comparable to limits on English freedom—and rightly so. The African slaves clearly did not have liberty, though they ought to be freed.

This protection of institutionalized freedoms was reinforced by his political realism. Wesley was skeptical of radical efforts because the knowledge of politics did not provide adequate guides to wise action. Most information about politics was regarded as one-sided. Political action often provided surprising results in the push and pull of counterforces. Most politics was self- or party-interested. The political desires and actions of political actors were hard to determine because most lied about their political aims. Wesley's political essays, suspicious of motivations, lacking a reliable political science, and set in dangerous, rebellious times, guarded the monarchy and the real liberties of England. His commitments to reform and change for the sake of liberty are seen particularly in the struggle to abolish slavery and in economic reform for the poor.

The essays were philosophical. They represented the political work of the intellectual. The first of this series of essays, "Free Thoughts on the Present State of Public Affairs," from 1768, was to defend George III. Most of the essays were to defend George III's reign from London rioters or American revolutionaries. He wrote it plainly: "That I have heard it affirmed with my own ears, 'King George ought to be treated as King Charles was!' "[1] He wanted his king neither overthrown nor assassinated.

If Wesley's conservatism in the face of radical challenges is to be understood, it must be in terms of his love of liberty and his respect for power: "Wesley's support for the established order in the period of 1772–82 was based not only on his residual and suitably amended Toryism, but also on his appreciation of the rights enjoyed by the free-born Englishman. This is also the framework within which his anti-French and anti-papist sentiments, especially evident in 1778, are best understood."[2] At the same time, he was implicitly subverting the authority of the established church, a church that was generally regarded in England as one entity with the state. His respect for appropriate power meant no radical change of the monarchy or the church.

On Power

Wesley believed, as have all Christian political writers, that power comes from God. He also believed, as have most Christian theorists until the modern age, that the supreme earthly power is usually vested in one person. In this most fundamental of his political treatises, "Thoughts Concerning the Origin of Power," he preferred monarchy as a form of government. In classical fashion he suggested three forms of government: aristocracy, democracy, and monarchy. Democracy had existed in Greece and in Rome in his view, but he thought it had in his time disappeared. His contemporaries of the Enlightenment, Montesquieu and Rousseau, assumed that republican forms of government were for small states. In fact, Sweden, Geneva, and Switzerland could have been regarded as republics.

The rest of his essay was an attack upon the idea that as all are equal, they must consent to be governed, and that therefore power derives from the people. His first line of attack derived from the question: "Who are the people?" If the proposition were true, women and children were people and should vote. But they did not vote. Moreover, only freeholders with an income of forty shillings a year could vote in England. The number of people in England who could vote was only half a million from the original population of eight million. The others were excluded by laws, which they neither made nor consented to formally or freely. That was certainly not government by the people. Furthermore, he argued that history provided no example of rulers in England being chosen by the people and very few being so chosen in history. He mentioned one elected by the people in Naples in the preceding century. So, in his judgment, neither reason nor history witnessed to power being from the people. Rather, it was from God. He came close to the divine right of kingship as claimed by the Stuarts. He had, in his own mind, overthrown Locke's government by consent of the people. Susanna and probably his brother Samuel could have drawn Jacobite divine right support from his essay, but he, following his father, did not. He recognized the legitimacy of the kingship of the one who was monarch. His theory of government then was quite theocratic, as he concluded: "There is no power but of God."[3]

The intense persecution of the Methodists reinforced Wesley's loyalty to the king. Finding freedom of religion supported by the monarch, he also hoped for the king's protection. He experienced stoning frequently; he learned of Methodist preachers being beaten; he objected to their being impressed into military service; he saw the burned and looted houses of Methodists; and he alternatively avoided and suffered at the hands of anti-Methodist mobs. In 1744, he swore the oath against the pope when ordered to do so, and as some of his persecutors decried him as a Catholic, he wrote a letter to the king distinguishing himself from Catholicism. To be accused of Catholicism in 1744 was to be guilty of sedition. Wesley's unsent letter declared his group to be loyal Protestants seeking justice, mercy, truth, the glory of God, peace, and goodwill while abhorring the doctrine of Rome. The monarch was promised financial support, prayers, and subjection for "conscience sake."[4]

On Liberty

John Wesley's critique and analysis of liberty were inspired by the Wilkite riots of the 1760s and 1770s. John Wilkes was part of the agitation by radical London elements against George III. Wilkes was sentenced to the Tower for libeling the king. Upon his release, the crowd chanted "Wilkes and Liberty," as they would intermittently for several years. The mob protested the public burning of Wilkes's libelous paper the *North Briton* at the Royal Exchange. Wilkes was expelled from Parliament, and he fled to Paris. When he returned, he was reelected to Parliament from Middlesex, initiating London riots. Wilkes was again jailed, which resulted in more riots ending on 10 May 1768, with the army killing eleven and wounding others.

On his release from prison further riots occurred. He was denied his place in Parliament again. Parliament and the City of London entered a struggle, which resulted in the Lord Mayor being jailed. George III became the subject of protest, and three years after that riot John Wilkes was elected mayor, leading to further rioting. Wilkes was permitted to take his seat in Parliament, and gradually, his connections with those inclined to riot faded.

A few years later the passage of the Catholic Relief Act led to riots instigated by a Protestant association. A week of rioting left 285 dead rioters and almost 200 wounded. After a trial, twenty-five were hanged, ending the worst of the London riots during Wesley's lifetime. The disorder that Wesley feared in the Wilkes rebellion had destabilized London, creating a context for the more extreme riots of 1780. In comparing the Wilkite troubles to the

English revolution as King George was being compared to King Charles, he noted the Wilkite rebellion was secular, whereas the previous outbreak had been in part religious. The religious outrage reappeared four years later in rebellion. Both riots also revealed some class hostility, as the property targets of the mobs were those of the rich.[5]

John Wesley's love of peace and order as well as his preference for monarchy led him to stand against John Wilkes's rebellion. He wrote against the claims of Wilkes's followers for liberty. In Wesley's view he possessed more freedom to follow his religious conscience and to utilize his property as he saw fit than at any previous time in English history. He had the essential liberties he wanted. He derided the rebellious calls for liberty as calls for the liberty to kill, or to take others' property, or to violate women. The need for liberty is a human need that found particularly strong expression in the English nation. In Wesley's view, the prevalent clamor for liberty in association with the rebellion of Wilkes needed philosophic examination. His examination was to analyze several different meanings of liberty, rejecting liberty to kill, plunder, steal, or rape, and to affirm liberty of property and religion. In his affirmations of liberty he stood clearly upon Lockean philosophy, even though he elsewhere rejected Locke's myth of the social contract to consent to government.

Only recently the Acts of Uniformity and the acts to suppress conventicles under King Charles had restricted religious and property rights. John's grandfathers had suffered under such threats. But under George I and George II these rights had been well protected. To Wesley, the freedoms that Englishmen had wanted had been won, and they needed protection from mobs clamoring for liberty: "Have we not in England full liberty to choose any religion, yea or no religion at all? Whoever therefore in England stretches his throat, and bawls for more religious liberty, must be totally void of shame, and can have no excuse but want of understanding."[6] For all this liberty, he exalted, "Let us be thankful for it to God and King!"[7]

The "Free Thoughts" of 1768 was noteworthy for its circumspect reserve about political comment. Of course, such reserve served his purpose of mocking those who were sure they knew better than people involved in politics. He regarded politics as complicated and the sources of action as hidden. It was characterized by a multitude of facts about which it was hard to be exact. The sources of facts could not be trusted, for they often were colored by political interest or passion. He further stated that he was no expert and that he did not know well people in politics. Yet as an Englishman, he claimed a right to a political opinion. As he was not beholden to any political party or interest, he thought he could offer opinion relatively free of self-interested bias. He could present his "naked thoughts," but he was "sure of nothing."

He defended the king from criticism, suggesting George III conducted himself as an Englishman, Christian, and king should. He praised the king for his family life and his life as a Christian. He mentioned that some questioned the king for being without skill in the political arts, and he countered by praising him for not being skillful in the arts of politics as recommended by Machiavelli.[8] He suggested that libeling the king smacked of high treason, and he quoted at length the speech of Judge Lord Mansfield that denied Wilkes his seat. He thought that the citizenry was not particularly able to render discriminate political judgment. He raised the suspicion that Wilkes had been in the pay of the French. In any case, Wilkes was pursuing his own ambition, and Wesley approved of the government's not giving in to the rioters' demands. Wesley in his realism did not expect that a dissolution of Parliament would lead to the election of a better Parliament. Wesley did not expect much from government; he certainly had no utopian expectations of government; and he distrusted the foes of order. Meanwhile, as Wesley wrote, he feared for the state from the madness of passionate rioting. His final word was that England should humble itself before God.

The outworking of the Wilkes crisis contributed to English freedom in two ways. Wilkes won a case of false imprisonment against the secretary of state and an award of £4000. William Pitt led the attack against the general warrants under which Wilkes had been arrested, challenging the draconian power of Parliament. Judges responded, according to Winston Churchill, with statements on liberty, governmental powers, and freedom of speech. Churchill credits the responses to Wilkes as increasing the liberty of the

English in freedom to publish as well as freedom from unlawful arrest.[9]

These same arguments against sedition and rebellion in the name of liberty written in 1772 would be used against the American Revolution of 1776. The colonies had problems of misgovernment, but they were not best addressed through a revolution for liberty in his perspective.

The American Colonies

Charles Wesley had heard radical talk of revolution during his stop in Boston on his return to England in 1737. John watched the anger of the colonies mount during the reign of George III. The Peace of Paris of 1763 granted an interlude in Britain's century-long conflict with France. The attempt to raise taxes to pay for the war that had added Canada to the British Empire set the stage for the colonial revolt of 1776. The French support of the colonists would eventually lead Louis XVI to try to raise taxes from the French Parliament to pay for the colonists' victory over Britain in the American War of Independence. Louis XVI's attempt ignited the French Revolution, which would lead again to French-English warfare.

John also read the stirrings in the colonies as part of the opposition to George III in England. At first he appealed to Parliament to meet some of the colonists' demands and appease their claims. In 1768, he had seemed sympathetic to the colonists in "Free Thoughts." He criticized the treatment of the colonies by George Grenville, who was opposed by George III. Some of the Americans' demands he regarded as their legal due and as being presented fairly.[10]

By 1775, Wesley seemed to have completely changed his mind with his publication of "A Calm Address to Our American Colonies." Actually, the times had changed as the Americans were approaching full rebellion. Also Samuel Johnson's "Taxation No Tyranny" had persuaded him that the levying of taxes on the colonies was appropriate. Opponents criticized him for plagiarism of Johnson. In the next edition he pointed out his source, and the report was that Johnson was pleased to be used by Wesley to criticize American complaints. Wesley sold the "Calm Address" for a penny a copy; the government distributed it free outside churches, and its distribution reached more than 100,000 copies.

The arguments of "A Calm Address," plagiarized from Johnson, drew a storm of protests. He was accused of writing to earn a pension as well as inconsistency. He admitted to changing his mind on the issue. Augustus Toplady could not resist the chance to attack. His twenty-four-page tract, "An Old Fox Tarr'd and Feather'd," featured a picture of a fox in clerical dress for a frontispiece. He proclaimed Wesley "a low and puny tadpole in divinity who wants to be a high and mighty whale in politics."[11] He accused Wesley of literary theft and mistaken judgment. John Fletcher and Thomas Olivers defended Wesley with their publications. He defended his motives in a letter to *Lloyd's Evening Post*, proclaiming his aim was to help calm the rising clamor toward independence and war. He believed that all should see that the American claim for exemption from taxation was not a just cause but an excuse for agitation.

He wrote to the prime minister and colonial secretary expressing his fears and pleading for the withholding of force against the Americans. In those letters Wesley avoided expressing his opinion that the Americans were totally in the wrong. He feared that force would lead to a war that would not be easy to win. He argued against those English who thought the Americans would be easily defeated, and he warned of European intervention on the side of the Americans or even invasion of England while her forces were busy killing their American cousins. Then he expressed his fears that there could be an uprising in Britain. He knew by his travels of four thousand to five thousand miles per year that the population was exasperated. Inflammatory papers had done their work, he said, and reverence for the king was gone: "So that first despising him, they were just ripe for open rebellion. And I assure your lordship so they are now. They want nothing but a leader."[12] In addition to the politics, two economic conditions seemed to him to contribute to the revolutionary situation: (1) the decline of business and (2) the high expense of commodities. Multitudes of hungry unemployed might join any who could promise bread.[13]

Wesley concluded his letter appealing for the avoidance of force with an appeal for faith in God to be taken seriously and the injustice of "the astonishing luxury of the rich" be corrected. Perhaps, he threatened, it was already too late. Perhaps the Lord had decided to destroy the state. His last word of warning was that the ministers of state would remember kings defeated by the populace, particularly Rehoboam, Philip II, and Charles I.

Economic recession, the possible defeat in war, a suffering population, and a division in the ruling class are indeed ingredients for revolution, and Wesley was correct to utter dire warnings and to plead for prudent peacemaking policies. England had experienced civil war in 1745–1746 with the Jacobite pretender bringing his army to within 145 miles of London. Wesley's fear of civil war can be seen in his description of the aftermath of the Battle of Culloden in 1746. English memories of their own revolution of the 1640s would produce actions to avoid the folly breaking out at home. These memories were insufficient, however, to sustain the bonds with their American cousins. The war would be a civil war, a revolution, and a war of independence all rolled into one struggle.

Wesley, sensing the approach of civil war, deepened his attack upon the American arguments. To him as an English monarchist seeking peace, the approaching conflict violated his values in dividing the country, threatening the king, and engaging in war.

But other issues drew his attention at the same time, and a chief one in connection with liberty was slavery. Having addressed the question of the liberty of slaves in his 1774 publication, "Thoughts upon Slavery," he responded vehemently to the attacks on Johnson's "Taxation No Tyranny." His opponents had written that taxation without representation was *slavery*. He responded that as he had no vote, he had no representation. In fact, most in England had no votes. But they certainly were not slaves. In his opinion they were very free people. He argued, under government we are obligated to obey laws and pay taxes whether or not we are represented in Parliament.

He returned to his discussion of the actual condition of the Africans in America and said, "This is slavery." The English and the Americans generally go where they want, worship as they will, and receive money for their labor. That, he said, was liberty. He recognized that most English would never be able to own a freehold. "But be that as it may, they have no vote now; yet they are not slaves, they are the freest men in the whole world."[14]

Wesley attacked the arguments that supported the rebellious colonists. Wesley never praised the Baron Montesquieu. In his 1775 essay he referred to him as the fanciful Montesquieu, who asserted that all in England had the right to vote. Not so, claimed Wesley, as the empirical evidence showed. He accepted that the English Parliament had a right to tax and to demand obedience to its laws. It was rather rare, Wesley argued, for one to be represented in Parliament by anyone a person has voted for. Moreover, most laws were passed before one was born, so there was no consent to them. All were born subjects of some state, and in Wesley's theology passive obedience was required. Wesley agreed that colonists had the rights of Englishmen, but he added, unless they forfeited those by moving to colonies that did not vote for Parliament.

Wesley then proceeded to list taxes that various parliaments had enforced upon the colonies, establishing the precedent for taxation. He also repeated the argument that by right England could assess new taxes to pay for the protection of the colonies in the war against France.

Wesley's point eleven revealed another level of his fear of the colonies' secession. He attributed the rising of rebellion in the colonies to the same forces that objected to monarchy in England. There were those who wanted to replace monarchy with commonwealth. He believed there was no gain to be won in a commonwealth. The consequences of struggling to win a commonwealth in either England or America were fearsome to him. He confessed love for both America and England and appealed for peace and respect for the king.

By 1776, the claim of the colonies had moved to independence. Still, they hid the demand for independence in the demand for liberty. Wesley argued that the colonies have liberty and against independence as a just claim. To Wesley, the demand for liberty beyond what both the English and the Americans enjoyed was to neglect reality and to seek anarchy. If human nature contained the right to directly govern, then it applied to twenty-year-olds, children, and women as well as to twenty-one-year-old male freeholders. He repeated the arguments of his essay on the origin of power rooting it in its source, God.

On 5 February of that same year he wrote "A Seasonable Address to the More Serious Part of the Inhabitants of Great Britain" signed "By a Lover of Peace." The division had come, and he saw a bitter civil war before them, yet he called for reason and peace: "A kingdom divided against itself is an evil, of all others the most dreadful; inasmuch as an innumerable train of evils necessarily follow; no inconsiderable part of which are the sword, fire, plunder, and famine."[15]

Civil war would destroy homes and relatives. It might rage not only in America, but also in England. As these peoples fell upon each other, perhaps a third party would intervene and pick up the spoils. The cost of war was so high that it revealed a total lack of wisdom in people who had permitted it. He quoted what must be one of the most poignant passages written against civil war. The quotation he chose was reminiscent of the great scene in India's *Bhagavad Gita* of Krishna contemplating civil war.

> See! Here are some thousands of our brave countrymen gathered together on this plain; they are followed by the most tender and feeling emotions of wives, children, and an innumerable multitude of their thoughtful, humane, and sympathizing countrymen. Then turn your eyes and behold a superior number at a little distance, of their brethren, "flesh of their flesh, and bone of their bone," who only a few years since emigrated to the dreary wilds of America. These also are followed with the most tender feelings of wives, children, and countrymen. See, they advance towards each other, well prepared with every instrument of death! But what are they going to do? To shoot each other through the head or heart; to stab and butcher each other, and hasten (it is to be feared) one another into the everlasting burnings. Why so? What harm have they done to one another? Why, none at all.... But brother goeth to war against brother; and that in the very sight of the Heathen. Surely this is a sore evil amongst us. O how are the mighty fallen! How is wisdom perished from the wise! What a flood of folly and madness has broke in upon us![16]

The contemplation of civil war in the *Bhagavad Gita* produced nervous breakdown, religious vision, and a wholesome search for salvation. About 150 years later than Wesley, Gandhi would find a call to pacifism in the Indian text. Here Wesley, contemplating the civil war, called for peace. Now there was no assigning blame, but the cry of the religiously sensitive soul for peace.

He found war so deplorable that his theodicy drove him to look for the reason in England's sin. What secret sin could be so judged that the country would be subject to this judgment of blood and division? The source could have been in England's lack of vital piety, but he estimated that had been increasing. So he ascribed it to England's participation in the slave trade and to imperialism in the East and particularly in India. The dispute that fueled the colonial war might have been a party affair, but beneath it Wesley believed was a national sin, and it was the "blood that we have shed in Asia, Africa, and America." He asked his readers to turn from the sin of their neighbors to their own sin. Repentance was needed as well as a turning away from the conflict. He called for fasting, worship, and repentance; even if those measures failed and destruction continued, he assured his readers that they would be remembered for their humility and service.

Throughout the year he observed the ways of the American rebels and repeated a tale of a shameful, deceptive attack upon a British ship. He welcomed the sight of the British slave ships forced to dock at Liverpool because there was no market for slaves, given the war. He wrote political letters beseeching British leaders to seek a negotiated end to the conflict. On 17 February 1778, he wrote "A Serious Address to the Inhabitants of England with Regard to the State of the Nation" to assure the people that the war was not the ruin of England. He followed the arguments of Josiah Tucker, the dean of Gloucester, in this essay.[17] Tucker had shown that in population, agriculture, manufacture, transportation, fisheries, taxes, and debt, the country's state of the nation was secure. Wesley wanted to argue the case for calming the population. He undertook such efforts several times during the war to prevent panic and provide support for the authorities.

To Wesley, the empirical state of England was not a cause for fear. After his facts presented from Tucker, he returned to the religious argument criticizing the English for their profanity. The people of England should fear God, Wesley argued, for their speech was more profane than that of other peoples. England was sloth-ful, but he thought other nations were also. In their blasphemous use of the holy name, he thought they were particularly sinful. God should be feared, but the English treated God with contempt in their speech. They should, therefore, fear evil consequences in their affairs: "Whoever spends but a few days in any of our large towns, will find abundant proof, that senseless, stupid profaneness is the true characteristic of the English nation."[18] He called for England to make its peace with God and to be thankful for all it had. His reference to the repentance of Nineveh points toward his combination of rationalistic use of the best empirical data of his day with a quite literal sense that God judged England as biblical authors portrayed the judgment of Israel in the Hebrew Scripture.

A few months later, on 10 May 1778, he likewise wrote from Limerick to the Irish, commending calmness to them. He admitted England had panicked a few months earlier over the course of the war. He urged his readers to regard some of the claims of Washington's army as exaggerated. He also discounted the fears of a French invasion of England. He thought England could stand against France and Spain if she joined the war. He reasoned that Spain would hesitate and that Portugal would refuse to join Spain against England. Nor did he fear Irish conspirators because he regarded the militia and the Irish authorities as adequate to main-tain order. The one to fear was God. But even here, John did not think that God was yet disposed to destroy England. There were more good people in England than the ten needed to save Sodom. On the whole, vital piety in England was increasing, and England was not slaying the prophets as Jerusalem had done. To the extent that England was at peace with God, there was no need to fear.[19]

Later in 1778, Wesley published "The Late Work of God in North America" in sermonic form with the text of Ezekiel 1:16: "The appearance was as it were a wheel in the middle of a wheel."[20] His brief introduction noted that the wheels within the wheel referred to the complications of God's providence. This providence is hid-den, but he undertakes to provide an explanation of how provi-dence has worked within the history of the American colonies.

The first wheel was the movement of evangelical Christianity in America from his own mission to Georgia, the New England awakening with Jonathan Edwards, George Whitefield's preaching, to the growth of the Methodist societies to three thousand members. But the increasing wealth of America led to luxury, pride, idleness, sloth, and wantonness that hindered the spread of true religion.

The second wheel was the growth of the spirit of independence through the same time period. He quoted John Witherspoon's speech to the Continental Congress to illustrate that the goal of the Americans was really independence. Wesley thought, however, that the cutting off of America's trade would reduce American wealth, pride, and rebellious spirit. Wesley thought God's providence would return the Americans toward humility, industry, and temperance. So, the outcome would differ from Dr. Witherspoon's intentions. The spirit of *independence* would have been overcome by the overrunning and impoverishment of the land by armed forces. In all of this, Wesley thought God intended the return of the Americans to spiritual blessings and the curtailment of independency. With that outcome they could receive the blessings of life, including the blessing of "true British liberty such as they enjoyed before these commotions."[21] This Wesley expressed as the "glorious liberty of the children of God."[22]

Wesley's history in this sermon or essay is peculiar and uniquely from his experience and perspective. His speculations about God's providence failed to be realized, and John Witherspoon's words and cause prevailed. It is strange to have the outcome of the words of these two great theologians of Calvinist and Arminian persuasion depend upon the intervention of the French Catholic forces at Yorktown. Maybe great events can be interpreted theologically after the fact. It is certainly imprudent to attempt such an interpretation in the midst of a shifting armed struggle.

The French-Spanish fleet threatened an invasion of the Isle of Wight in July 1779, and Wesley assured the people that it would be well with them if they were righteous. The French-Spanish disorganization was as bad as the British lack of preparation, and the combined fleet left without a landing or engagement. Significantly, at his Conference of preachers that year, the preachers were enjoined not to challenge the governing authorities.

He continued the same message through his January 1782

publication "How Far Is It the Duty of a Christian Minister to Preach Politics?" His published view was the same as his view at the time of the Wilkes affair: that it was difficult, if not impossible, to know the details or motives of public officials. Moreover, obviously, the duty of the preacher was to "preach Jesus Christ and him crucified." However, it was also a duty to refute false slanders against the king. Generally, the preachers were to remain silent on political issues. But if the king or his government was unjustly censured and if the preacher were certain of his case, he should refute the false charges. The occasion for such preaching would be rare, remembering always the "main business to preach repentance towards God, and faith in our Lord Jesus Christ."[23]

John did not just write his own tracts and encourage his preachers to support the king; he also edited and published the work of other Loyalists.[24] Furthermore, he enlisted particularly John Fletcher and Thomas Olivers to counterattack Augustus Toplady, Caleb Edwards, and others who attacked his defense of the monarch and Parliament. Quite detailed political tracts were published by Wesley's publishers and sold at his preaching houses throughout Great Britain.[25]

Wesley's political philosophy of monarchy and established church was overthrown in the colonialist revolt by Enlightenment and Calvinist ideas. Wesley's synthesis held in England but was lost in the protracted war in America, which he had hoped to avoid. The combination of Enlightenment and Calvinism in political order was more creative than Wesley could comprehend. But it was to prove less creative than evangelical Anglicanism in overcoming slavery; and in France, the Enlightenment without its Calvinist realism would soon lead to evils Wesley had feared for America. Wesley's ideas of liberty did not demand the same political participation that was required by his American cousins. His movement would contribute to the expansion of liberty in both America and England but in the different manner required by the different politics.

10. Slavery

The early mission of the Wesley brothers to Georgia failed. However, it brought them into direct contact with three of the great evils of the violent eighteenth century. Great Britain was expanding its empire, exterminating the Native Americans, and forcing Africans into slavery for sale in the Americas. Wesley remained somewhat oblivious to the evils of colonization in the Americas, and while he observed the extermination of the American indigenous population, he did not focus his critique on it systematically or prophetically. But the enslavement and exportation of the African he studied and denounced. British imperial policy other than in America also received his condemnation. These two denouncements of his nation's major policies are a clear refutation of the widely held interpretation of Wesley as simply an endorser of his government's practice.

Slave Trade

In calling for an end to slavery, Wesley rejected the triangular trade from England to Africa, to America, and return to England on which some of the wealth of his country, particularly Liverpool, depended. Since the 1566 raids by Sir John Hawkins to capture and enslave Africans, England had been robbing Africa of its productive people. Wesley argued that neither law nor history justified evil.

At this point of his abolitionism Wesley is akin to liberation theology. In his writing on this degrading economic institution Wesley let the ethical agenda of liberation pull the arguments along. His passion and his method are shaped by the need to abolish the demonic system. How ironic that it was at this very point that the founder of North American liberation theology would criticize Wesley. James Cone, a leading Methodist theologian, probably had not read Wesley on slavery when he wrote: "John Wesley also said little about slave holding and did even less." In his note he elaborated, "The Wesley that has come to us seems very white and quite British, and that ain't no good for black people who know that the Englishmen are the scoundrels who perfected the slave trade." He also indicated in "reading his sermons and other writings, one does not get the impression that slavery was one of the burning issues on Wesley's mind."[1]

The enormity of the slave trade is hard to grasp, and the number of slaves exported to the Americas is under debate. Two sources of differing ideologies estimate 10 million slaves imported in three centuries into the Americas,[2] and another respectable source estimates half as many died in Africa through forced march and mistreatment.[3] This eighteenth-century crime is of the same magnitude as the Nazi horrors of the twentieth century. A figure of 10 to 15 percent of the slaves dying on the voyage from Africa to the Americas is a low estimate, and maybe another 15 percent died during the early seasoning process in the islands before transshipment. If the low estimate of 10 million imported slaves is accepted and most are regarded as human beings taken in wars and raids, it is reasonable to think of another 10 million as casualties of the process.

The English companies prospering in the trade made profit three times: (1) in the profit made on trade goods from England or Africa for the purchase of slaves at the "slave factories" along the coast, (2) in the sale of the slaves in the Americas, and (3) in the resale of the American molasses, rum, sugar, and cotton in England. These profits could be great on an economically successful voyage. The revenues contributed to British family fortunes and significantly to the development of the seaport cities. But the more significant economic enrichment during the eighteenth century was this world-reaching expansion of the British market while experiencing the beginnings of the industrial revolution. The building of wealth from the massive warring on Africa, which totally disrupted its life, generated an ideology of justification. The racism took shape denying the humanness of both the indigenous Americans and the Africans who were enslaved to replace them. The gaining of wealth produced a spiritual sickness in the conquering English. Jack Gratus's study of slavery moves explicitly through that dynamic. He quotes the English businessmen of the eighteenth century as to the origins of their wealth in slavery. Malochy Castlethwayt, an economist, was typical of his sources: "As the present prosperity and splendour of the British colonies have been owing to Negro labour, so not only their future advancement, but even their very being depends upon our pursuing the same measures in this respect as our competitors do."[4]

Tracing the arguments of the slave interests, Gratus noted the opposition of Adam Smith on economic grounds and Wesley and the Quakers on religious grounds. Because some of Wesley's fellow evangelicals and some leading Quakers, including William Penn, owned slaves, the opposition seems rooted in particular ethical insights and not in the centers of their theologies. After Lord Mansfield's ruling in 1772 made slavery illegal in England, the force of the reformers' efforts turned particularly against the slave trade. It was during the controversy surrounding the case of James Somerset before Lord Mansfield that Wesley read Anthony Benezet, and he attended more fully to the slavery question. For those opposing either the slave trade or slavery itself on religious grounds, it was one of the clearest examples of religious-ethical insight opposed to economic gain. For Granville Sharp, the Quaker abolitionist, the souls of the masters were to be judged for "their want of brotherly love."[5]

The abolitionists of note came from three quarters: Quakers, evangelicals, and humanists. The Quakers were among the most politically active in both North America and Britain, exerting influence far beyond their numbers. But some Quakers owned slaves and defended the practice. The evangelicals also were divided; George Whitefield encouraged slavery in Georgia and acquired slaves to support an orphanage. John Wesley's "Thoughts upon Slavery" was at the time the most influential written piece against slavery. John Newton would at a later date become a leading abolitionist, but when he wrote his evangelical autobiography, he was seemingly quite naive about the evil hidden behind his individualistic-evangelical piety.

According to John Newton, "During the time I was engaged in the slave trade, I never had the least scruples to its lawfulness. I was, upon the whole, satisfied with it as the appointment of Providence had marked out for me."[6] His letters, which go into extreme detail about meditations on his spiritual life and his relations with others in the business, hardly mention his cargo. There is one reference to the threat of slave insurrection, but other than that, his cargo could have been inert matter. He refers to trading, but never to those whose lives he is trading. His letters describe the sea, sky, and ships but not the purpose of his trading voyages. Except for the one reference to the threat of insurrection, it is only the trajectory of the voyage, Liverpool to the West African coast, to the West Indies, and home to Liverpool that suggests the meaning of his shipping.

Whereas some of the abolitionist movement in the English-speaking world can be attributed to humanism, in France the humanists took the lead. Condorcet, Montesquieu, Voltaire, Rousseau, and Robespierre were the intellectual leaders in France, though they lacked a program. In England the philosophy of human sympathy of David Hume and Adam Smith permeated eighteenth-century letters, and provided a background in naturalistic-utilitarian humanism to fertilize ethical arguments. Frank J. Klingberg sees the abolitionist movement as largely an awakening of humanitarianism. He particularly stresses the influences of Lord Shaftesbury, James Thomson, and a general inclination toward reform, which Samuel Johnson celebrated in 1758.[7]

Wesley derived his arguments from all three sources of Quakers, evangelical witness, and humanist argument. In his correspondence with and encouragement of the abolitionist cause, he consistently reminded the leaders of the movement of the need for realistic assessment of their opponents' money and power. He encouraged the religious enthusiasm nurturing humanist arguments that were present. The ethic of "Thoughts upon Slavery" could be appreciated by a wide variety of readers because it did not depend on any particular christological distinctiveness or any particularly Methodist arguments. It did not presuppose any particularly developed church community, or a personally developed character for its reception or its writing. It was a public ethic based on widely held views representing a mixture of humanist and Christian arguments.

In 1772, Wesley read Anthony Benezet's writing on slavery, and he was profoundly moved. Benezet, a refugee from France, had lived in Holland and England before settling in Philadelphia in 1731. He spent his mature life teaching and agitating for the abolition of slavery. His *Historical Account of Guinea* (1771), though perhaps not his first book to influence Wesley, was to contribute significantly to Wesley's tract. Benezet had written to the British abolitionist Granville Sharp, informing him that he had incorporated material from Sharp's book into his own *Historical Account of Guinea*. As Benezet had incorporated the work of Sharp along with many other accounts into his work, so Wesley incorporated Benezet, including portions of Sharp's work. The correspondence among the three supports this borrowing. Warren Thomas Smith's analysis concludes that Wesley employed Benezet's text for roughly 30 percent of his own.[8]

The Ethics of "Thoughts upon Slavery"

Wesley's monograph on slavery is presented in five sections with numbered paragraphs. On receipt of the volume, the abolitionist Granville Sharp recognized its clear organization and Wesley's incisive condensing and summary of previous works. He predicted its power and great effect. As one of Wesley's social ethics treatises written at the height of his powers, it reveals a method of Christian ethical analysis.

Section I defined the problem to be addressed. He addressed the fact of obligations of perpetual slavery in which humans were reduced to the same treatment as domestic animals with the extension of the obligation to the following generations. He saw its roots extend into ancient times. Although he mentioned the Jews, Greeks, Romans, and Germans, he did not mention Islamic or African slavery. He believed slavery to have declined until its revival by Portugal and Spain in the sixteenth century. Other nations followed as they acquired stakes in the Americas. Here he paraphrased Granville Sharp, and he referenced the case of James Somerset, which did so much to encourage the abolitionist movement. The form of presentation is still seen in church policies on social issues: definition, brief history, and current practice in the opening paragraphs of policy statements.

Section II drew mostly from Anthony Benezet's presentation of the reports of others on West Africa and the qualities of the Africans. In contemporary analysis, this is the social science section of the study. His sentences were often direct but uncredited quotations from Benezet—though he attributed the whole section to the accounts of others. Among the authorities consulted was Monsieur Adamson, a correspondent for the Royal Academy of Sciences in Paris, in the early 1750s. The quality of life in Africa from Senegal to South Africa was portrayed as Edenic prior to the Europeans' encroachment. Wesley, who had few illusions about the life of Native Americans, accepted a "noble savage" view of Africa. He described kingdoms without reference to power struggles, slavery, and war. He commented on their religion as a belief in one God with no references to the possibility of alternative practices. The description of Whidah, known for its prosperity derived from slavery and as a center for witchcraft, was presented as ideally as the rest.

Martine de Souxa, an African of partial Portuguese descent who provides guide services and serves as a local coordinator for slavery research, laughed heartily on learning of Wesley's opinion that the African peoples had been peaceful until European slave traders arrived. After suppressing her laughter, she said on 3 August 1998, "Our African kingdoms have bloody histories. Visit the Royal Palace at Abomey and learn the history." The oral and artistic histories of the kingdom of Dahomey bear out her perspective. Dahomey, with its port of Ouidah, was a major exporter of slaves to Brazil, Haiti, and Cuba. The voodoo, centered in Ouidah, spread to these American countries where the connections with Dahomey are still understood.

Dahomey's history is one of pride in conquest of neighboring peoples. The kingdom seemed to have been no more pacific than Italian city-states or ancient Britain. The first law of their legendary constitution was that each ruler was to increase the borders of Dahomey. Beyond a history of realpolitik, the kingdom's militant history is enriched by stories of mass sacrifice, a brigade of women warriors, and slavery. Certainly, here an Enlightenment romanticism about the innocent African has displaced Wesley's rather rigorous views of human sinfulness based on Christian orthodox interpretations. Still, the most obvious fault rests with the eighteenth-century science on which he drew. He concluded the description with the surprising twist that true justice and honesty were found in Benin, Congo, and Angola, and not in Europe. The polemic of the section was directed at the argument that Africans were better off being removed from Africa to Christian, white civilization in the Americas.

Section III used material from both Sharp and Benezet to establish the evil ways in which slaves were acquired and punished.[9] The apologists for slavery argued that prisoners of war and criminals who would be executed were sold as slaves, and that the export of slaves saved lives. Without addressing the slavery apologists directly, Wesley detailed how slaves were acquired by fraud, European slave raids,[10] the incitement of Africans to war for slaves, kingly enslavement and sale of the population, and the kidnapping of children and others. One of the battles to acquire slaves, to which Wesley referred, left 4,500 men dead on the battlefield as recorded by a New York surgeon. He used his sources to paint a picture of slaves forced to naked display, packed into slave ships like lumber in a hold, dying on the voyage, displayed naked again before purchasers, families separated, and massive dying in the seasoning processes of the arrival islands. He estimated that about 10,000 died aboard English ships out of about 100,000 shipped per year and another 25,000 in the island process of conditioning, or maybe a total of 30,000 murdered in addition to the destruction in Africa.

He then went on quickly to show that the laws of punishment of the slaves varied in their cruelty from island to island and the mainland, but that generally, the slaves had almost no legal protection. These paragraphs denied the slavers' arguments that slaves were protected by British justice. Wesley's descriptions of how slaves were taken, transported, worked by the lash, tortured, and punished led any reader to weep or scream. He concluded the discussion with testimony he had gathered in his mission work in America of a slaveholder burning his slave to death.

Section IV moved beyond the published debates of 1774, which were on the legality of the slave trade, to the deeper question of the impropriety of slavery itself. Wesley here denied, by implication, the practice of the monarchy, the legislation of Parliament, the economy of Liverpool, the major reason for the British merchant marine, and the ethics of his fellow evangelists, Jonathan Edwards and George Whitefield. Wesley was a leader of a movement, a publisher, the controller of meeting halls, a theologian, an established academic; here, he moved out from all of that security to join the ranks of the radicals.

He set aside the necessity of biblical answers: "setting the Bible out of the question."[11] He turned to criteria of justice and mercy, asking if the practices described could be reconciled with them. Recognizing that slavery had the force of law, he persisted that it was unjust: "Notwithstanding ten thousand laws, right is right and wrong is wrong. There must still remain an essential difference between justice and injustice, cruelty and mercy."[12] He recognized the African as having "the same natural rights as an Englishman." So, here the argument was a natural law argument. Murder and the deprivation of liberty were wrong on the grounds of natural rights.

He then turned to Blackstone to show that prisoners of war were not by justice rendered slaves. The very grounds of a just war presupposed that beyond the right of self-defense, war prisoners were to be freed at the end of the conflict. Likewise, the very justice of buying and selling presupposed an equivalence in value. One cannot sell oneself because nothing was returned to oneself but only to the master as purchaser. Such a sale could not be valid. So, again, on just-price, natural-law considerations, slavery failed. As one could have been rendered a slave neither by war nor by self-sale, so there was no just way one could have been born a slave. All natural justice was denied to the institution of slavery in itself. As for mercy, Wesley denied that any slaver ever operated a slave voyage for mercy, rather than for profit.

The typical defense for slavery was necessity. But Wesley denied that the production of the slaves was necessary. The end of the production of coffee and sugar was not necessary. Besides, Wesley argued from his own experience, white people could farm the tropics. He rejected the argument that only black people could work those areas, for English people and Germans had so worked in Georgia.

Finally, he argued against the slavers that the opinion that the slaves were rebellious, stubborn, and wicked rebounded onto the slavers. Africans in Africa were at least the equal of Europeans in Europe, and the warring upon and enslavement of Africans gave them any undesirable qualities they possessed in their slavery. In some ways, it was a simple observation, but how true Wesley's argument was. The oppressed will act like the oppressed. Then he turned again explicitly against the slavers and asked if they had carefully taught slaves Christian morality, including that God would judge all the evil ones. In paraphrasing the final judgment of Matthew 25, Wesley was actually threatening the slave owners while asking about their pedagogy.

He concluded Section IV, "What wonder, if they should cut your throat." He chastised the defenders of slavery: "You act the villain to enslave them, then you brutalize them and fail to educate them, then you blame them for lacking education as a reason for using them as 'brute beasts.'" Here Wesley went beyond polite speech, and the words applied to the sovereign as well as to the establishment. The Prince of Wales was particularly deep into the slave trade and personally, emotionally defensive of it.

Section V concluded the essay in application primarily to the sea captains, the merchants, and the planters. Wesley's realism made him skeptical of Parliament's willingness to respond, and the English nation was too general a target to be of use. In the end, it became a matter of conscience appealing to business. The histories of the issue still struggle over whether in the end, conscience prevailed or changed business practices produced abolition. In fact, Parliament acted against the trade in thirty years and against slavery in six decades. Of the three—business, politics, and conscience—business was of the least use in ending slavery.

Wesley urged the sea captains out of humanity, sympathy, compassion, and fear of God to give up their vile profession. Likewise, he addressed the traders, "Be you a man! Not a wolf, a devourer of the human species! Be merciful that you may obtain mercy!" To anyone who had an estate in the colonies, he wrote that "man-buyers" were as guilty as "men-stealers." The owners of the plantations were guilty of murder and "men-stealing." He pleaded with them to stop their practice.

Before he concluded with a prayer, he returned to the theme of natural rights. All are by nature free, and liberty should not be denied them. Liberty is the law of nature, and no human law could deny it. He pleaded, "Render unto all their due," and added, "Give liberty to whom liberty is due, that is to every child of man, to every partaker of human nature.... Away with all whips, all chains, all compulsion. Be gentle toward all men. And see that you invariably do unto everyone, as you would he should do unto you."[13]

The controlling ethic of the argument is a natural-law argument. The problem was defined, a version of history of the problem was presented, eighteenth-century social science was used, biblical arguments were downplayed, but the ethics of justice, mercy, compassion, and love had expression. The Golden Rule was echoed, as was the judgment-apocalypse of Matthew 25. The humanity and to a lesser extent the Christianity of the slavers were both appealed to as a resource for sympathy and justice. "Men-stealing" was left as the charge against the slavers, but with no explicit reference to "Thou shalt not steal" or "Thou shalt not covet." In the end, it seems best to regard John Wesley's ethic in this tract as a liberation ethic grounded in natural law. It was reconcilable with a biblical ethic or a double love commandment ethic, but it was not formulated as either. The motivation for the essay was in his closing prayer: it was his own love for God, who loved all and desired all to be loved by one another.

Contemporary African interpretation of slavery points to the fact that it was a *slave trade*. Africans sold other Africans to the Europeans. Although slavery existed before Europeans reached Africa, and its practice and even transport of slaves vis-à-vis Islamic traders predated the European encroachment, the European practices exploded the exploitation, extent, and horror of the practice. Certain African rulers profited from the practice while the masses suffered. Wesley saw clearly that greed was at the root of slavery. He may have been naive about the pacific nature of African kingdoms,[14] but he was correct that European encouragement and trade multiplied the ferocity of African cruelty to other Africans. The masses of slaves traded and exported were captured by slave raids and wars to acquire slaves. Estimates are that for every slave exported, another three died as casualties of the raids, wars, transportation, and social disruption—a figure even higher than that suggested earlier in the chapter. If we accepted Hugh Thomas's estimate of eleven million transported, that ratio would mean thirty-three million killed in addition.[15] The figures support Wesley's recognition that slavery was the worst crime of Europe. Ironically, today little is known in Ghana about Wesley's abolitionist writings, but chapels bearing his name and Methodist schools proliferate. The British took over the Dutch Castle-Dungeon at Elmina in 1862 after they had abolished slavery. They named their chapel in the Castle-Dungeon the John Wesley Memorial Chapel.[16]

Wesley's letter from his deathbed to William Wilberforce encouraged him to stay the course, though the resistance to ending slavery was fierce. Wesley himself saw no improvement in the African's fate. Through his writing, speaking, and organizing, he provided some of the steadfast religious enthusiasm that with other forces would in forty years end slavery in the British Empire, if not in the Americas. Anxiety about the French Revolution joined the fears aroused by the slave revolution in Haiti in 1791 to shelve the development of British reform movements. In 1807, finally, the abolitionists in both Britain and the United States would win the victory with the bill abolishing the transatlantic trade. Slavery itself would continue through 1833 and forced apprenticeship for another five transition years. Elsewhere, it persisted, and the English cotton industry would depend on slave labor from the United States until the Civil War of 1861–1865. Thereafter, the fervor of the evangelicals of the abolitionist Clapham Sect would contribute to the colonization of Africa and to further misuse of African labor. Reginald Coupland, an Oxford historian of imperialism who stressed the humanitarian contributions of colonization, commented on the sorry crime of African slavery: "It is difficult not to regard this treatment of Africa by Christian Europe, following Moslem Asia, as the greatest crime in history."[17]

11. "God Is with Us" (1780–1791)

The Elderly Wesley

Wesley's last decade continued the deep trajectories of his early years: he still itinerated, preaching as often as there was opportunity, sometimes four times a day. He remained healthy, which he credited to rising at 4:00 A.M. and traveling continually. He often remarked that he felt as well as he had forty or fifty years earlier, and indeed his weight remained steady at 122 pounds. His *Journal* made it clear that his primary vocation was preaching, though counseling, facilitating, and organizing the society also occupied him.

He considered that his theological thinking had not changed over the years, even though he acknowledged reading "five or six hundred books" over the forty-five-year period, and that he had learned quite a little history and philosophy: "Forty years ago, I know and preached every Christian doctrine which I preach now."[1] He mused on the news that he had heard at Tiverton of the preacher who burned all his sermons every seven years and began anew. He concluded that he could not write better sermons than he had forty-five years previously. The political philosophy of the previous chapters was occasioned by threats to the political order. It was new in that he had not written much on this subject before his seventieth year, but the principles were consistent with his earlier thought. His occasional political activity was marked by letters to Prime Ministers North and Pitt and by attendance at George III's opening of Parliament speech. His literary production on social issues dealt primarily with poverty, but he kept active in the abolition movement, and the church issues of ordination and women preaching occupied him until his death.

Poverty and Wealth

Prior to 1781, Wesley had labored consistently on behalf of the poor. The publication of his sermon "The Dangers of Riches" in the

Arminian Magazine made his economic radicalism more apparent. John Locke's philosophy and the government of England were both committed to the security of property. Adam Smith's *Wealth of Nations* was winning converts. Wesley urged that wealth be not pursued and that property be given away. The plain message of the sermon was that the pursuit of riches drew people into hell. To pursue riches meant to act to obtain more than one needed for a modest provision for one's household. The purpose of property was that it was to be shared according to the will of the proprietor, God. Other selfish purposes pursued with money were denying God's will.

In the sermon, he dealt with his economics of giving away his unexpected earnings from book and tract sales, advising his readers to give not 10 percent or half but all beyond what was needed to preserve life. He explicated the psychology of how pursuing riches led to the neglect of faith, hope, and humility, noting that he feared that the pursuit of money was robbing the Methodists of their early zeal and commitment. He concluded with the warning of how difficult it was for the rich to be saved. But he promised, with God, it was still possible.[2]

Wesley retained the sharing of goods in common from Acts 2 as an eschatological goal of Christian faith. He maintained sharing all one can as the normative prescription for his followers. In his sermon of April 1783, the eschatological nature of the community of goods was clear. When the grand Pentecost fully comes and all shall be filled with the Holy Ghost, the grand stumbling block of the love of money will be overcome.[3] Then, as in the beginning of the Christian church, all will be held in common. It will be a time when love drives the whole of humanity. Wesley had some hope that such a day was coming; even the growth of the revival could be seen as a sign of the coming millennium. He could write of the coming time, "There will be no Ananias or Sapphira to bring back the cursed love of money."[4]

John Walsh has done more than anyone to make the case for the persistent hope of John Wesley for the koinonia sharing of goods in common.[5] The trail of evidence extends from Wesley's mentor, William Law, urging the community of goods through Wesley's preference for primitive Christianity, particularly that of Acts.

There were already traces of the community of goods in Holy Club activities, in Wesley's hopes for Native Americans, and in conversation with friends. These evidences were enhanced by his repeated denunciations of the corrupting influence of wealth in private hands. He said in a sermon as late as 1789 that the Methodists could care for their own poor and provide for everyone as they had need if they would only share. Wesley himself could, and often did, give away his resources spontaneously—most would probably add charismatically. But the majority of his followers withheld their wealth.

His vision from Acts from each according to gifts and to each according to need was a perennial expression of human hope. His fervently and persuasively argued norms of radical sharing and avoidance of loyalty to mammon were appropriate, as were his pleas for changed national policy. His vocation, political realism, and political weakness, even at the height of his influence, prevented him from detailed community political organization to reform the poor laws or to achieve policies for justice for the poor.[6]

In a letter to Prime Minister William Pitt, Wesley pleaded for a pension for Lieutenant Webb and made several recommendations on tax policy. He criticized taxes not collected on the wealthy, customs evasion by smugglers, and tax evasion by distillers. The letter's significance was in its specificity on tax policy. Wesley not only preached against smuggling; he disciplined his church members for cheating the king of his customs tax. In this letter, he petitioned the prime minister to act. Likewise, on several issues of tax policy on which he had written in "Thoughts on the Present Scarcity of Provisions," he petitioned the leader of Parliament to act.

Tyerman argued that Wesley's tract society established in January 1782 to place reading materials into the hands of the poor was the first such society founded.[7] How typical of Wesley to found such a society. It expressed his priority for the poor in spreading both education and real religion. In this act, as in his editing of the fifty volumes of the *Christian Library,* the concerned Christian and the humanist scholar are uniquely synthesized.

His free medical services, loan funds, poor houses, and educational services have been mentioned earlier. His passion, though, to relieve people's suffering became especially obvious when he walked through the snow of London begging for provisions for the poor when he was in his early eighties. In the *Arminian*, he warned that the religious revival assisted people to become industrious and frugal, traits by which they prospered. With prosperity, their faith cooled, and so to some degree the revival was self-defeating. To preserve vital religion, it was necessary to give away everything beyond the resources that one needed to maintain life.

His polemics against wealth became more frequent and powerful in the later years. The evangelical revival had grown, but the love of money threatened it at the core. His sermonic essay "The Mystery of Iniquity" described the corruption of the world from the Garden of Eden to the present. He developed the theme of love of money as the corruption of the church. Yet he was not romantic about the purity of the church in any period. Even the early communism of the church was immediately corrupted by Ananias and Sapphira. Constantine particularly contributed to the corruption by the favors he bestowed upon the church. The medieval church was quickly dismissed by Wesley as almost totally corrupt. But the Reformation had not cleansed the church either. Only a few escaped the corruption. God would achieve the final victory, and creation would be freed of its groaning condition. He found very little evidence that Christianity had made a positive difference. Greedy English Christians had acquired a new empire in India without benefit to the people of India.

> Look into that large country, Indostan. There are Christians and heathens too. Which have more justice, mercy, and truth? The Christians or the heathens? Which are most corrupt, infernal, devilish in their tempers and practice? The English or the Indians? Which have desolated whole countries, and clogged the rivers with dead bodies?
>
> O sacred name of Christian how profaned![8]

Establishing a Church

Wesley, at age eighty-one, spent seven months traveling in 1784. The year was momentous for establishing the independency of Methodism. In England, the Conference agreed to the Deed of

201

Declaration that established the Conference of one hundred preachers as the ruling body of Methodism. It guaranteed the continuity of Methodist chapels and property under the ownership of the Conference. The limiting of the Conference to one hundred offended many and led to some withdrawals, however. The Deed established the Conference's authority, thereby assuring continuity after the aging Wesleys. The Conference, through various changes, would remain the collective bishop for English Methodism.

The thousands of Methodists in America had neither established church nor king. They were in all but name an independent church by fact of revolution. Samuel Seabury failed to receive consecration from English bishops after being elected Episcopal bishop in an American convention. He secured consecration in November of 1784 by three Scottish Episcopal bishops at Aberdeen. Wesley, frustrated in his efforts to get English bishops to ordain ministers for his American work, under pressure from America and from Dr. Thomas Coke, finally went ahead and ordained Richard Whatcoat and Thomas Vasey as ministers and Dr. Thomas Coke as cosuperintendent with Francis Asbury for America. Later, Coke and Asbury as superintendents would claim the authority of bishops for themselves and for Wesley as bishop in England. Though Wesley regarded himself as coequal with bishops as an elder, he had not intended to ordain Coke as a bishop or for Coke to ordain Asbury. Correspondence indicates that Coke would have rejoined the Episcopal Church either in America or in India if he could have received ordination as an Episcopal bishop.[9] Charles Wesley broke with his brother over these ordinations and withdrew even farther from influence in the Conference. Within a few years, John had proceeded to ordain ministers for Scotland, for Newfoundland, and three for work in England.

Charles took John's ordination to be separation from the Church of England and had secured the opinion from the justice Lord Mansfield that this was correct. John dissented and refused to concede that he had separated from the Church of England. After much correspondence, John pleaded, we disagree, leave it alone. His position was that he varied from the Church of England but that he had not separated.

John's character trait of domination had early beginnings and continued throughout his life. John Whitehead, his early biographer, saw Wesley as authoritarian and even absolute in his control of Methodism. As a boy at Charterhouse, he was reputed to have exclaimed when queried about why he played with the younger boys: "It is better to rule in Hell than to serve in heaven." He did not tolerate challenges to his authority in his Methodist society. His general outlook was patriarchal; he understood the king to receive power from God, and then this power was mediated downward. Whitehead, who caustically criticized Wesley for his assumption of episcopal power in ordination, quoted Charles Wesley:

> So easily are Bishops made,
> By man's or woman's whim:
> Wesley his hands on Coke hath laid,
> But who laid hands on him?[10]

But Whitehead went on to answer Charles's question: "The answer is nobody. His Episcopal authority was a mere gratuitous assumption of power to himself, contrary to the usage of every church, ancient or modern, where the order of bishops has been admitted."[11]

Whitehead seemed to think Wesley ordained Coke bishop. I do not think he did; rather, Wesley appointed him superintendent in a liturgical act. But in either case, Wesley regarded his standing as elder as equivalent to that of a bishop; and he had a high view of his own authority. Whitehead commented on the exercise of that authority: "During the time that Mr. Wesley strictly and properly governed the societies, his power was absolute."[12] Whitehead, of course, did not mean Wesley used his absolute power for his personal interest. He saw Wesley using that power for the good of the Methodist society and the peace of the nation. Personal interests of Wesley were surrendered, according to Whitehead, for "the general purpose of doing good."[13]

Last Years

Several important events marked the last years of John's long life. John's beloved hymn-writing brother, Charles, died in 1788. Even at the end, John and Charles expressed their love without needing to agree. Charles insisted on being buried, and his wish was honored, in Church of England consecrated ground. John had hoped Charles would be buried at the City Road Chapel grounds where later John was interred. It provoked John to publish an article attacking the whole concept of consecrated ground as being contrary to reason and Scripture.

Perhaps the most remarkable event of 1788 for John occurred in New Chapel, Bristol. A large crowd attended his announcement of speaking on the slavery issue. In the middle of the sermon, he recorded a large noise arose, scaring the congregation. For six minutes, terror and confusion ensued, and several benches were broken as the crowd panicked. Then calm followed, and he finished his sermon on slavery. The next day was set aside for fasting, prayer, and petitions to God to free the slaves. He continued to advise the abolition movement and to print, at his own expense, his treatise against slavery for the movement.

Organizationally, he struggled to hold his preachers within the Church of England. He refused to separate, though he found many in the Church of England pushing the Methodists to separate. His *Arminian* published a sermon about Lazarus on the dangers of becoming wealthy. Industrialization, providing riches to some, was also lifting up Methodists, many of whom were employed in the new industries. Wesley feared the corruption of wealth; he was proud that in his will he had no money to leave. The next year, he would close his account book, after almost seventy years, convinced that he had given away as much as he could. Dr. Whitehead, his physician and friend, estimated that over his lifetime, Wesley had given away between £20,000 and £30,000. On reading Wesley's accounts, Henry Moore thought the estimate could be increased by several more thousand pounds.[14] It should be noted that he did leave property to the movement and some income from his book business to relatives.

Times had changed for John, and he recorded the change on 18 August 1789:

> We procured leave to drive around by some fields and got to Falmouth in good time. The last time I was here, above forty years ago, I was taken prisoner by an immense mob, gaping and roaring like lions. But how is the tide turned! High and low now

lined the streets from one end of the town to the other out of stark love and kindness, gaping and staring as if the King were going by.[15]

By 1 January 1790, he was still able to "do a little for God before he dropped into the dust." But he was decaying: "I am now an old man, decayed from head to foot. My eyes are dim; my right hand shakes much; my mouth is hot and dry every morning; I have a lingering fever almost every day; my motion is weak and slow. However blessed be God, I do not slack my labour. I can preach and write still."[16]

Death for Wesley was both biological fact and a new beginning. The realism of it was that his friends were dying, and he recorded the losses as matters of fact. A few days before analyzing his own decay, he had written of Edward Perronet's forthcoming demise: "I returned to Canterbury and spent half an hour with my old friend Mr. Perronet, the last of the six sons, and nearly worn out, and just tottering over the grave."[17]

The Conference in 1790 indicated that growth in Methodism had exploded; they recorded 134,549 members with 57,631 of those being in America. Immediately after presiding at Conference, John left for preaching in Wales. He was able to continue preaching until 23 February 1791. His last sermon at Leatherhead was on the text "Seek ye the Lord while He may be found; call upon Him while He is near."[18]

A few days earlier, John had again addressed the issue of women preaching. An Irish Methodist woman, Alice Cambridge, had been criticized for preaching, and she inquired of Wesley. He replied:

> London, January 31, 1791.
> My dear Sister,—I received your letter an hour ago. I thank you for writing so largely and so freely; do so always to me as your friend, as one that loves you well. Mr. Barber has the glory of God at heart; and so have his fellow labourers. Give them all honour, and obey them in all things as far as conscience permits. But it will not permit you to be silent when God commands you to speak: yet I would have you give as little offence as possible; and therefore I would advise you not to speak at any place where a preacher is speaking at the same time, lest you should draw

away his hearers. Also avoid the first appearance of pride or magnifying yourself. If you want books or anything, let me know; I have your happiness much at heart. During the little time I have to stay on earth pray for

Your affectionate brother.[19]

The letter encouraged her, and her preaching in Ireland met a hearty response. Her membership in the Conference was denied in 1802, but she was admitted in 1811. She led a revival in Limerick and was accepted by both Methodists and Presbyterians in Ulster. There are reports of her speaking to 10,000 people in later years.

Wesley kept his diary to within six days of his death. The entry for 22 February 1791, indicates he was reading Gustavus Vassa's *Interesting Narrative of the Life of Olaudah Equiano or Gustavus Vassa.* Vassa had been born in Africa in 1745, kidnapped, and sold into slavery in Barbados. He regained his freedom in England and was baptized in 1759. Wesley's last letter to Wilberforce, urging him to persist in his work against the slave trade, was motivated by his reading of this African's book:

> Unless God has raised you up for this very thing you will be worn out by the opposition of men and devils; but, *if God be for you, who can be against you?* Are all of them together stronger than God? O! *be not weary in well doing.* Go on in the name of God and in the power of His might till even American slavery—the vilest that ever saw the sun, shall vanish before it.[20]

Miss Elizabeth Ritchie, who attended Wesley's last days, provided an account of his dying. Whitehead read it to the congregation after preaching Wesley's funeral sermon, and it was printed by Wesley's colleagues on 8 March 1791.[21] She had come in November 1790 to visit Hester Ann Rogers, who had become too weak to continue serving John Wesley. Elizabeth Ritchie moved into the City Road Chapel House and was persuaded into service as Wesley's helper and companion. The Rogerses continued to live in the house and were also present at John Wesley's death.[22]

He declined quickly on returning from preaching at Leatherhead about eighteen miles away. He lingered for a week saying good-bye to visitors, directing the settlement of business affairs, occasionally singing and praying by himself or with others. He questioned his beloved niece about her faith. Confirming himself a sinner, he proclaimed the necessity of faith and then going onto sanctification. He declined other medical advice other than what Dr. Whitehead would provide. He embraced his sister-in-law, Sally. Among his closing phrases was the twice-repeated affirmation: "The best of all is God is with us!"

He has been hailed as the most significant private citizen of his age and as the greatest social reformer of the eighteenth century. We have seen that he was a public, if not a political, person, and also that the eighteenth century resisted social reform. Wesley resisted revolutionary or radical social reform except for the abolition of slavery. The witness of his sometime opponent the *Gentleman's Magazine* at his death provides a fair accounting.

> "Whatever may be the opinions held of his inspiration it is impossible to deny him the merit of having done infinite good to the lower classes of the people," the *Gentleman's Magazine* commented in April 1791. "By the humane endeavors of him and his brother Charles a sense of decency in morals and religion was introduced in the lowest classes of mankind, the ignorant were instructed and the wretched relieved and the abandoned reclaimed....He met with great opposition from many of the clergy and unhandsome treatment from the magistrates....He was one of the few characters who outlived enmity and prejudices, and received in his later years every mark of esteem from every denomination....His personal influence was greater perhaps than any private gentleman in the country. All the profit of his literary labours; all that he could receive or could collect (and it amounted to an immense sum) was devoted to charitable purposes. Instead of being an ornament to literature he was a blessing to his fellows: instead of genius of his age, he was the servant of God."[23]

12. Ethics

The tracing of the ethical themes through the complexities of John Wesley's life reveals seven emphases of his ethic. Against the predestinarians and other determinists, he argued for *human freedom* or liberty as a necessary precondition of the gospel and of ethical discourse. His insistence on human freedom in theology had ethical consequences in his passion for the abolition of slavery and his toleration of other religious opinions or systems. His difficulties in defending the teaching on Christian perfection were rooted in his passion for understanding Christian life as a *life of love*. Creation, redemption, and eschatological fulfillment were all from God's will of love. Christian ethics was based on the double love commandment rooted in God's love. His exposition of the Sermon on the Mount and his understanding of the Ten Commandments expressed the rule of the love-oriented direction of his ethics. Likewise, whether ethical guidance was taken from the example of Jesus or the life of the early church, it was to express the love of God and of humanity.

A third theme was his *realism*. His volumes of history and his tracts on social-ethical themes never underestimate the resistance of the world to love. Some commentators have missed the realism and chided Wesley for not proposing more systematic programs of political-social reform. Wesley did not propose schemes for parliamentary action because they were not relevant to his time of the eighteenth century. The landowners in the eighteenth century controlled Parliament as well as the other organs of government, including the army and the Church of England. There were riots and much social discontent in the eighteenth century. But fundamentally, England was organized to defend the rights of the property owners, and they were not allowing systematic political reform that would change the political economy. England under the Hanoverian kings might not have been governed much, and it certainly was not governed justly, but it was stable in its protection of the privileges of the privileged class. Wesley asked for tax reform, not expecting it. The area where he expressed his passion for systematic structural reform and supported organizing for it was in the abolition of slavery. In this area, there were sufficient divisions in the ruling class to make it a possibility. Where there were this division and the chance for change, he moved, though even here his politics were realistic as witnessed in his deathbed letter to Wilberforce.

The sources for Wesley's ethic were broad. He could write a whole social-ethical tract like his famous thoughts on slavery without relying directly on biblical argument; instead he went to freedom rooted in *natural law*. In the same essay, he relied more on the fledgling social science of his day than he did upon Scripture or theological argument. This breadth must not be forgotten in a consideration of his ethic. Similarly, his writings on the American Revolution are full of natural law reasoning and the dependence upon an analysis of events for recommendations for social policy. In writing on war, he used the Christian tradition of natural law as exemplified in just war theory.

However, *Scripture* was normative for him. Although Christians were not beholden to the ceremonial law or even the Mosaic institutions of the Old Testament, the law of the Bible was to determine Christian practice. This law, discussed below, is the expanded meaning of love found in the Ten Commandments and, even more clearly, in the Sermon on the Mount. Also, whereas he did not follow Thomas à Kempis thoroughly, the imitation of Christ, as found in the Gospels, remained an ethical pattern, as did William Law's following of the example of Jesus. Following Jesus meant applying love to new situations with reference to examples of Jesus. Wesley also carefully pursued many of the *early church patterns* in Acts. From his friends teasing him as Mr. Primitive Christianity to his never abandoning a vision of sharing property in common as each had need, Acts continued to influence him. He distrusted mysticism, and so he sought the plain meaning of Scripture as it was available to him for ethical reflection. All of Scripture was interpreted by Scripture in its ultimate meaning as the love of Christ known in faith. Moreover, he used and provided for others what he regarded as the best commentators on Scripture to clarify its meaning. There was neither obfuscation of Scripture nor protection of esoteric readings of Scripture from the higher or lower criticism of Scripture as it was available in his day.

It was not only reason that came to bear upon Scripture to determine its meaning, but *experience* illumined the interpretation of Scripture. Wesley experienced successful preaching by women, so he could not deny it, though his peers would because of selected biblical texts that seemed to forbid it. Likewise, he would not have continued through the debates to claim perfection for Christian life as perfect love unless he had heard testimony that it was so. Their testimony reinforced his stubborn conviction that the promise of the gospel included perfect love. Actually, he could have saved himself a lot of difficulty and ridicule by insisting that Christians can act out of love without willing sin. Nothing in his doctrine meant that they acted unambiguously freed from their corrupt institutions. He certainly rejected the idea that Christians were freed from ignorance, mistakes, or ambiguity in history. All he needed was that the will when one with Christ in ecstatic love willed love. This is experienced. The perfection language occurs infrequently in the Greek New Testament. It probably cannot even be articulated in Jesus' language of Aramaic. Wesley did not need the term, but he needed a term for moral rigor. Once the debates started, he would not surrender it. W. E. Sangster's impressive study argues that Wesley's own term of *perfect love* was his main meaning and that *Christian perfection* confused the debate.[1]

Before we enter into a detailed discussion of the particularly Christian ethical dialogue on law and love, his realism or pragmatism deserves more elaboration. He was a pragmatist. The word had not been coined yet, and no one would mistake Wesley for his heirs in universal benevolence, the British utilitarians. He directed his movement successfully and made financial and personnel decisions. Charles Wesley would have destroyed the movement several times over, but John fit his leadership to pressures within the movement. He would use lay preachers, and he would resist their ordination until the American Revolution made it necessary. When it was necessary, he would bend. He would cast out extreme preachers who would discredit or ruin the society, but he would not cut off the Americans from an ordained Methodist ministry. Nor would he leave the Church of England. He knew how Dissenters from the

Church of England were declining. He wanted to remain a society within the Church of England. England and its church were one. If he wanted to reform England, he had to reform its church. Charles declared John to be outside the Church of England. John was more realistic or pragmatic (here the terms mean the same thing); he would differ from the Church of England, but he would not leave. John's pragmatism is seen in his success in maintaining his own movement despite ferocious opposition to it. As a pragmatist or realist in politics, even in his last letter to Wilberforce, he warned the abolitionist of the intense opposition to their cause. His preferences were to look at historical realities rather than ideal policies for historical change. In an Age of Reason, he tempered reason with historical experience. He had good instincts as to who controlled England in the eighteenth century, and he adjusted to those realities, generally, while pushing for specific reforms.

Love and Law

Two of the best interpretations of John Wesley's ethic disappoint because they subsume his ethic under other categories. James Logan is in too much of a hurry to relate Wesley's ethic to a theology of creation and eschatology.[2] He presents Wesley's natural law theory briefly, but he does not get to the heart of Wesley's ethic in the love commandments.

Marquardt's excellent book *John Wesley's Social Ethics* understands that the twofold commandment of love is both the initial basis and the cardinal point of his ethics.[3] Neither Marquardt nor Logan references the other, so one cannot determine how each would view the other's work. Marquardt, it seems to me, is so much under the influence of liberation theology that he treats Wesley's ministry to the poor as his central focus. The book begins and ends with strategies for ministering to the poor. My focus on ethics means that the love, which Marquardt recognizes as central, must be made central. Wesley did not find his way to love by consideration of the poor. In his ethics, the double love commandment comes first. He learned it from Susanna, and ministry to the poor soon followed at Oxford. It is not only that a focus on the intractable problem of the poor in the eighteenth or the twenty-first century burns us out; it is also that ethics must be considered in primarily ethical categories. Ethics cannot be surrendered to a preferential option for the poor or to the demands of either psychological or sociological sciences. Ethics needs to be related to the biographical-historical context of the thinker as this study has attempted, but it must also understand the power of its own categories. Wesley wrestled particularly with the categories of law and love in sermonic essays.[4] Wesley is not always clear about the place of moral law in the Christian life, but this systematic presentation in terms of Paul's theology in Romans can be taken as a definitive summary for Wesley.

The *law* that Paul declares to be good in Romans 7:12 is to Wesley neither the law of Rome nor the moral or ceremonial law of the Mosaic institution. Christians are dead to all that law. This is a radically freeing statement. Here the dominance of the New Testament faith in Wesley is very clear. The *moral law* of which Wesley speaks is the divine will given before creation to a supposed *group* of intelligent beings who served God in their natures. Then it was placed in humanity's inmost nature. Humanity overthrew this moral law in its rebellion, but God, to a lesser extent, "reinscribed the law on the heart of his dark sinful creature." Then it was given again to the particular people of Israel and written on two tablets of stone, and later it was to be put "in their inward parts."[5] But the law praised by the apostle is not the Mosaic law but the more internal law: "It is the heart of God disclosed to man."[6] From another perspective: "If we survey the law of God in another point of view, it is supreme unchangeable *reason*."[7] The moral law is the will of God, so it cannot be the cause of sin. Furthermore, this moral law is just: "It renders to all their due."[8]

This law, which is from before time, is also relational: "It is adapted in all respects to the nature of things, of the whole universe and every individual. It is suited to all the circumstances of each, and to all their mutual relations.... It is exactly agreeable to the fitness of things, whether essential or accidental.... 'Thy will be done' is the supreme universal law both in earth and heaven."[9]

All of the particular laws are from God's love through the darkened understandings of humanity. Finally, God through God's love confirms it all in Christ. It is as if Wesley relativizes all of the particular writings while asserting their goodness and their foundation in the eternal law. The eternal law fits all particulars for they, too, are particulars in God's world for which the law is the expression. Present fashion is to show the disunity in various legal teachings, whereas Wesley refuses to be bothered by the particularities seeking the universal will of God's love.

Wesley concludes his sermon by saying that the law has three uses. First, the law convinces one of sin. It reminds one of one's unworthiness. Wesley urged his preachers to preach the law so that the listeners would be aware of their need of the gospel. He is much more brief and also less clear on the second use of the law. He says, "It is to bring him unto life unto Christ that he may live."[10] He does not say *how* this is a function of the law. Its essential meaning seems to be contained in the first use. Is he trying to round out a threefold pattern to follow Calvin and not Luther? The third function of the law is to keep Christians alive in Christ. It seems to mean to inform Christians as to their way to live close to the model of Christ and, thereby, enhance their fellowship with the second person of the Trinity. He repeats that the entire Mosaic dispensation is replaced by the Christ. The Christian is both finished and not finished with the law because now it becomes the way to walk freely in the love of God. Wesley's sermon is very bold in overthrowing the morality of the Old Testament, but then he returns: "Therefore I cannot spare the law one moment, no more than I can spare Christ; seeing I now want it as much to keep me to Christ as ever I wanted it to bring me to him."[11]

The law does not atone, but it keeps one close to the Lord. If one is already maturely at liberty and one with Christ, then Wesley urges one to celebrate. One can be free not only from Jewish guilt and law, but also from the fear of hell. Elsewhere, I have noted Wesley's use of the fear of hell as a theme in his preaching; here he acknowledges its irrelevance to the truly free Christian. Still, he urges the mature Christian to use liberty to avoid sin.

Wesley's threefold use of the law is less clear than John Calvin's, which was (1) to convict of sin; (2) to restrain wickedness; and (3) to inform Christian conscience. His second use had a public function. Wesley certainly used the law this way, particularly natural law, but in this discussion he failed to mention it.

The second sermon in the series adds nothing to the first since it is only a very strong warning against antinomianism or the disregard of the law by neglect, by dismissal through faith, or by sins of omission.

In the third sermon, he asserts that as important as faith is, "Still it is only the handmaid of love. Love is the end of all the commandments of God."[12] He continues, "Love existed from eternity in God, the great ocean of love. Love had a place in all the children of God, from the moment of their creation. They received at once from their gracious Creator to exist, and to love."[13] Faith is the means by which humanity is reestablished in love. The faith in Christ leads to the knowledge of the love of God that produces the love of neighbor. In this love, both the negative law of doing no harm to the neighbor, as in the second tablet of the Ten Commandments, and the positive law of doing good to the neighbor are contained. This love is for Wesley established most importantly in hearts and lives. The conclusion of the "sermon" is that the law of love is established: "So shall you continually go from faith to faith. So shall you daily increase in holy love, till faith is swallowed up in sight, and the law of love established to all eternity."[14]

In these three sermons, Wesley expanded Paul's writing and used John's theology to establish what he had already explicated from Matthew, that the Christian ethic is fundamentally an ethic of love. H. Richard Niebuhr's *The Responsible Self* characterized Christian ethics as belonging primarily to the end-oriented type, the rule-oriented type, or the fitting response type.[15] Clearly here, whereas there are elements of end ethics or teleological ethics in the eschatological and personal hope of love being fulfilled, these elements are not dominant. It is basically a rule- or command-oriented ethic, though the command reflects original or essential human nature. This expression of the ontology or metaphysical nature of love reminds all students of Christian ethics of the ontology of love in Paul Tillich's *Love, Power and Justice*[16] and *Systematic Theology*, volume 3.[17] In those works, Tillich shows how love becomes a command ethic because of the estranged nature of humanity. Wesley made the point two hundred years earlier than Tillich. A final word about the contemporary relevance of this presentation of Wesley's ethic of love is that in its claims for the absoluteness of love and the presupposition of social realism, Wesley's ethic prefigures Reinhold Niebuhr's great chapter on justice in the *Nature and Destiny of Man*.[18] Even in their claims for the requirement of personal ethical character in the Christian and the sure knowledge of the fallenness of human social organization, the two are similar.[19] Wesley's ethic here is loosely based in an exegesis of Paul, and its similarities to contemporary insights of H. Richard Niebuhr, Paul Tillich, and Reinhold Niebuhr in their philosophical writings are at first surprising. But Wesley was pushing his exegesis of Paul into philosophical concepts, and the philosophical concepts of the three mentioned were all grounded in theology indebted to Paul.

Type of Ethics

Students of Wesley's ethic would be wise to recognize it as a form of "rule-agapism."[20] This recognizes the central role of love in Wesley's theology and ethics and in their combinations. It also credits Wesley with his seriousness in combating antinomianism. His morality is characterized by obedience to God's will expressed in Scripture and in moral principles. The terms focusing on love also claim the particular Christian character of Wesley's ethic. Christian ethics is an ethic of love before it is assigned either a teleological or a deontological type. It is not enough to say Christian ethics is representative of a kind of philosophical ethics as Christian ethics is grounded in given imperatives regarding both the divine and the human.

Throughout the study of Wesley's life, responsiveness to situations can be found. Prudence governs many situations, but he governs his own life and the lives of his preachers through rules. To the extent possible, he extends the discipline of rules over his societies. The well-known tendency toward moralism in the later Methodist churches owes its origins to Wesley himself. Frankena, in his recognition of the Christian type of ethics called agapism, worried about the place of justice in such an ethic. It seems to me that justice was part of the essence of humanity, as created, and known through reason, guided by prevenient grace it is the expression of love for the neighbor. To love the neighbor is for Wesley to give the neighbor what the neighbor deserves.

The recognition of the rule-agapism of Wesley's ethic would have spared as good a student of Wesley as Leon Hynson a lot of confusion. In Wesley's "Thoughts upon Slavery: A Declaration of Human Rights," he argues, following Clarence Bence, that Wesley's ethic is teleological or end-oriented, even though Wesley is using principles of natural law to destroy the arguments for slavery.[21] The actuality is that out of love for the poorest of the poor whom he had met, instructed, and baptized, he used principled arguments to attack inhuman greed represented in the slave trade. In his earlier book, Hynson attempts to discuss Wesley's moral law of unchangeable reason under Edward L. Long Jr.'s categories of deliberative ethics.[22] Actually, in *A Survey of Christian Ethics,* Long regards the ethic of Wesley as of the prescriptive type.[23] Hynson's work is very useful, and the concept of Wesley's ethics as rule-agapism would have reinforced Hynson's correct conclusion that "what matters is faith that works through love" (Gal. 5:6 TEV). If any biblical passage may be normative as crucial to Wesleyan ethic, this is it.[24] Elsewhere he had correctly written, "Wesleyan social ethics is an ethic of love."[25]

Wesley wrote so much that it is best not to be too certain of one's interpretation of the whole Wesley. However, authors who try to impose theological formulas on Wesley's ethic often do it without many supportive quotations from Wesley. I hesitate to impose schemes of creation, redemption, or eschatology, or trinitarian formulas, or christological categories upon his ethic. It is true that Wesley was christological, trinitarian, and committed to orthodoxy regarding creation, redemption, and eschatology. But it is also true that he was as concerned—if not more concerned—about how his followers lived their lives than he was about their theological opinions. He is fundamentally an evangelist; but when it comes to Christian thought, his concerns and originality are as likely to be on the subject matter of ethics as theology, though no absolute dividing line is possible. His fight against antinomianism is one of three major theological controversies of his life. The second is over predestination, which in its more stark Calvinist forms doomed both ethics and evangelization in his view. The third was over the meaning of Christian perfection, also primarily an issue of ethics and of the consequences and possibilities of Christian love.

216

Character

The central motif of Wesley's ethics is love. His ethics include other models related to love. Justice, law, and sanctification are important ethical concepts for Wesley, and they are all related to love. Stanley Hauerwas suggested the need to relate character and virtue to sanctification. He recognized that "character and virtue" are traditionally more central in Roman Catholic ethics and that he was "attempting to rethink Protestant theological ethics from the point of view of the traditional Catholic stress on virtue and character."[26] As an eighteenth-century thinker, Wesley regularly referred to character. There are 344 uses of *character* in the standard edition of his works. Most of these uses are in reference to the moral character of human beings and to their selves as moral agents. Wesley repeatedly refers to his personal self-examination and, through interviews, to the character of members of his classes. Character is very important in his thought, as in other eighteenth-century authors like Henry Fielding's novel *Tom Jones*.

Early Methodist writers on John Wesley also study his character. Yet Wesley, familiar with the Aristotelian-Thomistic emphasis on character and virtue, as both Oxford and Anglicanism stressed it, refused to bring it into the center of his ethics. Character is too humanistic, goal-oriented, and works-oriented for Protestant ethics. To try to bring it into the center of Protestant ethics is to overthrow the justification-sanctification dynamic of God and the human in Protestant ethics. I would suggest both Wesley and Hauerwas knew this. Wesley refused the option and built a movement; Hauerwas accepted the option and remained an acute critic of Protestant ethics. Some of Hauerwas's criticism of Wesley may be due to the absence of his reflection on Wesley's writing on character. He chose to focus on Wesley's writing on perfect love and neglected, as far as we can tell from his text, Wesley's work "The Character of a Methodist." The reading of the text would force qualification of as bold a statement by Hauerwas as this: "Even Wesley, who was so insistent on the experiential aspects of grace, makes no attempt to clarify the kind of self that is determined to display these effects."[27]

"The Character of a Methodist" (1742) is a relatively early

document similar to other summary statements of Wesley on the type of character he was attempting to mold in his societies.[28] It well illustrates Wesley's authoritative use of primitive church tradition as it is based on Clement of Alexandria's (ca. 150–215) *Miscellanies*.

It is here that he identifies John Bingham from Christ Church as the one to coin the term *Methodist* for the group of serious young men at Oxford. In the document, he lays out the *principles* and *practices* of this particular Christian group. For Wesley, both thought and action produce the character of the Methodist. Whereas I regard most of Wesley's ethics to be in a prescriptive mode here, he sets out to describe the thought and moral practice of his society. He does not claim, however, that it is descriptive of himself or what everyone in his group has achieved. The principles and practices in their lofty aspirations retain a degree of both teleological pull and prescriptive attainment.

1. Scripture as given by God is the *only and sufficient* rule of faith and practice.
2. Methodist language is scriptural and plain, not distinctive.
3. Methodist practice in clothing, customs is not unique.
4. Methodist belief does not stress one aspect of religion at the expense of others; it is holistic.
5. A Methodist is one who loves God with the whole heart.
6. One is happy rejoicing in God.
7. One cheerfully accepts hope in immortality and is thankful to God.
8. One prays without ceasing.
9. One loves the neighbor and strives to promote the neighbor's welfare.
10. One is pure in heart.
11. One designs one's life according to the law of Christ.
12. One fulfills the commandments of God with all one's might and energy.
13. One's whole life is directed toward God's will.
14. One denies the customs of the world to pursue the good.
15. Finally, one does all the good one can for all people serving both their physical needs and their souls.

Wesley fills in more detail elsewhere than in this short outline. If one were within reach of his preaching, class visitation, or correspondence, it was quite easy to grasp his picture of the Christian's character and what one should be doing to sanctify it. His recommendations were for the active practice of piety and the active serving of the neighbor. He engaged the self, the religious society, and the wider church and society to remold them all toward the love that God would have them exhibit. The Christian life to him was an active molding of self, religious society, and society. My reading of Hauerwas's study of Wesley sees it as weak in explicating the particular importance and techniques of the self's being formed in solidarity in the religious society and even weaker in understanding the self's need to be engaged in the wider social reform and philanthropy. We learned from Wesley there is no adequate Christian self disengaged from others in religious society and there is no adequate Christian character not involved in the social reform of its day.

Reform and Revolution

Wesley's followers were not inclined to revolution. John himself had opposed both the Jacobite rebellion of 1745–1746 and the American Revolution of 1776. The radicalism of the French Revolution would split the English Whig Party and was opposed by the Tories, but by that time, John was declining in health and social comment. He had consistently opposed the French philosophers whose thought encouraged French and British radicals; he had attacked Rousseau, Montesquieu, and Voltaire, finding nothing of value in their thought. The British philosopher who could be regarded as revolutionary, John Locke, had already had his thought confirmed by the Glorious Revolution of 1688. As far as John Wesley was concerned, that was the last revolution of his time to be approved. Radicals, whether they be atheists like Thomas Paine or Calvinists like John Witherspoon, were to be resisted. John's opinions are illustrative of his ethics, but historians have sometimes exaggerated their social influence. Though, according to social historian Roy Porter, Wesley's followers outnumbered any other religious bodies in England except the established church, by the time of his death, they were still too few to prevent or cause a revolution: "Methodism's importance must not be predated. There were only 24,000 Methodists in 1767 and 77,000 by 1796. Hence it is only through an optical illusion that certain historians see Methodism as having 'saved England' from a 'French Revolution'—or indeed as having almost caused one. Nor did it remain unified."[29]

Porter rightfully sees Wesley as encouraging, despite his authoritarianism, democratic spirit and self-dignity among his religiously awakened, disciplined people. Wesley should be seen as encouraging devotion to the sovereign, but without deeper divisions in the ruling class and splits within the military after the loss of the American Revolution, there was no opportunity for revolution. British hatred for the French prevented the wholesale importation of French radicalism, even though there were Francophiles among the British aristocracy and intelligentsia. The execution of the French monarch evoked too many memories of chaos in British minds of the anarchy of the British civil war to provoke emulation. Wesley would have worked to stamp out revolutionary spirit among Methodists in the 1790s if he had been healthier and if he had needed to. But he did not need to, and he was declining. The cause of the abolition of slavery was his concern at the end.

This is not to say that in the nineteenth and twentieth centuries Methodism could not encourage radicalism. It did encourage unionism and social criticism, particularly among some sections of the Primitive Methodists. Clement Attlee, the labor prime minister following Churchill after the war, told me personally in 1959 that he would never have been elected as a socialist member of Parliament if it had not been for the support of the Methodist Chapels. But the ethic of John Wesley himself was directed to Christian philanthropy and reform.

Wesley's study of the history of England provided no examples of revolution improving the living standard of the poor. Even twentieth-century Communist revolutions carried out in the name of the proletariat or the peasant are very mixed in terms of gains for either class. In Wesley's day, the political power that could have effected change for the poor was in the relatively stable aristocracy that controlled the land, trade, army, and church, and in some of the emerging industrialism in the later part of the century. A new economic theory was being elaborated in Glasgow. There is no evidence that Wesley, despite his breadth of reading, ever read Adam Smith. Still, comparison and contrast between the rational optimism of Smith and the passion for assisting the poor of Wesley help locate Wesley's ethic.

The Harmonious Society of Adam Smith

Adam Smith's moral theory presupposed that people were primarily self-interested. They also possessed virtues of sympathy for other creatures in as much as they were like themselves. From this mixture of self-interest and sympathy the use of reason could derive morality. Economics was understood as part of the moral philosophy that Smith taught at the University of Glasgow (1751–1764). The moral philosophy also encompassed the philosophy of religion. Smith's religion, like his life, lacked the passion of a John Calvin, but it sufficed for his membership in the Church of Scotland, an heir of Calvin. As was the case for Calvin and Wesley, the love of God and the love of neighbor were central pillars for Smith, but the details of his morality on worldly matters rested on appropriate behavior as appreciated by the reason of an eighteenth-century gentleman-scholar.[30]

Smith as a person was a somewhat distracted, eccentric scholar of immense knowledge, which he organized systematically and rationally.[31] First as a teacher of logic, then as a writer on astronomy, he was impressed with the regularity and harmonious nature of life. These harmonies were grounded in nature of the heavenly bodies of astronomy or the human nature expressed in the social studies he undertook. All were grounded in God, but God did not interfere often with the regularities of the created order.

So as he described how the self-interested person gathered wealth, he noted how this maximizing of each individual of wealth contributed to the total accumulated wealth of the society. The individual who by nature accumulated, bartered, and traded did not necessarily intend the good of society. But as long as one promoted the purpose of self-accumulation rationally and appropriately, the entire wealth of the community was increased. "One is in this, as in many other cases led by an invisible hand to promote an end which was no part of one's intention."[32] The assumption was that one traded or sold one's labor at the highest possible rate of return in a competitive society according to the principle of marginal utility. As long as people so engaged to mix their labor with the available capital and resources of a society, the wealth of the society grew. He had used the phrase earlier in his moral philosophy to mean not the maximization of wealth, but the distribution of the necessities of life by the wealthy through their employment of others. The phrase was used more naively in the moral theory to assert that all have roughly equal access to equal peace of mind, if not to all the necessities of life. "The beggar, who suns himself by the side of the highway, possesses that security which kings are fighting for."[33] In its usage in the moral philosophy, *the invisible hand* was used in parallel construction with the divine providence, which, dividing the world unequally, still provided for the happiness of the poor. The blithe assumption that people were treated roughly equally needed to be tested by more empirical observation of the squalor of eighteenth-century England and the cruelty of its developing mines and factories. In his earliest reference to the invisible hand in his writings on astronomy, it had been to the non-interference of the invisible hand of Jupiter in the regularities of nature. The other use of the term in *Wealth of Nations* is similar to the assertion of rough human equality in *The Theory of Moral Sentiments*. It is only in the use of the invisible hand to mean the results of the maximization of marginal utility that the term has cogent meaning for economic ethics.

Smith's revolutionary goal in his *Wealth of Nations* was to show that the natural laws of human nature would, if allowed to flourish, meet utilitarian goals of greater happiness for more people. The principles of the division of labor joined to the increasing productivity of machines would increase the wealth of a society. The market worked better than planning for the maximization of the wealth of a nation. The market's natural functioning to increase wealth would be undone if the government, serving business interests, tried to direct the market or to prevent international trade by restrictive practices. Generally speaking, the people, that is, the consumers, would be best served by less government interference for particular business interests. Similar to the possibility of government corruption of a market was monopolistic corruption of a market. Both had to be exposed as irrational impediments to the good of the consumer and the growth of wealth.

There are great moral blinders on Smith in contrast to his contemporary John Wesley. Wesley pleaded for and organized the poor, fought to abolish slavery, and worked to reform the prisons. Smith was transcendent of these causes and rather naive about the corruptions of the human spirit. Nevertheless, he optimistically projected human economic development and increasing human happiness through rational choice in economic matters.

England of 1776 corresponded in many features to what Smith saw, but there was much unrelieved misery that he did not comprehend. He was correct that rational, economic competition implies cooperation, which can increase the wealth of all. He had little sense of the limits of nature, but at least he did not ascribe all value to labor and capital; he recognized natural resources as contributing to wealth. Our contemporary world economy reflects his analysis and confronts his thought with issues of which he was little cognizant. His analyses of division of labor, industrial development adding to labor, unplanned cooperation as the function of a market, need for world trade for wealth development, the dangers of particular interests dominating government or business and corrupting the market are all fruitful contributions to ongoing agonizing over economic injustice. Smith's Enlightenment optimism regarding harmony stemming from pure competition seems quaint to a generation raised on Karl Marx, Charles Darwin, and Sigmund Freud. It appears as an assertion close to economic autonomy without the disordering reality of sin and the orienting reality of the kingdom of God.

Evangelical Economics

John Wesley's passion rang through his writing on economics. Whether he was describing the inexcusable suffering of Africans forced into slavery by Europeans or the vile conditions of the English poor imposed by government and establishment, he was never temperate. His language, syntax, and argument called for fundamental economic changes. Some of his writing was descriptive, but with his eye on the kingdom of God, he saw clearly and described the squalor of human life. Africans were thrown off slave ships to the depths of the Atlantic and English were forced to find their food among dung heaps because of sin expressed in greed.

Wesley knew of the harmonious aspect of society as Smith knew of the conflictual nature of society. Both thirsted for order and for sufficiency for the people of eighteenth-century England. But Wesley, with a longing for perfection and deep awareness of sin, hoped for more transformation of people and society than Smith. He seemed also to see the need for transformation more clearly than Smith. Smith's human nature was inclined toward morality because of natural human sympathy for other beings like oneself. Wesley's human nature was driven toward morality because of divine imperatives.

Wesley's demands for mercy and justice in the economic world followed from his observations, study, and work with the despised of the world. There was an immediacy to his pleas for justice that in the contemporary world has resonated in the theologies of liberation. Yet most of his pleas were for reform. He did not expect the king and Parliament to be overthrown; in fact, he dreaded revolution, whether in America or in France. His specific recommendations were for reform, and in most cases they could be achieved without revolution. Historically, most of them have been approximated, even if not sustained, without revolution.

His advocacy of the abolition of slavery was the most far-reaching of his reforms as some of the prosperity of England rested upon the wretched practice of the triangular trade. Whether wealth would be served or not, slavery was wrong, and all were admonished to end it. Europeans were guilty of worse practices than any of the pagan empires Wesley knew about, and economic necessity was not a valid argument for maintaining slavery. The fact that it was supported by human law was irrelevant in the confrontation with God's law. As with Bartolomé de las Casas and Pope Paul III in the sixteenth century, those subject to slavery were potentially subject to Christ, and they had to be freed for their evangelization. For Wesley and the best of sixteenth-century

Spanish Catholicism, humanity was free by nature, and freedom was sought out of the evangelical thrust of the gospel. The arguments of the establishment for keeping slaves were argued in terms of economic necessity; in fact, slavery stemmed from greed, not need.

Monopolies in agriculture and the consumption of grain by horses desired by the wealthy as a sign of luxury drove food prices for the poor to formidable heights in Wesley's analysis. The monopolies in agriculture needed to be broken up and the luxurious keeping of horses ended by legislation to restore small agriculture and fair food prices. In Wesley's eyes, unnecessary military expenses, especially unneeded fortifications, had pushed up the national debt, raising interest rates. The wasteful military expenditures needed to be curtailed and the national debt retired. Hence, he recommended policy changes for employment. His particular passion was to reduce the price for food, which consumed nearly everything the poor could earn. Taxes, prices of land, prices of food, and so forth, he reduced to governmental expenses and resultant government debt accrued in military expenditures.

Wesley wrote of thousands in England starving, and their starvation was rooted in unemployment. Without funds for anything but food, the poor could not buy the goods that the unemployed might have produced. Because he regarded all property as subject to the will of God for its wise stewardship, the luxuries of the rich were regarded as both unnecessary and a drag on the economy. He advocated steep taxation of luxuries. Believing in the wisdom of the day regarding supply and demand, he advocated getting resources into the hands of those whose demand would create more products. Thwarting the needs of the poor was the establishment's passion to live in luxury and the use of the government toward that end. He knew that certain practices (e.g., the overuse of grain in the overconsumption of alcohol) needed to be stopped, and other privileges of the rich (e.g., luxury, size of estates, and horse consumption of grain) limited to achieve a healthy economy. He was skeptical of the Christian establishment's will to change. So he advocated for his own religious compatriots lives of economic discipline and effort with the goals of earning all one could without harming self or others, saving all one could without deprivation of family, and the giving away through the church and then to the broader population all one could after family needs had been modestly met.

Wesley did not make contributions to economic theory. He did not, at length, present a systematic perspective on economics. But he had no reservations about relating faith and its consequences directly to contemporary economic practice. His calls for economic change toward justice and for the poor were very bold. He knew that Christian economics was about getting scarce resources in an abundant land to those without economic power. Furthermore, on each page of his economic writing one feels the dialectic of organization and self-help for the poor and the criticism of the powerful establishment for failing to practice just stewardship.

In fact, the Wesleyan-organized cell movements provided the discipline, hope, organization, learning, and networks that lifted many of the early Methodists out of poverty. Religiously inspired communities of economic, ethical orientation, and education may still be one of the greatest antidotes to poverty for many societies.

Reform Self, Church, and Society

Wesley's evangelical practice was to reform the self, church, and society. The pages of his magazine, the *Arminian,* are full of testimonies of lives changed by evangelization and social solidarity within the Methodist society. The Methodist society was to reform the established church, and that would have reformed the society. But the established church, whether it opposed Wesley by mob action, legal harassment, and intellectual debate, or accepted and tolerated him, would not transform itself. So, his society simmered and waited until four years after his death when it became independent and thereby forfeited its chance to reform church and society.

A methodological point raised by Alasdair MacIntyre indicates why to understand Wesley's ethic, one must comprehend his practice.

> Theory is the articulation of practice and good theory of good practice. Moral debate is therefore not primarily between theories as such, but rather between theories that afford expression to

rival forms of practice. And we do not understand any theory adequately until we've understood in concrete detail the form of practice of which it's an articulation. Theory, when it is recognized to be the articulation of practice, enables practice to be reflectively thoughtful and so to remedy what have been its defects and limitations.[34]

A summary of Wesley's moral practice shows the breadth of his moral concern:

1. Evangelical preaching of the moral law, human failure to achieve it, and the atoning love of God in Christ appropriated by faith.
2. The binding of the religiously awakened in classes, bands, and a religious society related to the Church of England for their growth toward sanctification. Regular examination of converts' characters by class leader, lay preachers, or Wesley himself. Enforcement of strict Christian discipline through group pressure and expulsion.
3. Frequent practice of the ordinances of the church: Communion, fasting, scripture study, church attendance.
4. Education in class meetings, Methodist schools, Sunday schools, and reading of literature, secular and sacred, produced for Methodists and others.
5. Employment centers, loan funds, clothing, and food provision by societies.
6. Prison visitation, payment of prisoners' debts, publishing of criticism of prisons, raising of provisions for prisoners.
7. Active peacemaking through preaching, preparation of tracts, publication of books, criticism of war, letter writing, preaching, and witnessing to soldiers.
8. Arguing and writing for tax reform, reduction of national debt, preventing unnecessary pensions, closing unnecessary military installations, taxes on horses, and opposition to distilled spirits.
9. Support for the sovereign through preaching and

writing and encouraging preachers to support monarch. Criticism of selling of votes or acceptance of food or liquor for vote. Criticism of misrepresentative districts. Encouragement of voting conscience.

10. Evangelization, baptism of slaves. Acceptance of slaves and freed slaves in societies. Lobbying for end of slave trade. Preaching and writing on behalf of abolition of slavery. Lobbying political leadership on behalf of abolition. Committing Methodist society to ending of slave trade movement and publishing antislavery documents.[35]

Can we explain Wesley's accomplishment? He was a gifted individual of great health and intelligence. He came from a religiously driven family, and the drive was embedded in him with a powerful mother's conviction that he was "a brand plucked from the burning." Yet he could not find satisfaction, and he refused to quench the nagging discomfort. He lived the religious question through Oxford, the Georgia disappointment, and the Moravian challenge. It came together for a relatively distraught, celibate priest in a warm acceptance of forgiving grace. The rest of his life expressed his robust health, energy, and intellect in sharing this warm acceptance (the gracious, feminine side of the divine) with others of an acceptance that he never could establish with a woman. His authoritarian nature permitted him to override objections to his particular Puritan,[36] Moravian, Church of England synthesis and to weave his movement together. He could make the compromises and exercise authority to mold this movement, which met some of the people's religious needs of the day as it met his.

Notes

1. Origins (1703–1714)

1. John A. Newton, *Susanna Wesley and the Puritan Tradition in Methodism* (London: Epworth Press, 1968), p. 93. See also Robert C. Monk, *John Wesley: His Puritan Heritage* (Lanham, Md.: Scarecrow Press, 1999), pp. 10-11.

2. Newton, *Susanna Wesley*, p. 107.

3. Ibid., p. 63.

4. Ibid., p. 161.

5. Ibid., p. 200.

6. Charles Wallace Jr., ed., *Susanna Wesley: The Complete Writings* (New York: Oxford University Press, 1997), pp. 365-76.

7. Colin Ella, *Historic Epworth: The Heart of the Isle of Axholme* (Stadhampton: Rural Publications, 1994), p. 84.

8. Newton, *Susanna Wesley*, p. 111.

9. Frederick E. Maser, *The Story of John Wesley's Sisters, or Seven Sisters in Search of Love* (Rutland, Vt.: Academy Books, 1988).

10. The discussion of the sisters is from Ella, *Historic Epworth*, pp. 42-45. Full research on the family is in the Doncaster, England, public library.

11. Maldwyn Edwards, *Family Circle: A Study of the Epworth Household in Relation to John and Charles Wesley* (London: Epworth Press, 1949), p. 182.

2. Oxford (1720–1735)

1. V. H. H. Green, "Religion in the Colleges, 1715–1800," in *The Eighteenth Century*, ed. L. S. Sutherland and L. G. Mitchell, vol. 5, *The History of the University of Oxford*, ed. T. H. Ashton (Oxford: Clarendon Press, 1986), p. 425.

2. Ibid., pp. 436-37.

3. V. H. H. Green, *The Young Mr. Wesley* (New York: St. Martin's Press, 1961), pp. 1-12.

4. Quoted in ibid., p. 22.

5. Felix Markham, *Oxford* (London: Weidenfield & Nicholson, 1967), p. 116.

6. Ibid., p. 125.

7. L. G. Mitchell, "Introduction," in Sutherland and Mitchell's *Eighteenth Century*.

8. Susanna Wesley, "Letter to John Wesley" (June 8, 1725), in *Letters* I, ed. Frank Baker, *The Works of John Wesley*, vol. 25 (Oxford: Clarendon Press, 1980), p. 165.

9. Ibid., p. 185.

10. Nehemiah Curnock, "Introductory," in *The Journal of the Rev. John Wesley, A.M.*, vol. 1 (London: Robert Culley, 1909), pp. 3-77.

11. Green, *Young Wesley*, is the major source in addition to Wesley's letters for 1725–1735.

12. G. Elsie Harrison, *Son to Susanna: The Private Life of John Wesley* (Nashville: Cokesbury Press, 1938), pp. 69-72.

13. Green, *Young Wesley*, pp. 130-34.

14. *Journals and Diaries* I, ed. W. Reginald Ward and Richard P. Heitzenrater, *The Works of John Wesley*, vol. 18 (Nashville: Abingdon Press, 1988), p. 134.

15. *Letters I, Works*, 25:346-47.

16. John Wesley, *Sermons* I, ed. Albert C. Outler, *The Works of John Wesley*, vol. 1 (Nashville: Abingdon Press, 1984), p. 172.

17. Ibid., p. 173.

18. Ibid., p. 176.

19. Ibid., p. 178.

20. Albert C. Outler, in ibid., p. 113.

21. Ibid., p. 114.

22. Richard P. Heitzenrater, *Wesley and the People Called Methodists* (Nashville: Abingdon Press, 1995), p. 214.

23. Frank O'Gorman, *The Long Eighteenth Century: British Political and Social History 1688–1832* (London: Arnold, 1997), pp. 165-66.

3. Georgia (1735–1737)

1. "Mr. Andrews" identified as the Reverend Mr. William Andrews in the note to *Letters* I, ed. Frank Baker, *The Works of John Wesley*, vol. 25 (Oxford: Clarendon Press, 1980), p. 464.

2. Ibid., p. 466. Published in *Gentleman's Magazine*, May 1737, pp. 318-19.

3. Ibid., p. 474.

4. *Journals and Diaries* I, ed. W. Reginald Ward and Richard P. Heitzenrater, *The Works of John Wesley*, vol. 18 (Nashville: Abingdon Press, 1988), p. 201.

5. Ibid., p. 202.

6. Ibid., pp. 175, 466.

7. *Letters* I, *Works*, 25:467.

8. *Journals and Diaries* I, *Works*, 18:180.

9. Ibid., p. 181.

10. Ibid., p. 482.

11. Ibid., p. 195.

12. "The Life and Conversation of that Holy Man Mr. John Wesley during his abode in Georgia: The Affidavit of Mr. Robert Williams of the City of Bristol, Merchant," June 22, 1741, in the Bodleian Library, Oxford, with reply by John Wesley.

13. *Journals and Diaries* I, *Works*, 18:214.

14. Rupert E. Davies, ed., "Introduction" in *The Works of John Wesley*, vol. 9 (Nashville: Abingdon Press, 1989), p. 9.

4. Moravians (1738–1739)

1. *Journals and Diaries* I, ed. W. Reginald Ward and Richard P. Heitzenrater, *The Works of John Wesley*, vol. 18 (Nashville: Abingdon Press, 1988), p. 227.

2. Ibid., p. 228.

3. Ibid., p. 237 n.

4. Ibid., p. 239.

5. Ibid., p. 250.

6. Ibid., p. 254.

7. John Wesley, "Salvation by Faith," in Albert C. Outler, ed. *Sermons* I, in *The Works of John Wesley*, vol. 1 (Nashville: Abingdon Press, 1984), pp. 117-30.

8. Ibid., p. 125.

9. *Journals and Diaries* I, *Works*, 18:255, n. 7.

10. Ibid., p. 272.

11. *Journals and Diaries* II, ed. W. Reginald Ward and Richard P. Heitzenrater, *The Works of John Wesley*, vol. 19 (Nashville: Abingdon Press, 1990), p. 29.

12. Ibid., p. 30.

13. John Wesley, *Explanatory Notes upon the New Testament* (New York: T. Mason and G. Lane, 1839), p. 151.

14. *Journals and Diaries* II, *Works*, 19:51.

15. Ibid., p. 97.

16. Ibid., p. 125.

17. Martin Schmidt, *John Wesley: A Theological Biography*, vol. 1 (New York: Abingdon Press, 1962), pp. 244-45.

18. Rupert E. Davies, ed., *The Works of John Wesley*, vol. 9 (Nashville: Abingdon Press, 1989), p. 6.

19. Ibid., p. 10.

20. Ibid., p. 11.

21. Ibid., p. 13.

22. G. Osborn, ed., *The Poetical Works of John and Charles Wesley* (London: Wesleyan-Methodist Conference Office, 1868), p. xiii.

23. Ibid., p. xix.

24. Ibid., p. xxii.

25. Ibid.

5. Reform (1740s)

1. Leon O. Hynson, *To Reform the Nation* (Grand Rapids: Zondervan, 1984), p. 34.

2. *Journals and Diaries* II, ed. W. Reginald Ward and Richard P. Heitzenrater, *The Works of John Wesley*, vol. 19 (Nashville: Abingdon Press, 1990), p. 221.

3. *Letters* II, ed. Frank Baker, *The Works of John Wesley*, vol. 26 (Nashville: Abingdon Press, 1982), pp. 24-31.

4. Ibid., pp. 34-35.

5. *Journals and Diaries* II, *Works*, 19:155.

6. *Sermons* I, ed. Albert C. Outler, *The Works of John Wesley*, vol. 1 (Nashville: Abingdon Press, 1984), p. 224.

7. Ibid., p. 222.

8. Ibid., p. 232.

9. John Wesley, "Principles of a Methodist" (Bristol: Felix Farley, 1742).

10. Ibid., p. 13.

11. John Wesley, "The Character of a Methodist" (Bristol: Felix Farley, 1742), p. 16, italics in original.

12. Ibid., p. 20.

13. John Wesley, "The Appeals to Men of Reason and Religion and Certain Related Open Letters," in *The Works of John Wesley*, vol. 11, ed. Gerald R. Cragg (Nashville: Abingdon Press, 1989), p. 82.

14. John Wesley, "Letter to the Mayor of Newcastle," in *Letters* II, ed. Frank Baker, *The Works of John Wesley*, vol. 26 (Nashville: Abingdon Press, 1982), p. 101.

15. *Journals and Diaries* III, ed. W. Reginald Ward and Richard P. Heitzentater, *The Works of John Wesley*, vol. 20 (Nashville: Abingdon Press, 1991), p. 16.

16. Ibid., p. 37, n. 78.

17. Ibid., p. 47.

18. Rupert E. Davies, ed., *The Works of John Wesley*, vol. 9 (Nashville: Abingdon Press, 1989), p. 277.

19. Ibid., p. 278.

20. John Wesley, *Primitive Physic: or, An Easy and Natural Method of Curing Most Diseases*, 24th ed. (London: G. Paramore, 1790).

21. John Wesley, "A Short Account of the School in Kingswood Near Bristol" (Bristol: Felix Farley, 1749).

22. John Wesley, "An Account of an Amour of John Wesley," in Umphrey Lee, *The Lord's Horseman* (New York: Century Co., 1928), pp. 267-351. This remarkable document with corrections in John Wesley's handwriting was published in the first edition of Lee's work and removed from later editions. It was copied from the original in the British Museum. It had been in the possession of Noah Vazeille, the son of Mrs. John Wesley. It was first published by Augustin Leger, as *Wesley's Last Love* (London: Dent, 1910).

23. Frank Baker regarded the twice-repeated vows in 1749 between Wesley and Murray as more binding than the 1748 engagement. Baker followed the nuances of the debate and still concluded: "Throughout it all I am convinced that Wesley believed Grace Murray was in some sense his legal wife" (*Methodist History*, October 1977, p. 43). Beyond the disputes over the status of a *de praesenti* pledge in the 1740s, English law is a general recognition, at least, of their engagement.

24. Lee, *The Lord's Horseman*.

6. Sermon on the Mount (1748–1750)

1. "On the Wedding Garment" in *Sermons* IV, ed. Albert C. Outler, *The Works of John Wesley*, vol. 4 (Nashville: Abingdon Press, 1987), pp. 140-48.

2. Ibid., p. 147.

3. Ibid.

4. "The Circumcision of the Heart," in Albert C. Outler, ed. *The Works of John Wesley*, vol. 1 (Nashville: Abingdon Press, 1984), pp. 401-16.

5. "On the Wedding Garment," *Works*, 4:148.

6. "Upon Our Lord's Sermon on the Mount, I," *Works*, 1:482.

7. "Upon Our Lord's Sermon on the Mount, II," *Works*, 1:496.

8. "Upon Our Lord's Sermon on the Mount, III," *Works*, 1:516-17.

9. "Upon Our Lord's Sermon on the Mount, IV," *Works*, 1:533.

10. Ibid., p. 534.

11. Ibid., p. 539.

12. Ibid., p. 548.

13. "Upon Our Lord's Sermon on the Mount, V," *Works*, 1:552.

14. Ibid., p. 571.

15. "Upon Our Lord's Sermon on the Mount, VI," *Works*, 1:582.

16. Ibid., p. 583.

17. "Upon Our Lord's Sermon on the Mount, VIII," *Works*, 1:616.

18. Ibid., p. 618.

19. Ibid.

20. Ibid.

21. Ibid., pp. 628-29.

22. Outler, *Works*, 1:634, n. 10.

23. "Upon Our Lord's Sermon on the Mount, IX," *Works*, 1:640.

24. Ibid., p. 641.

25. Ibid., p. 649.

26. "Upon Our Lord's Sermon on the Mount, X," *Works*, 1:658.

27. Ibid., p. 660.

28. Ibid., p. 661.

29. Outler, ibid., p. 675.

30. "Upon Our Lord's Sermon on the Mount, XIII," *Works*, 1:698.

31. See Tore Meistad, *Martin Luther and John Wesley on the Sermon on the Mount* (Lanham, Md.: Scarecrow Press, 1999), pp. 311-15.

7. Marriage and War (1750s)

1. *Journals and Diaries* III, ed. W. Reginald Ward and Richard P. Heitzenrater, *The Works of John Wesley*, vol. 20 (Nashville: Abingdon Press, 1991), p. 379.

2. See Richard Heitzenrater, *The Ellusive Mr. Wesley* (Nashville: Abingdon Press, 1984), pp. 174-94 for Wesley's letters to Mary and others.

3. *Journals and Diaries* III, *Works*, 20:481.

4. Ibid., p. 482.

5. *Letters* II, ed. Frank Baker, *The Works of John Wesley*, vol. 26 (Nashville: Abingdon Press, 1982), p. 533.

6. *The Works of the Rev. John Wesley, A.M.*, vol. 12 (London: John Mason, 1830), p. 205.

7. John Telford, ed., *The Letters of the Rev. John Wesley, A.M.* (London: Epworth Press, 1931), p. 89.

8. Ibid., p. 102.

9. Ibid., 6:321-22.

10. Transcribed copy of letter to Molly Wesley, 9 December 1771, in London's Museum of Methodism.

11. Transcribed copy of letter to Molly Wesley, 15 July 1774, in London's Museum of Methodism. Also in Telford, *Letters*, 6:98.

12. Telford, *Letters*, 6:321-22.

13. *Journals and Diaries* IV, ed. W. Reginald Ward and Richard P. Heitzenrater, *The Works of John Wesley*, vol. 23 (Nashville: Abingdon Press, 1995), p. 225.

14. John Wesley, *Explanatory Notes upon the New Testament* (Bristol: Graham and Pine, 1760), p. v.

15. Ibid., p. vii.

16. John Wesley, "Predestination Calmly Considered" (London: Foundry, 1752).

17. Ibid.

18. Ibid., p. 81.

19. John Wesley, "A Plain Account of Genuine Christianity" (Dublin: S. Powell, 1753).

20. Ibid., p. 9.

21. Ibid., p. 10.

22. John Wesley, "The Dignity of Human Nature" (1762), p. 41. The same pages were published also as part of "The Doctrine of Original Sin."

23. Eric Robson, "The Armed Forces and the Act of War," in *New Cambridge Modern History*, ed. J. O. Lindsay (Cambridge: University Press, 1970), p. 167.

24. Reinhold Niebuhr, *The Nature and Destiny of Man*, 2 vols. (New York: Charles Scribner & Sons, 1941–43).

25. Wesley published an extraction of the writing on the Ten Commandments by Bishop Hopkins, which explicitly affirmed just war teaching, and his own writing on the Sermon on the Mount allows for just defense.

26. Wesley, "Dignity of Human Nature," pp. 41-45.

27. Kenneth N. Waltz, *Man, the State and War: A Theoretical Analysis* (New York: Columbia University Press, 1959).

28. John Wesley, Preface and Extracts of *A Short Exposition of the Ten Commandments: Extracted from Bishop Hopkins* (London: G. Paramore, 1792).

29. Ibid., pp. iii-iv.

30. The author hopes his *Ultimate Imperative: An Interpretation of Christian Ethics* (Cleveland: Pilgrim Press, 1999) succeeds in exposition and illustration of the Ten Commandments without becoming "legalistic."

31. The discussions of the themes of sin and perfection in love are central to Wesley's theological ethics, and they are presented in chapter 9.

8. Maturation (1760s–1770s)

1. John L. Peters, *Christian Perfection and American Methodism* (New York: Abingdon Press, 1956), pp. 15-18.

2. See Henry D. Rack, *Reasonable Enthusiast: John Wesley and the Rise of Methodism* (Nashville: Abingdon Press, 1992).

3. John Wesley, "A Discourse on Sin in Believers" (London: Foundry, 1763), p. 11, italics in original.

4. John Wesley, "Christian Perfection," in *John Wesley*, ed. Albert C. Outler (New York: Oxford University Press, 1964), p. 270.

5. John Wesley, "The Scripture Way of Salvation," in *John Wesley*, p. 274.

6. Ibid., p. 275.

7. Wesley, "Thoughts on Christian Perfection," p. 284. Ted A. Campbell in *Methodist Doctrine: The Essentials* (Nashville: Abingdon Press, 1999) says Methodists have always defined perfection "by repeating the great commandment" (p. 61).

8. Wesley, "Thoughts on Christian Perfection," p. 299.

9. John Wesley, *A Plain Account of Christian Perfection* (London: Epworth Press, 1952), p. 107.

10. Joseph Galloway, *Reflections on the Rise and Progress of the American Revolution* (London: Foundry, 1780).

11. John Wesley, "Thoughts upon Necessity" (London: R. Hawes, 1774), pp. 22-23.

12. Ibid., p. 33.

13. John Wesley, "Predestination Calmly Considered" (London: R. Hawes, 1776).

14. John Wesley, "Thoughts upon God's Sovereignty" (London: R. Hawes, 1777), p. 10.

15. John Wesley, "Doctrine of Absolute Predestination Stated and Summarized" (Bristol: William Pine, 1770), p. 12.

16. John Telford, *The Letters of the Rev. John Wesley, A.M.*, vol. 5 (London: Epworth Press, 1931), p. 252.

17. *Arminian Magazine* 1 (London: J. Fry & Co., 1778).

18. John Wesley, *A Survey of the Wisdom of God in the Creation or a Compendium of Natural Philosophy* (Bristol: William Pine, 1763), p. i.

19. John Wesley, *A Concise History of England: From the Earliest Times, to the Death of George II*, vol. 1 (London: R. Hawes, 1775), p. ix.

20. John Wesley, *Concise History*, vol. 4 (London: R. Hawes, 1776), p. 102.

21. Ibid., p. 286.

22. Ibid., p. 287.

23. Ibid., p. 290.

24. Ibid., p. 248.

25. John Wesley, *Explanatory Notes upon the Old Testament* (Bristol: William Pine, 1765).

26. Ibid., p. 1.

27. L. Tyerman, *The Life and Times of the Rev. John Wesley, M.A.* (London: Hodder & Stoughton, 1870), p. 399.

28. Samuel Johnson, quoted in James Boswell, *The Life of Samuel Johnson*, ed. John Canning (London: Methwin, 1991), p. 91.

29. Leslie White, *More About the Early Methodist People* (London: Epworth Press, 1949), pp. 136-76. See Earl Kent Brown, *Women of Mr. Wesley's Methodism,* (Lewiston, N.Y.: Edwin Mellen Press, 1983).

30. White, *More About the Early Methodist People,* p. 159.

31. Ibid., p. 163.

32. Ibid. The reference in White is to Z. Taft, *Holy Women* (London: Kershaw, 1825–28), 1:84. It is not in Telford's *Letters* and is not known to be extant.

33. Ibid., p. 170.

34. "Use of Money," in *Sermons* II, ed. Albert C. Outler, *The Works of John Wesley,* vol. 2 (Nashville: Abingdon Press, 1985), p. 268.

35. Ibid., p. 271.

36. Ibid., p. 280.

37. John Munsey Turner, "Wesley's Pragmatic Theology," in *Windows on Wesley: Wesleyan Theology in Today's World,* ed. Philip R. Meadows (Oxford: Applied Theology Press, 1997).

38. Robert Hughes, *The Fatal Shore* (New York: Alfred A. Knopf, 1987), pp. 22-23.

39. Rack, *Reasonable Enthusiast,* p. 10.

40. Ibid., p. 14.

41. John Wesley, "Thoughts on the Present Scarcity of Provisions" (London: R. Hawes, 1773). The title page does not list Wesley's name, but it is regarded by Henry D. Rack and others to be John Wesley's authorship. The neglect of it has led to some of the judgments criticizing that Wesley did not think in terms of relevant social policy. Neither the journal references nor Tyerman's biography ascribes it to Wesley.

42. Kenneth J. Collins, *A Real Christian: The Life of John Wesley* (Nashville: Abingdon Press, 1999), p. 122. Another recent essay in a respected series inexplicably omits reference to Wesley's essay. David Deeks, "Economics from a Wesleyan Perspective," in *Windows on Wesley.*

43. Manfred Marquardt, *John Wesley's Social Ethics: Praxis and Principles,* trans. John E. Steely and W. Stephen Gunter (Nashville: Abingdon Press, 1992).

9. Liberty

1. *The Works of John Wesley,* vol. 11 (Grand Rapids: Zondervan, 1958), p. 16.

2. David Hempton, *The Religion of the People: Methodism and Popular Religion c. 1750–1900* (London: Routledge, 1996), p. 82.

3. "Thoughts Concerning the Origin of Power," in *The Works of the Rev. John Wesley, A.M.,* vol. 11, 3d ed. (London: John Mason, 1830), p. 53.

4. *Journals and Diaries* III, ed. W. Reginald Ward and Richard P. Heitzenrater, *The Works of John Wesley,* vol. 20 (Nashville: Abingdon Press, 1991), p. 16.

5. George Rudé, *The Crowd in History: A Study of Popular Disturbances in France and England 1730–1848* (New York: John Wiley & Sons, 1964), pp. 52-62.

6. "Thoughts upon Liberty," *Works,* 11:41.

7. Ibid., p. 45.

8. Wesley's references to Machiavelli in his writing are all negative. Shortly after studying Machiavelli in Georgia (24 February 1737), he referred to him as "the first born of Hell."

9. Winston S. Churchill, *A History of the English Speaking Peoples*, vol. 3 (New York: Dodd, Mead & Company, 1957), pp. 167-68.

10. See "Free Thoughts," *Works*, 11:24.

11. L. Tyerman, *The Life and Times of the Reverend John Wesley, M.A.* (London: Hodder & Stoughton, 1870), p. 190.

12. Quoted in ibid., p. 199.

13. Ibid.

14. "A Calm Address to Our American Colonies," *Works*, 11:81.

15. *Works*, 11:119.

16. Ibid., p. 125.

17. *Journals and Diaries* VI, ed. W. Reginald Ward and Richard P. Heitzenrater, *The Works of John Wesley*, vol. 23 (Nashville: Abingdon Press, 1995), p. 176, n. 75.

18. *Works*, 11:148.

19. See ibid., p. 154.

20. "The Late Work of God in North America," in *Sermons* III, ed. Albert C. Outler, *The Works of John Wesley*, vol. 3 (Nashville: Abingdon Press, 1986), pp. 594-608.

21. Ibid., p. 607.

22. Ibid., p. 608.

23. *Works*, 11:155.

24. Anonymous, *An Account of the Rise and Progress of the American War* (London: n.p., 1780), Charles Wesley's personal copy at Wesley's London House, 56 pp., and Anonymous, *Reflections on the Rise and Progress of the American Rebellion* (London: J. Paramore, 1780), copy at Wesley's London House.

25. Anonymous, *An Extract of a Letter to the Right Honourable Lord Viscount Howe on His Naval Conduct in the American War* (London: J. Paramore, 1781). Anonymous, *An Extract from a Reply to the Observations of Lieut. Gen. Sir William Howe* (London: J. Paramore, 1784).

10. Slavery

1. James Cone, *A Black Theology of Liberation* (Philadelphia: J. B. Lippincott, 1970), p. 72.

2. David S. Landes, *The Wealth and Poverty of Nations* (New York: W. W. Norton, 1998), p. 117. Walter Rodney, *How Europe Underdeveloped Africa* (Washington, D.C.: Howard University Press, 1974). A figure as high as 40 million transported is given in *The Great White Lie*, by Jack Gratus (London: Hutchinson, 1973), p. 11. Hugh Thomas's conclusion is that the figure of 11 million is about correct with an error margin of .5 million (*The Slave Trade* [New York: Simon & Schuster, 1997], pp. 861-62).

3. Jared M. Diamond, *Guns, Germs, and Steel: The Fates of Human Societies* (New York: W. W. Norton, 1997), p. 80.

4. Quoted in Gratus, *Great White Lie,* pp. 34-35.

5. Ibid., p. 56.

6. John Newton, *The Life of the Rev. John Newton* (New York: American Tract Society, n.d., first published in 1764), p. 69.

7. Frank J. Klingberg, *The Anti-Slavery Movement in England* (New Haven: Archon Books, 1968).

8. Warren Thomas Smith, *John Wesley and Slavery* (Nashville: Abingdon Press, 1986), p. 91.

9. Smith notes here that Wesley is following the original *Representation* of Granville Sharp and not the excerpt in Benezet. See *John Wesley and Slavery,* p. 93.

10. Note that Wesley corrects Benezet's date of John Hawkins's raids from 1556 to 1564. A contemporary history dates his three voyages as 1562, 1564, and 1568 (Thomas, *The Slave Trade,* pp. 156-58). The description in Wesley seems to correspond to the expedition of 1564, which produced a profit of 60 percent with the cooperation of the queen. He was knighted for his raids and sale of slaves, and he took the emblem of an African female for his coat of arms (p. 157).

11. "Thoughts upon Slavery," IV, 1, in Smith, *John Wesley and Slavery,* p. 136.

12. Ibid.

13. Ibid., V, 6, p. 147.

14. One may need to discount Wesley's published views on the nobility of Africans. After all, he was engaged in a bitter polemical argument for their liberation. In his review of a book on native islanders discovered off the coast of China he returned to his theology. He argued that if the islanders were as innocent as Captain Wilson affirmed, the doctrine of original sin was false, and there was no need for Jesus Christ. On the basis of the doctrine of the fall of humanity he denied that Wilson's account of the islanders could be true. In the same review he rejected Captain Cook's account of the innocence of the natives of Hawaii. See John Wesley, "Thoughts on a Late Publication," in *The Works of John Wesley,* vol. 13 (Grand Rapids: Zondervan, 1958), p. 413.

15. Thomas, *The Slave Trade,* p. 477.

16. In the summer of 1998, I visited two major sites in West Africa that John Wesley described in his eighteenth-century writing against slavery. Interviews were conducted among a few Methodist pastors and at two theological seminaries. Among those I contacted, very little was known precisely of Wesley's campaign against slavery. Research on the subject was welcomed at two seminaries. One Methodist woman pastor administering a school in the bush near Abomey, Benin, had read the "Thoughts upon Slavery" in French at her seminary in Porto Novo. She was skeptical of the spiritualized, allegorical interpretation put on the text by her instructor. My major learning from Africans was that they generally regarded it as a slave trade. That is, some Africans traded other Africans to Europeans for trade goods and cannons. Wesley's somewhat sentimental interpretation of African society was challenged by the Africans I interviewed.

One slave fort or factory that Wesley described was Ouidah. On the road from the fort to the beach is a small tree, a replacement for the original forgetting tree. The inscription in French indicates that while slaves circled this tree several times, they were instructed to forget their families, their villages, and their previous lives. The tree symbolizes the destruction of identity that was enforced through the practice and wrong of slavery. The still living presence of Ouidah voodoo in Brazil, Cuba, and elsewhere indicates that neither the forgetting tree ritual nor the lash completely succeeded in driving Africa out of the Africans, but the heartless attempt is remembered.

17. Reginald Coupland, *The British Anti-Slavery Movement* (1933; reprint, New York: Barnes and Noble, 1964), p. 35.

11. "God Is with Us" (1780–1791)

1. John Wesley, *Journals and Diaries* (1776–1786) II, in *The Works of John Wesley*, ed. W. Reginald Ward and Richard P. Heitzenrater, vol. 19 (Nashville: Abingdon Press, 1990), p. 105.

2. *Sermons* III, ed. Albert C. Outler, *The Works of John Wesley*, vol. 3 (Nashville: Abingdon Press, 1986), pp. 228-46.

3. *Sermons* II, ed. Albert C. Outler, *The Works of John Wesley*, vol. 2 (Nashville: Abingdon Press, 1985), pp. 494-95.

4. Ibid., p. 495.

5. John Walsh, "John Wesley and the Community of Goods," in *Protestant Evangelicalism: Britain, Ireland, Germany and America c. 1750–c. 1950*, ed. Keith Robbins (Oxford: Basil Blackwell, 1990), pp. 25-50.

6. John Walsh, in private conversation on 17 November 1999, in Oxford, pointed out that the lack of any reference in Wesley to the poor laws of England is puzzling.

7. L. Tyerman, *The Life and Times of the Rev. John Wesley* (London: Hodder & Stoughton, 1870), pp. 369-70.

8. John Wesley, "The Mystery of Iniquity," in *Sermons* II, *Works*, 2:468.

9. Tyerman, *Life and Times of Wesley*, p. 434.

10. Quoted in John Whitehead, *The Life of the Rev. John Wesley M.A. and the Life of the Rev. Charles Wesley, M.A.* (Philadelphia: John E. Potter & Co., n.d.), p. 532.

11. Ibid.

12. Ibid., p. 553.

13. Ibid., p. 554.

14. Tyerman, *Life and Times of Wesley*, p. 616.

15. John Wesley, *The Works of John Wesley*, vol. 4 (Grand Rapids: Zondervan, 1958), p. 468.

16. Ibid., p. 478.

17. Ibid., p. 477. Edward Perronet was the author of "All Hail the Power of Jesus' Name." His father, Vincent Perronet, had introduced John and Molly Wesley.

18. Tyerman, *Life and Times of Wesley*, p. 650.

19. John Wesley, "Letter to Alice Cambridge," in John Telford, *The Letters of the Rev. John Wesley, A.M.*, vol. 8 (London: Epworth Press, 1931), p. 259.

20. Augustine Birrel, ed., *The Letters of John Wesley* (London: Hodder & Stoughton, 1915), p. 489.

21. Reprinted in Nehemiah Curnock, ed., *The Journal of the Rev. John Wesley, A.M.,* vol. 8 (London: Charles Kelly, 1916), pp. 133-44.

22. See Earl Kent Brown, *Women of Mr. Wesley's Methodism* (Lewiston, N.Y.: Edwin Mellen Press, 1983), for the details of the friendship between Mrs. Rogers and Miss Ritchie, pp. 199-217.

23. Quoted from V. H. H. Green, *John Wesley* (Stanford: Stanford University Press, 1964), p. 152.

12. Ethics

1. W. E. Sangster, *The Path to Perfection* (London: Epworth Press, 1957), pp. 77-92.

2. James C. Logan, "Toward a Wesleyan Social Ethic," in *Wesleyan Theology Today,* ed. Theodore Runyan (Nashville: Kingswood Books, 1985), pp. 361-71.

3. Manfred Marquardt, *John Wesley's Social Ethics,* trans. John E. Steely and W. Stephen Gunter (Nashville: Abingdon Press, 1992).

4. Sermonic essays have the form of sermons, but they may never have been preached as sermons. Three of them on law and love were written in 1750 and published to follow his thirteen sermons on the "Sermon on the Mount," *Sermons* II, ed. Albert C. Outler, *The Works of John Wesley,* vol. 2 (Nashville: Abingdon Press, 1985), pp. 1-43.

5. Ibid., p. 8.

6. Ibid., p. 9.

7. Ibid., p. 10.

8. Ibid., p. 12.

9. Ibid.

10. Ibid., p. 16.

11. Ibid., p. 18.

12. Ibid., p. 38.

13. Ibid.

14. Ibid., p. 43.

15. H. Richard Niebuhr, *The Responsible Self* (New York: Harper & Row, 1963).

16. Paul Tillich, *Love, Power and Justice* (New York: Oxford University Press, 1954).

17. Paul Tillich, *Systematic Theology,* vol. 3 (Chicago: University of Chicago, 1963).

18. Reinhold Niebuhr, *The Nature and Destiny of Man,* vol. 2 (New York: Charles Scribner's Sons, 1943), pp. 244-86.

19. See Reinhold Niebuhr, *Moral Man and Immoral Society* (New York: Charles Scribner's Sons, 1932).

20. William K. Frankena, *Ethics* (Englewood Cliffs: Prentice-Hall, 1963), pp. 42-45.

21. Leon O. Hynson, "Wesley's *Thoughts upon Slavery*: A Declaration of Human Rights," *Methodist History* 33 (October 1994): 46-57.

22. Ibid., pp. 47, 55.

23. Edward L. Long Jr., *A Survey of Christian Ethics* (New York: Oxford University Press, 1967), p. 113.

24. Leon O. Hynson, *To Reform a Nation* (Grand Rapids: Zondervan, 1984), pp. 54-55.

25. Ibid., p. 56.

26. Stanley Hauerwas, *Character and the Christian Life: A Study in Theological Ethics* (San Antonio: Trinity University Press, 1975), p. 2.

27. Ibid., p. 194.

28. Similar purposes are served by "The Character of a Methodist," "The Principles of a Methodist," "The Nature, Design, and General Rules of the United Societies," and "Rules of the Band Societies" all published in *The Works of John Wesley*, vol. 9, ed. Rupert E. Davies (Nashville: Abingdon Press, 1989), pp. 31-79.

29. Roy Porter, *English Society of the Eighteenth Century*, rev. ed. (London: Penguin Books, 1991), p. 177. Tyerman's larger number of 135,000 from the Conference of 1790 does not materially alter Porter's point.

30. The following pages on Smith and Wesley are an edited version of pages from my *The Ultimate Imperative: An Interpretation of Christian Ethics* (Cleveland: Pilgrim Press, 1999). Pages 145-49 are used with the permission of Pilgrim Press.

31. See Robert L. Heilbroner, *The Worldly Philosophers* (New York: Simon & Schuster, 1972), for the presentation of Smith's eccentricities.

32. Adam Smith, *An Inquiry into the Nature and Causes of the Wealth of Nations* (Indianapolis: Liberty Fund, 1981), p. 456.

33. Adam Smith, *The Theology of Moral Sentiments* (Indianapolis: Liberty Fund, 1982), p. 185.

34. Alasdair MacIntyre, "The Recovery of Moral Agency," *Harvard Divinity Bulletin* 2, no. 4 (1999): 8.

35. The summary itself refutes James Gustafson's critique of Wesley's ethics. Gustafson had focused on Wesley's works on perfection and on his sermons on perfection. His student, Stanley Hauerwas, seems to have made the same mistake. Gustafson wrote: "He is a preacher, and the whole of theology becomes focused on human existence itself and largely in individualistic, subjective terms" (*Christ and the Moral Life* [New York: Harper & Row, 1968], p. 81).

36. The scholarship on the Puritan contribution to the Wesley synthesis is particularly well summarized by Robert C. Monk's, *John Wesley: His Puritan Heritage*, 2d ed. (Lanham, Md.: Scarecrow Press, 1999), pp. 5-8.

Index